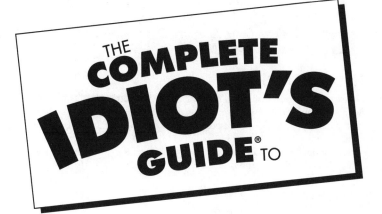

THE
COMPLETE
IDIOT'S
GUIDE® TO

Solaris 9

D1361751

by Martin C. Brown

ALPHA

A Pearson Education Company

To Sharon, who managed to keep Oscar, Leon, and Darcy supplied with mice and food whilst I completed the book.

For marketing and publicity, please call: 317-581-3722

The publisher offers discounts on this book when ordered in quantity for bulk purchases and special sales.

For sales within the United States, please contact: Corporate and Government Sales, 1-800-382-3419 or corpsales@pearsontechgroup.com

Outside the United States, please contact: International Sales, 317-581-3793 or international@pearsontechgroup.com

Publisher: *Marie Butler-Knight*
Product Manager: *Phil Kitchel*
Managing Editor: *Jennifer Chisholm*
Acquisitions Editor: *Eric Heagy*
Development Editor: *Michael Koch*
Production Editor: *Billy Fields*
Copy Editor: *Ross Patty*
Illustrator: *Chris Eliopoulos*
Cover/Book Designer: *Trina Wurst*
Indexers: *Angie Bess, Brad Herriman*
Layout/Proofreading: *John Etchison, Rebecca Harmon*

Contents at a Glance

Contents

Appendixes

Introduction

This book is about Solaris—the Unix-like operating system from Sun Microsystems.

Whether you've picked up the book deliberately or by accident, I'd like to tell you a story about Unix.

My first ever work-experience interview during college was at a company in London's financial district. They handled the computers for share trading, actually using big Hewlett-Packard boxes running the HP version of Unix, HP-UX. I'd seen some wonderful things, including a computer twice the size of a car in a massive, super-cooled room, and enough computer equipment to keep even me happy for days, possibly even weeks.

Of all the impressions that I got at the interview, only one stuck in my mind. I decided on my return that I wasn't cut out for a job in computers because I neither wore sandals nor planned on growing a beard, and that nearly ended my career right there. Of course, since then I've learned that things are not quite as black and white as all that.

Whom This Book Is For

You don't need to use braces (suspenders) instead of belts, wear glasses, or know the works of Tolkien and Pratchett back to front to be able to use Solaris. A working knowledge of the technology from *Star Trek* or *Star Wars* isn't required. Despite what you may think, there are no Jeffries tubes in Solaris, and you won't have to crawl through confined spaces or use a Hydrospanner either!

Solaris is in fact very easy to use, and I've tried my hardest to make this book as easy to use and read as possible. You've probably had some experience using other computers, and in essence there aren't many differences between them at a basic level. There are some specific elements which I need to cover—and that's what this book is about.

The book is aimed at people who are new to Solaris, but familiar with computers and other platforms such as Windows or Mac OS. Although I cover the basics of the operating system, and some more advanced topics, you'll be expected to know basic computer terminology.

The book will also be useful for those familiar with other Unix variants such as Linux, AIX, or HP-UX, although I haven't made specific comparisons between these operating systems and Solaris.

How to Use This Book

Depending on how you intend to use Solaris and how much you already know about Unix will determine the best way of using the book.

If you are a user of Solaris, I recommend you read at least:

1. Chapters 1, 2, and 5.
2. All of Part 4.

If you are a system administrator, new to Solaris or Unix, you should read:

1. All of Part 1.
2. All of Part 2.
3. All of Part 4.

If you are a system administrator and already know Unix, then you can more or less read the book from cover to cover.

Of course, reading the whole book, whether administrator or end user, will give you more information and tips on understanding and using the system. If you get itchy feet and need more information, check the resource guide in Appendix A or my website (www.mcwords.com), where you'll find more information and links about Solaris.

How This Book Is Organized

This book is divided into five parts:

Part 1, "The Solaris Operating Environment," covers the basics of the Solaris operating system, including comparisons to other operating systems, tips on the installation, a complete installation walk-through, and an instant guide to using your newly installed Solaris operating environment.

Part 2, "Basic System Administration," deals with the common tasks expected of all systems administrators, from creating users and adding hard disks to printing and software management.

Part 3, "Networking," goes into the mechanics of connecting your machine to the network, sharing information through disks, and setting up email and web services.

Part 4, "Using Solaris," is a quick guide to using Solaris for performing different tasks, such as basic file management, text processing, and using the command line shell and graphical Common Desktop Environment (CDE).

Part 5, "Tuning and Diagnostics," provides information on how to monitor, identify, and fix problems that either affect your machine's operation or reduce its performance.

Conventions

To make life easier, there are a few conventions that I've used in the book to help you identify different components. *Items in italic (like this)* are the names of commands or entries that you type, or the names of files or directories. In addition, you'll find the following extras:

Sun Lotion

These boxes contain tips and hints on how to improve your experience, or ways of making the process easier.

Solingo

These boxes fill you in on a new piece of terminology that you might not have come across before.

A Postcard From ...

These boxes provide extra nuggets of information that fill you in on some background data, useful real-life examples, or a useful sideline from the main text.

Sun Screen

These boxes warn you about potentially dangerous operations, or areas where there might be a problem that you should be aware of before continuing.

Contacting the Author

I'm always happy to hear from readers, whether the feedback is good or bad; and you'll always be able to find the latest information and updates on my website at www.mcwords.com. If you have a problem that is not covered in this book, check the website—I might have added an article or update on what you are looking for. I'm always happy to help, up to a point, if you are having a problem. If you want to contact me directly, either use the contact form on the website or email me at mc@mcwords.com.

Acknowledgments

First and foremost, thanks to my agent, Vicki Harding at StudioB, who recommended me for the job and tirelessly promoted me as the ideal author for the role. Second, thanks to Eric Heagy at Alpha Books who trusted Vicki and me to complete the book on schedule.

Thanks also need to go to Nick Barron (nikb), who managed to help me out right at the start when somebody else had failed—that was the first time he'd saved my life. Somehow, during the course of the book, I managed to up that debt to two. I'll pay you back the favors, I promise!

Of course, I must thank the production team at Alpha Books for turning my manuscript into something useful, and to Michael Koch for doing the preliminary work of reading my chapters and getting them ready for production.

Finally, I must give the biggest thanks to my wife, Sharon. Once again, she survived cold beds and frustrated cats missing their usual playtime and affection to allow me to get the book out the door. Just a week after completing the book was our 7th anniversary, and I love her now as I did then.

Special Thanks to the Technical Reviewer

The Complete Idiot's Guide to Solaris 9 was reviewed by an expert who double-checked the accuracy of what you'll learn here, to help us ensure that this book gives you everything you need to know about Solaris. Special thanks are extended to Richard Baker McGee.

Trademarks

All terms mentioned in this book that are known to be or are suspected of being trademarks or service marks have been appropriately capitalized. Alpha Books and Pearson Education, Inc., cannot attest to the accuracy of this information. Use of a term in this book should not be regarded as affecting the validity of any trademark or service mark.

Part 1

The Solaris Operating Environment

Before I get into the full details of how to use and administer a Solaris system, you first need to understand what Solaris is, and how Solaris compares to and fits in with other operating systems that are available. It's also important to understand what's involved in installing the operating system and what steps are required to get there.

Included in this section is a complete walk-through of the installation of a Solaris system, on both Intel and SPARC platforms, and a quick overview and guide to using the system for the first time.

Introducing Solaris

In This Chapter

- ◆ A brief history of Unix
- ◆ Introducing the Solaris operating system

You're at the office looking up some information on a website, shopping for some books and CDs, and downloading some music files to keep you amused if the workload ever decreases. Without realizing it, you've probably just used a number of machines running Unix. Unix is the backbone of the Internet, providing fast and reliable services over the network. More significantly and precisely, you've probably been using Solaris—a flavor of Unix—somewhere along the line. You've probably heard of Unix, and possibly even Solaris, and how it's this really complicated and powerful operating system that has one of those "quaint" command line interfaces and that takes years of beard growing and the breaking in of countless pairs of sandals.

Don't worry though, Unix is not nearly as complicated as the people in beards and sandals make out. Strange though it may seem, the beard and sandals are actually optional, and they aren't a required element to learn how to use Unix, or to keep it running once you've mastered the techniques.

In this chapter I discuss the basics of the Unix operating system, how Solaris fits in to the collection of Unix operating systems, and some specific elements of the Solaris implementation.

Introducing Unix

Unix was developed by Ken Thompson and others at Bell Laboratories in 1969. Unix was the successor to the MULTICS (Multiplexed Information and Computing System). MULTICS was large, unwieldy, and generally very unstable, but it planted an idea and some enthusiasm and lead, with the help of some other programmers, to the development of Unix. Amongst those other programs was Dennis Ritchie, who developed the C programming language with Brian Kernighan. C and its object-oriented brother C++ is one of the most popular languages available and is used to write lots of operating systems, including Unix, Windows, and Mac OS.

The early versions of Unix were written in assembly language—the raw assembler codes that a processor uses to execute any instruction, and the element that makes any computer work. Within a year Unix had been completely rewritten using C and made one of the first major steps for any operating system—Unix was now capable, through C, of being used to compile and build itself. This meant that updating and improving Unix could be performed right within the operating system itself.

Solingo

You may see **Unix** in a number of different capitalizations. The proper format is Unix, leading uppercase character, lowercase everything else. The reason is quite simple, Unix is *not* an acronym. The U, N, I, and X do not actually stand for anything, they are just letters used in a name. The confusion comes from AT&T, who trademarked the name UNIX using small capital letters.

By 1970 one of the critical steps to the Unix phenomenon was taken. Unix was distributed to universities. Both tutors and students found the operating system powerful, practical, versatile, and easy to use. If you took the time to learn C, you could also improve and expand on the operating system very easily, making Unix an ideal platform on which to learn about computers. Those students who did learn, took their experience into the commercial marketplace.

Back at the home of Unix, steps were being made to supply Unix as the operating system platform for a new venture by the U.S. government which would provide a network during times of war. The network was designed at a hardware level to survive a nuclear attack and to solve the problem of using a single computer to provide military support—knock out that one computer, and the way is lost. The idea was to connect sites together and then allow the computer (a single computer was so expensive, nobody had more than one) at each site to talk to the others connected to the network.

The "internetwork" was achieved through the use of linking multiple sites together and then allowing data to be routed through different sites and over a number of different links until it reached its destination. For example, if sites A, B, and C are connected to each other, it's possible to communicate between A and C either directly, or by sending the packets through site B on the way.

To support this network, the U.S. government already had a communications infrastructure—the telephone. What it didn't have was an operating system capable of supporting the needs and requirements of the network.

Unsurprisingly—considering that this is a book about Unix—the solution was ... Unix. Unix already had networking capability using a robust and expandable protocol called TCP/IP. Despite it being the early days of networking any sort of computer, TCP/IP had the ability to support hundreds of thousands of machines, and also to support different protocols and simultaneous communications channels. Unix also had a system for exchanging electronic messages between machines. We take these things for granted these days, but 30 years ago this was groundbreaking stuff.

A Postcard From ...

The number of machines that use the Internet is increasing at an exceedingly high rate each day. Although it's difficult to get precise figures, I was using the following comparison in 1994 (eight years ago) during presentations on the power of the Internet. Every hour, 1,387 new people sign up for the Internet—during that same hour, 916,666 Big Macs will be bought at McDonald's stores worldwide. The rate of Internet sign-ups today is probably 100 times what I quoted then!

Despite this increase, the bulk of these connections are clients—people in the home or office using the Internet to send emails and browse websites. On the back end—that is, the computers that are being used to provide those services—Unix is still the market leader with about half of the machines on the Internet running some flavor of Unix.

A high proportion of those are running Linux, largely because it's free and therefore cheap and easy to deploy, particularly by web-hosting companies. The next most popular Unix operating system providing Internet services is Solaris.

The network developed by the U.S. government was called ARPAnet (Advanced Research Projects Agency Network) and was the precursor to what we call the Internet today. Unix was there first, providing the networking support and capabilities used by the U.S. government. The TCP/IP and other networking tools like File Transfer Protocol (FTP) for file transfer and Simple Mail Transfer Protocol (SMTP) for exchanging email were developed, used, and deployed first on Unix.

Although most people think that the Internet started only ten years ago and that the technology and facilities offered by Internet servers are new, the reality is very different. The Internet is over 20 years old—Windows PCs and Macs didn't even exist when it was created; the protocols and technology you use today existed on Unix long before Windows and Macs even supported networking.

More than 20 years later, just about every company that provides a hardware platform has tried to produce a version of Unix. Everybody from Sun Microsystems to IBM, SGI,

Digital (now part of Compaq), and even Microsoft have produced, and in many cases still do produce, Unix-based operating systems.

A Postcard From ...

Unless you've been off the planet or living in a box with no communication with the outside world, you have probably heard of Unix at least a few times over the last few years. For example, Linux is a version of Unix written by Linus Torvaulds, which is provided free of charge (or for a nominal fee) by a number of companies and has been responsible for a huge rush of interest in Unix. Linux runs on PCs, and is therefore a viable (if not always sensible) replacement for Windows.

Also, as people become more computer literate they are beginning to understand (and be told) that Unix is an operating system that is used to provide and support facilities, like their email service or database needs.

Why Use Unix?

Ignoring the specific hype and abilities of the Unix operating systems—particularly those that have surfaced in recent years—the core of the Unix operating system consists of the following features:

◆ **Multi-user:** Unix was designed to allow more than one person to connect to and use a computer at the same time. Unix also provides a secure model that allows different users to run different applications at the same time, and to protect them if they choose to share their files with other users on the system.

◆ **Multi-tasking:** Unix was the first operating system which truly allowed you to run more than one application at a time, and the ability to switch between those applications. On a normal Unix system there are more than 20 background applications helping to manage your machine and provide services and facilities that make your machine easier to use, or more accessible on the network.

◆ **Stable:** The Unix operating system model means that each application gets its own "protected" memory space. If an application suffers some sort of failure, then the application will terminate without crashing the entire machine. It is virtually impossible to crash a Unix machine and it's not uncommon to find Unix servers that have been up for many many months, and even many years without ever having been rebooted.

◆ **Secure:** You cannot get into a Unix machine with a login and password, and even if you have those details, you can only do what the administrator allows you to do. Without the right permissions you cannot modify the configuration of the system, access files, or control any applications or resources other than your own.

◆ **Powerful:** Unix is capable of working on anything from an old 386 PC up to massively parallel boxes supporting hundreds of processors, gigabytes of memory and terabytes of disk space. Unix is also lightweight—you can provide a powerful email server on that 386 PC with as little as 8MB of RAM. Windows doesn't even install on a machine with less than 16MB, and it prefers 32MB, even before you run an application, and Mac OS—Mac OS X in particular—likes 64MB or more to operate effectively.

With all of these features it's no wonder that Unix is being used to provide:

- **Internet services:** These need to be up 24/7 and often have to provide complex and extensive services in a timely fashion.
- **Network services:** Inside a typical company network, your email, file sharing, and other services may well be supported with Unix.
- **Database services:** Governments, banks, universities, research installations, and many others use Unix as the platform for their databases because a Unix machine can handle the size and complexity of the data so easily.
- **Research and computation:** With multiprocessor support and the ability to work with huge volumes of data, Unix is used for real-world simulations such as wind tunnels and crash tests for cars and other vehicles.
- **Design and architecture:** Your car was probably designed on a Unix machine before a single component was manufactured, and other systems like airplanes and the airports which they use were probably designed on a Unix machine.
- **Virtual Reality:** To create an entire world that you can move around in and interact with takes a lot of memory and computer power, and an operating system that can handle it.
- **Filmmaking:** This probably surprises most people, but filmmakers often use Unix machines to both design and compute the digital effects and sequences in films.

A Postcard From ...

Toy Story, the world's first completely computer-generated movie was produced using Unix machines. The machine design and sequencing was handled by SGI. The actual rendering—that is, converting the 3D information about the different characters and environments in the film into a flat, 2D image suitable for broadcast—was handled by a render farm running Unix.

More explicitly, the render farm was based on 87 dual-processor and 30 quad-processor Sun-based workstations running Solaris. It took 46 days for the farm to render the 110,000 frames which make up the movie. Seven years later (*Toy Story* was produced in 1995), Pixar and others are still using Unix workstations and Unix-based render farms to produce the images in our films.

To name but a few, the films that used Unix include *Starship Troopers*, *Titanic*, *Star Wars* (Special Editions, and *Episode 1*), *Toy Story*, *Shrek*, *Monsters Inc.*, and many many others.

The Unix Divide

There are two basic flavors of Unix, System V Release 4 (SVR4) and BSD (Berkeley Systems Division). The SVR4 version of Unix is based on the code used by Bell Labs (later to become part of AT&T). Once it was clear that Unix had a viable future, AT&T did what any company would do in the same situation—they started selling Unix as a commercial product and started making money from it.

The BSD flavor is based on the complete rewrite of the Unix operating system performed at the University of California, Berkeley, USA. BSD was designed specifically for use within universities and colleges and was free (or almost free) for research and development use.

Today, these two strands remain—most commercial companies will base their Unix on either SVR4, BSD, or a combination of the two. The differences between the two platforms are relatively minor in terms of abilities and facilities—both offer the same multi-user, multi-tasking, and secure platform. The shells and 99 percent of the applications that you can use on each platform are also identical.

The differences are largely related to the administration and core background services. For example, BSD and SVR4 flavors have different methods for starting and stopping services, different printing systems, and a different focus on security.

Migrating from BSD to SVR4 or SVR4 to BSD is not a major headache, and for most users (as opposed to administrators) the differences between the two will be hard to identify.

Introducing Solaris

So what is Solaris? Well, Solaris is an operating system based on Unix and supported on the SPARC (Scalable Processor Architecture) and Intel x86 (Pentium I/II/III/4 and Celeron) hardware platforms. Solaris itself is written by Sun Microsystems, one of the leading hardware and software manufacturers of computers, strong proponents of the Internet, and the original developers of the Java development language.

Solaris 9, the latest version, is the most recent addition to a long line of Solaris machines. Solaris 2, the first true version of Solaris, was released in 1992. Solaris 1 was actually the rebadged name for the former Unix operating system released by Sun. SunOS was the name of the previous system. It stopped at SunOS 4.3.1, which became Solaris 1.

New revisions of Solaris have been released every 12 to 24 months ever since. Solaris 2.6 introduced two versions of Solaris, the SPARC and Intel platform versions. The two versions are virtually identical in every respect—you can move from one platform to another without making too many mental adjustments—and those differences that do exist are directly attributable to the differences in the underlying hardware.

Perhaps the biggest reason to use Solaris is that it's one of the most stable and reliable operating system platforms available. Although there are many different versions of Unix out there, many were developed for a particular hardware platform—such as Digital, IBM, and SGI—and have become niche products.

Nobody, and I mean *nobody*, knows the Sun SPARC hardware platform better than Sun itself. This means that Sun can provide, support, and optimize the Solaris operating system to work the most effectively on its own hardware. Sun hardware is also well recognized as some of the most reliable and long-lasting hardware made by any computer manufacturer. I still use a Sun IPC workstation—a machine that's about 14 years old. It's slow for some tasks, but it works and has never once in its life crashed.

Sun also has years of experience in developing and supporting the Solaris operating system—it's been making a version of Unix for 20 years so the principles and technologies are not new to Sun.

Solingo

Sun's corporate motto is "The Network is the computer." This means that a network of computers is more powerful than the sum of its parts. A computer on its own is nothing more than a computational tool. Connecting computers together allows you to share information and resources and enables you to make use of the power and facilities of all the machines.

Extend this from the desktop and LAN environment to the Internet and you'll see that the network really is the computer. The Internet is building communities and providing services and information to a huge range of people—many of whom will never meet each other—while still allowing the sort of collaboration only seen when people are in speaking distance of each other.

Coined many years before the real power of the network and the Internet became truly recognized, there is no expression that more aptly fits how people are using their computers today.

Using Solaris over Windows/Mac OS

Suggesting Solaris as an alternative to Windows or Mac OS is really an impossible order without knowing what you are going to be doing with it. I have a really bad habit of not ever suggesting a machine or platform without knowing what it's going to be used for, but there are a few situations and generalities I can suggest where Solaris might be as useful, if not more useful, than a typical Windows or Mac OS solution.

In addition to the situations I've already mentioned where Unix in general is a good solution, Solaris is also useful in the following situations:

◆ **Web development:** Unless you need ASP—a Windows-specific technology for website development—Solaris is more than capable of providing you with a suitable platform for developing complex, content-rich, and dynamically driven websites. I do 90 percent of my website development under Solaris using Apache, Perl, Python, and mySQL.

◆ **Internet hosting:** Solaris machines already power much of the Internet, with many of the largest Internet service providers and hosting services using Solaris at some point in their network. Up until it was purchased by Microsoft, the entire Hotmail service, which provides free Internet email access for millions of users, was supported using Solaris servers.

In terms of replacing Windows and Mac OS clients, Netscape and its open source brother Mozilla are available for all versions of Unix, including Solaris. For office applications where you would normally use Microsoft Word or Excel, the best solution is Sun's very own StarOffice suite, which provides word processing, spreadsheet, database, and presentation application modules.

Solaris is also one of the most widely supported Unix offerings when it comes to commercial software in a variety of areas.

As to integrating a Solaris machine into an existing Windows or Mac OS environment, you should have few concerns. Solaris will integrate with these platforms—especially now that we all use the same basic communication protocols (Windows and Mac OS have adopted the Unix protocols, rather than the other way round!).

The Java Fix

It seems a little unfair to talk about Sun without talking about perhaps its biggest contribution to computing and in particular the Internet—the Java programming language and environment.

Java, in case you didn't know, has absolutely nothing to do with coffee, or a country in the southern hemisphere. Instead, Java is a programming language that offers "write once, run anywhere" facilities.

One of the biggest problems with computers on the whole is their relative incompatibility with each other. Sure, you can share files and data with each other, and you can transmit email and other information between computers, but the element that makes a computer useful in the first place is the application that makes use of that data.

Applications are not transferable, however—you cannot take a program written for Solaris and run it, verbatim, on a Windows PC. There are two reasons for this: one is the underlying hardware and the other is the operating system. The underlying hardware is a problem because different processors and hardware platforms have different ways of communicating between components, and completely different languages for executing the basic instructions that make a computer work.

The operating system is a problem because it's the operating system that provides the libraries and core interaction between hardware and software that allows a computer to operate in the first place. Windows and Mac OS, for example, use two completely different ways of drawing information on the screen, even though the two platforms now use the same hardware to do so.

Java fixes all this. It provides a simple language that shares some semantics and abilities of the C++ language. Java uses a common set of libraries and facilities, and you create a Java application by converting your source code into Java bytecode. Providing a platform that has had the Java Virtual Machine written for it, you can take your Java application and run it on any platform, irrespective of the underlying hardware or operating system.

In addition to providing an architecture-neutral platform for executing software, Java can also be embedded within other applications so that you can execute Java applets (little applications) within a document or more specifically within a web page.

Java is entirely written and developed by Sun, although everybody from IBM to Microsoft to Apple has jumped on the Java bandwagon to produce Java-compatible platforms and applications.

It goes without saying that Solaris is an excellent platform for developing Java applications. In fact, Solaris comes with the Sun Forte for Java development environment and new versions of Java and many of the libraries and extensions are released on the Solaris platform first.

Introducing Solaris 9

It would be impossible, in a book like this, to cover all of the new improvements that the engineers at Sun Microsystems have included in the latest version of Solaris. Solaris 9, still in beta in January 2002, with the final version expected before the end of the first quarter 2002, is another in a long line of extensions, enhancements, and updates which Sun applies to its operating system every 12 to 24 months.

For an example of the scale of the changes, you have to look no further than Sun's own change document (available from the Sun Documentation Server at http://docs.sun.com). It's over 100 pages in length and details all of the major changes in the system.

The highlights, extensions, and improvements include:

◆ **Linux compatibility:** Solaris 9 allows you not only to run applications pre-built for running under Linux through the *lxrun* utility, you can also now develop applications under Solaris that are compatible with Linux.

◆ **Directory services:** Solaris 9 includes iPlanet Directory Server, allowing you to provide a central directory system using the Lightweight Directory Access Protocol (LDAP) system.

◆ **Improved PPP support:** For connecting your Solaris 9 box up to the Internet over a modem or ISDN connection.

◆ **Resource Manager:** You can now manage the resources of your machine and track the resource usage.

◆ **Volume Manager:** The Solaris Volume Manager has been updated to allow you to create Redundant Arrays of Inexpensive (or Independent) Disks (RAID) levels 0, 1, and 5.

◆ **Patch management:** A new patch manager allows you to install patches directly from Sun's own SunSolve patch repository.

◆ **Solaris Management Console:** A new version of the Java-based GUI provides a usable interface to most of the management and monitoring tasks to make the process of managing your machines—and other Solaris machines in your network—from a single point.

◆ **Solaris Live Upgrade:** Live Upgrade allows you to update and install major system software upgrades on your machines without having to shut down your machines and thus reduce their availability to your users.

◆ **CD writing abilities:** For the first time, Solaris now comes with software to allow you to create data and audio CDs and to work with both CD-R and CD-RW media.

◆ **Gnome:** Solaris 9 now includes the popular Gnome desktop environment as an alternative to the Common Desktop Environment (CDE). Gnome is a popular environment used on Linux machines.

◆ **Extended third-party software:** Solaris 9 comes complete with a whole new suite of third-party applications, many of them provided by the Free Software community, including many of the development tools and libraries used for Linux software projects.

I'll discuss some but not all of these new features in this book, although the main focus is on Solaris in general, rather than a specific release.

A Postcard From ...

At the time of writing (January 2002) Sun had just announced that the Intel version of Solaris 9 (Solaris 9 for x86) had been put on hold, while Sun determined whether Intel was a viable platform for supporting Solaris. Solaris 9 Beta was already available in an Intel version, and many of the examples and screenshots from this book will come from the Solaris 9 Beta running on an Intel machine.

Solaris 8 on Intel will still be available, and if you want an endorsement of how good the product is, I use it as the operating system on my main server in the office. It provides all my DNS, web serving, mail (including mailing list), database, and file serving operations (supporting Unix, Mac OS, and Windows clients). Until a reorganization early in January, the machine had been up for 182 days without falling over, and the reason for the interruption at that point was for a hardware upgrade.

The Least You Need to Know

- ◆ Solaris is a Unix-based operating system.
- ◆ Solaris is based on the SVR4 flavor of Unix rather than BSD.
- ◆ Solaris provides a stable and powerful platform for providing web and other Internet services, database management, and file serving.
- ◆ Solaris is available for Sun's own SPARC hardware platform and Intel-compatible PCs.
- ◆ Solaris 9 was released in a beta form in January 2002.

Solaris and Other Operating Systems

In This Chapter

- ◆ Solaris and Windows
- ◆ Solaris and Mac OS
- ◆ Solaris and Linux, and other Unix variants
- ◆ Slotting in Solaris

Solaris is an operating system. However, just as oranges are not the only fruit, Solaris isn't the only operating system.

In this chapter I'm going to take a fleeting look at some of the alternative operating systems out there and how Solaris compares to them at both client (desktop) and server tasks. I'll also take a quick peek at how Solaris can be used to bridge the gap between operating systems and be configured to integrate into any existing network.

Computer Evangelism

Computer evangelism is not funny. It was once said that more than half the bandwidth on Usenet was taken up by "flame wars" with people arguing over which system was best. The simple fact is that the majority of people think the machine they use is the best, and any other platform is a poor second.

The simple answer to anybody harping about a particular platform is, "I've selected the system most appropriate for me and what I do." I'm not an evangelist (well, not often), and I don't believe for a second that there's a single machine and operating system that will ever suit all of my needs. In my office I have separate machines running Solaris, Mac OS, Mac OS X, Linux, and Windows 2000 and I use whichever machine is the most suitable for the job I'm doing. If I need to, I can run any of the Windows variants (from 95 to XP), BeOS, FreeBSD, HP-UX, and one or two others that most people will never have heard of.

For basic web work I use Solaris for deployment and Linux for development. For much of my business work I use the PC because of the range of software, and I do all my writing and creative work on Mac OS/Mac OS X. I could potentially do all of the work on one machine, but instead I choose to use the right machine for the right job.

Solaris and Windows

Windows, historically, is a desktop operating system designed by Microsoft to provide a multitasking and GUI-based environment for running applications. At the time it was introduced it provided a huge improvement over DOS, which was capable of running only one application at a time.

In time, of course, the abilities of Windows increased—Windows 95 was a major leap forward, and since then we've seen Windows NT, Windows 98, Windows Me, Windows 2000, and Windows XP. Windows NT and 2000 are available in both server and client variations, whereas all the others are client-specific solutions for running applications.

In terms of specific comparisons, it gets more difficult. The two target audiences are very different, although in recent years there has been a significant amount of convergence. Windows is the most popular desktop operating system by a significant margin. Windows is now used by universities, by research labs, and as a simple platform for business applications.

Solaris—and indeed any Unix variant—is primarily a text-based solution. Unix itself is specially tuned for providing services and raw processor power to other computers over a network; it's not really a client operating system. That doesn't mean you can't use it as such. Many research and technical applications are available for Solaris, and if you need basic business applications to compare with Word and Excel you need look no further than Sun's own StarOffice suite.

In the server arena, Windows 2000 has made significant advances as the most obvious and compatible choice for file sharing, and for service development and provision using tools on the client side. This is probably the way in which Windows has sneaked in the server's backdoor—the Windows client and its ease of interoperability with a Windows server has made website development, client/server data-base systems, and cohesive and expandable solutions much easier to implement and develop.

However, with all the improvements and advances in Windows 2000, Unix still leads the way in network service provision. Most of the Internet is still supported on Unix machines, and a great proportion of those are Solaris based. Where Microsoft has the advantage is in the single platform for server and client solutions used for the computers on every desktop in a business. Although Solaris will support Windows machines quite happily, it's easier from a systems administration point of view to have one platform to keep the cost of ownership and staffing costs down.

Sun Lotion

If you want a comparison of Windows 2000 and Solaris in a server environment, you might want to check out the Microsoft white paper at http://www. microsoft.com/windows2000/ server/evaluation/compare/ solaris.asp. Written by me in preparation for the release of Windows 2000, it covers everything from scalability and service provision down to the reliability and management facilities offered by the two systems.

Solaris and Mac OS

Mac OS and Solaris are about as different as you can get in the computer arena in terms of both servers and clients. Mac OS is a desktop operating system originally designed for the client (although server systems have been available for the past five years). The target group is publishers, design and print agencies, and other creative people. I'm writing this book on one right now, and in all likelihood the text will be typeset on a Mac before being sent to the printer.

Mac OS lacks the command line front end—which is one of the more powerful interfaces of any Unix machine—but makes up for that lack by having one of the most complete and usable GUI-based interfaces available on any platform, even Windows.

As a server operating system, Mac OS doesn't really cut the mustard at all. Mac OS was never designed for the task, even with specialist extensions from Apple, such as the Apple-Share IP software, or special hardware. Although the Mac OS is capable of multitasking, it's better to say that the OS supports cooperative execution. The application running in the "front" has the bulk of the CPU power, with background applications sharing the remainder (generally less than 10 to 15 percent). That makes supporting multiple services effectively very difficult. After 10 years of trying, the most effective way I found of supporting multiple services under Mac OS was to use a single machine for each task. Not an ideal situation by any imagination.

However, there are some similarities there. Apple has control over the hardware and operating system of the Macintosh platform in the same way that Sun has control over their

SPARC hardware and Solaris operating system. As with Solaris, this provides Apple with the unique ability to target and provide an OS highly optimized for the Macintosh platform. For image processing and desktop publishing it's hard to beat the Mac OS, and Macs often provide the front end for designing websites, graphics for films and TV, and for TV production in general. Most TV companies will use Macs to produce the graphics and sequences used to introduce programs, provide links, and create the graphics that appear during a newscast or other program.

A Postcard From ...

Apple and Microsoft are strange bedfellows, at one and the same time they are major competitors (because of Windows versus Mac OS, and Windows Media Player versus QuickTime) and collaborators (Microsoft Office, Internet Explorer).

They both know their strengths, though. For a while, Apple used PCs running Windows NT for some of their web servers, and Microsoft used Apple equipment to produce their advertisements and graphics. Even elements like the Windows logo, the original Windows 95 ads, and the animation used in some of Microsoft's applications were produced on a Mac first!

The distinctions between Solaris and Mac OS X, Apple's new operating system, are less significant. Mac OS X is based on FreeBSD Unix. Mac OS X provides both a powerful GUI for running applications like Photoshop and Quark XPress, and video manipulation tools and a Unix underbelly capable of running the majority of Unix applications including all the basic Unix tools and applications like MySQL, Apache, and others.

Mac OS X is still young—at the time of writing 10.1.2 is the current version and the entire OS in public form is less than a year old, but it's already showing that it's a powerful combination of desktop usability and server capability in a single package.

Solaris and Linux

There is a lot of confusion generally in the market about what Linux is and what sort of a role it can really play in a fairly cutthroat market. There is no doubting that Linux is popular, and that it has a number of dedicated followers, but where it fits into the overall OS picture is not quite clear.

First, the simple facts. Linux is ...

◆ A freely available version of Unix.

◆ Supported primarily on the Intel x86 platform, but also available for PowerPC (IBM/Apple), SGI, SPARC, Hewlett-Packard PA-RISC, and many other platforms.

- ◆ A loose combination of the "best" bits from both the BSD and SVR4 variations of Unix, with a slight tendency towards SVR4.

- ◆ Available in source form—in fact, modifying and improving on the source code is actively encouraged for all the components that make up Linux.

- ◆ Supported commercially by companies who provide a "Linux Distribution" and some aftermarket support.

- ◆ Supported for free by a huge array of websites, discussion lists, newsgroups, and organizations.

- ◆ Free; Linux has spawned one of the largest bandwagon jumps in computer history, with even IBM, HP, and Sun joining in the fun, and Microsoft feeling threatened!

What most people consider to be Linux is a complete, ready-to-run operating system incorporating all of the tools, commands, and facilities of a typical Unix distribution. In reality, Linux is really just a kernel, written primarily by Linus Torvalds, which provides all of the core functionality such as the multiuser, multitasking, and protected memory space capabilities.

Built around the Linux kernel are a set of components—all of them free—which are a combination of those provided by the GNU project at the Free Software Foundation and others distributed around the Internet. GNU, short for the recursive GNU's Not Unix, is a project to create free versions of the primary tools that make up a typical Unix toolset. These cover a range of services, including core tools like *ls* for getting file lists, versions of languages like *awk*, and the *nroff/troff* commands.

Solingo

The **nroff** and **troff** commands are part of a suite of applications that can turn a text document—marked up using special commands embedded in the text—into formats suitable for display onscreen or for printing from a variety of printing devices, including the film devices used to generate films for big printing presses.

In Unix, the **roff* system, as it's more commonly known, is used for the online help system provided through the *man* command. The online help is formatted in a derivative of **roff* which is then parsed in real time to produce a formatted version of the document on screen.

Linux itself is provided in a series of "distributions." These incorporate ...

- ◆ The Linux kernel.

- ◆ A suite of additional device drivers for supporting USB, SCSI, and other devices.

- The GNU toolset.

- The free X Windows System project called Xfree86.

- A selection of different Window managers such as KDE and Gnome for providing a Windows/Mac OS-like interface to the OS.

- Additional development tools, such as the GNU C Compiler, Perl, Python, and other languages.

- An easy to use installer to allow Linux to be installed easily onto your hardware.

These distributions are provided by companies like Redhat, SuSE, and many others.

Because the source code is available for both the kernel and the tools on which it relies, Linux is frequently being used by companies developing small technology devices; they can create a kernel that works on their hardware and add drivers for their devices just by modifying the source. The introduction of Linux has created all sorts of distributions, collections, and tools based on this idea—you can even get a variety of Linux to work on your Compaq iPaq handheld computer!

In essence, there is not a lot of difference between Solaris and Linux when it comes to capabilities; both are Unix variants and provide a similar range of features and functionality. Solaris is now available for free, and if you are willing to sign the papers you can even get hold of the source for free, too. Solaris is, however, only supported on SPARC and x86 platforms.

The big difference between the two only really becomes apparent when you move your platform from single, dual, and perhaps quad-processor environments up to 8, 16, or more processors. Linux is not yet geared up for very high CPU numbers or the sort of massive hardware solutions provided by Sun, IBM, and others. Certainly the support will come in time, but Linux as an OS is still relatively young. Solaris in its current incarnation is about twice the age of Linux, closer to four times if you count only the very recent popularity of Linux. Historically, Sun has almost another 10 years of experience with the Unix operating system to back it up.

Furthermore, ignoring the x86 variation for the moment, Sun also has the benefit of building both the hardware and software, allowing it much closer integration between these components and more opportunity to improve performance and throughput when providing a Sun solution based on both hardware and software. That's not to imply that Sun's Solaris x86 software is underpowered or reduced in capability, just that it is not as tuned as the SPARC version can be.

The other major difference is support. Opinion is divided on this—on the one hand you have an operating system which is backed up by a team of paid, dedicated developers working with a strict set of rules and a relatively narrow range of hardware on which to support their operating system. On the other you have a system that is driven by a few people, but potentially has hundreds of thousands, if not millions of developers identifying and fixing bugs and providing new features.

A Postcard From ...

As an example of just how big and powerful Sun equipment can get, you might want to check the specification of the Sun Fire 15K. It supports up to 106 SPARC processors and more than 0.5TB of memory—that's more than 512GB of RAM. Most people have a desktop PC with a 40GB hard disk and 128MB or 256MB of RAM!

As well as providing a single, supremely fast server, the same system can also be configured to operate as up to 18 individual systems, and the allocation can be changed dynamically without rebooting or powering down the system. You could, for example, provide 10 machines with 10 processors each and then midway through a job increase the number of processes in one machine to 20.

All within the same box, and with the same redundancy, the Sun Fire allows you to change hard disks or processors while the system is running—even if a CPU fails, you don't have to shut down to change the CPU over!

If you buy Solaris from Sun (rather than getting the free version) you get telephone hot-line support (at a cost), regular, easy-to-install updates, and on SPARC hardware provided by Sun, you get a very fast, reliable, and scalable environment for deploying services. Even the free version is supported by Sun with a reduced set of updates and patches and is one of the most widely used variations of Unix.

If you look specifically at the desktop and server environments then there really is little to compare. At the desktop both Linux and Solaris have capable, if perhaps not ideal, user environments built on top of the same system, X Windows. They also both support alternatives, so if you are not happy with one solution then you can use another. I regularly use KDE on Solaris over CDE purely out of personal preference, although I could just as easily use Motif, Gnome, WindowMaker, and a myriad of other solutions. Both platforms also support the StarOffice software provided by Sun, so your choice makes little difference in terms of the core business applications.

At the server end things are different. As I've already mentioned, Linux doesn't scale very well beyond 4 processors, although it will at a push support 16-way systems. Both offer fast and powerful bases though for Internet services. Oracle provides both Solaris and Linux alternatives, and as both systems are based on Unix there is little to choose between interoperability and other features. The one big advantage for Linux is that it's free, and although Sun still accounts for a larger proportion of web servers on the Internet, the use of Linux has allowed countless companies to provide cheap and easily expandable web server abilities at a fraction of the cost compared to using Solaris.

Solaris and Other Unix Variants

Although I've mentioned two of the more popular variants of Unix, there are a few others which I haven't mentioned. Most of these are platform- and often hardware-specific versions of Unix specially designed to work with the hardware released by the same company. The following list presents some details about these alternatives:

♦ **A/UX:** This is the early attempt by Apple to jump on to the Unix bandwagon. Originally designed for the Macintosh II series of machines back in 1988, A/UX has not been updated for some time. Although it was a complete release, incorporating the shells, tools, and an X Windows environment, it never really caught on as heavily as Apple would have liked. The Mac OS was more popular, and Apple, its hardware, and its software have moved on somewhat since A/UX. Interestingly, 10 years after A/UX was introduced came Mac OS X, which as you've already seen is based on a Unix core.

♦ **AIX:** AIX runs on the RS/6000 and PowerPC platforms available from IBM. AIX is not as popular as other Unix variants, partly because the interest was never there, and partly because the operating system competed head on with the larger and more scalable IBM S390 and other systems. AIX is still available, and is best described as an amalgamation of the BSD and SVR4 variants with a series of standards applied to bring it into line with other Unix variants.

♦ **BSD and Variants:** When AT&T provided a version of Unix to the universities, they originally expected it to be used as nothing more than a teaching platform, but the people at the Computer Systems Research Group and the University of California, Berkeley had other ideas. They expanded on the original code and then rewrote 90 percent, and later 100 percent of the code to produce the modern BSD distribution.

BSD is now available in a number of variants from a commercial solution (BSD/OS) optimized for Internet service provision down to free versions such as NetBSD and FreeBSD. NetBSD and FreeBSD "compete" with Linux for the free desktop Linux market and there are frequent arguments between the two sides. BSDs most powerful feature is its high emphasis on security; the NetBSD variant is one of the most secure operating systems available without going for expensive, fully government-certified alternatives.

♦ **Darwin:** Darwin is the free portion of the Mac OS X platform and is the core Unix operating system on which the Aqua- and Mac OS-specific interface elements are built. Darwin, surprisingly, is a freely available version of Unix supported on both PowerPC and Intel hardware. It's mostly FreeBSD and Mach based, but with a few Apple specifics.

♦ **Digital Unix:** Supported by Digital Equipment Corporation (which eventually became simply Digital, and was then purchased by Compaq), Digital Unix is a 64-bit implementation that runs on Digital's own Alpha processor. Like other Unix variants, it's a combination of both SVR4 and BSD alternatives.

Digital Unix is one of the most stable, and its 64-bit capability—which arrived before most other Unix variants—has made it an obvious choice for large database solutions. The Lycos search engine is supported on Digital Alpha hardware running Digital Unix, and it serves over 100 million searches every day.

♦ **HP-UX:** Yet another platform-specific Unix, HP-UX works with Hewlett-Packard's PA-RISC platform. It's based on System V Release 2, with a vast array of additions and features bolted on from both the SVR4 and BSD sides of the Unix fence. HP-UX is very powerful, especially on suitable hardware, and HP computers were early promoters of Unix as a desktop platform. In fact, my first Unix computer was an HP-UX cluster running on HP 9000 Series 300 machines, which used the same Motorola 680x0 chips used by the original Macintosh series.

♦ **IRIX:** IRIX is the Unix variant used on SGI (formerly Silicon Graphics International) hardware, which uses the MIPS R*000 series of CPUs. SGI is the most famous of the desktop Unix operating systems because of its popularity and use in special digital effects used in films and TV. While you saw in Chapter 1, "Introducing Solaris," that Sun machines running Solaris were used to render films like *Toy Story* and *A Bug's Life*, the donkey work of drawing and creating the movements of an animation is handled by SGI machines running IRIX.

The SGI equipment is exceptionally fast at creating complex 3D and 2D graphic elements and its high-end workstations and servers are capable of making changes to video and even generating 3D realizations in real time. If you've watched a documentary recently, you'll have seen the reconstructions of pyramids and worlds, and just about every film produced in the last five years, from *The Mummy* to *Monsters, Inc.*, has used SGI equipment in the process.

The Unix advantage here over other platforms is its ability to work with large volumes of data with relative ease. It's possible to have a Unix workstation based on SGI, Sun, or HP kit with GBs of memory. That memory is needed to hold a sequence of film instantly available instead of constantly swapping with the disk. In the case of computer animated films like *Monsters, Inc.*, that same memory is used to hold the information required to generate each frame of video before it's written to disk.

♦ **UNIXWare:** This was the first real x86-specific Unix that was heavily promoted as a commercial possibility. It is distributed by SCO, although previous owners include Novell and Unix System Laboratories. It's still available now, although it's lost a significant share of its market to Linux and FreeBSD.

♦ **XENIX:** It's unlikely that you'll [TE Comment: missing word(s)? RB] anything recent about this. It was Microsoft's attempt to muscle in on the Unix market designed for use on Intel machines. The problem was that at the time Intel machines were not really powerful enough to make Unix on Intel an alternative to the "big iron" available from Sun, IBM, and Digital. Microsoft soon realized it couldn't really make money from the venture and switched its attention to Windows—and we all know the history there.

Solaris Interoperability

Although all of the operating systems above have their differences from the Solaris platform, it doesn't mean that Solaris, or indeed any Unix, sits entirely on its own.

The majority of services and systems are now provided by a server on a network using the TCP/IP protocol. You can share files, view websites, and send/receive email through TCP/IP, among many other things, and Unix was handling TCP/IP before either Mac OS or Windows were a twinkle in their prospective developer's eyes.

Windows machines use their own file-sharing protocols for sharing files with each other, but any Unix machine is capable of sharing its files using the same protocol. Samba, a freely available solution, can share any Unix drive with a Windows client. The latest versions will even act as the equivalent of a Windows NT or Windows 2000 server, providing authentication for the entire network from a single machine—or multiple machines using the standard NIS/NIS+ system.

Macs also use their own file-sharing format, but Unix machines can talk AppleShare and Apple File Protocol (AFP) just as easily using the NetAt package, another freely available application.

For more serious applications, Sun provides a Windows migration kit and a complete set of tools to help you move and migrate your clients from using Windows NT/2000 servers to using Unix servers instead.

These lines of interoperability will be blurred even further as time goes on. Data sharing and communication are being standardized through systems like XML and SOAP, and web serving and deployment are already supported cross platform with or without standards like WebDAV.

The Least You Need to Know

- Solaris and Windows are more alike than people realize, and it's possible through products like StarOffice to use Solaris as a desktop alternative to Windows machines.
- Solaris and Mac OS are very different, as Mac OS does not have a command line, but Mac OS X and Solaris are closer alternatives.
- Solaris and other Unix variants are roughly similar, as any Unix is based around the same basic design principles, security model, and commands.
- Solaris can be made to interoperate with Windows, Mac OS, and other Unix machines through as series of applications like StarOffice, NetAt, and Samba.

Preparing for Installation

In This Chapter

◆ Verifying your hardware environment

◆ Verifying disk space

◆ Preparing network information

It's no good leaping into an installation before thinking about exactly how you are going to set the machine beforehand. Although Solaris is almost as easy to install as Windows or Mac OS, it does require a little bit more planning up front. I know it's tempting to rip the cellophane off those disks and start plugging away. However, the planning and preparation you do now will save you time both during the installation and after the installation has completed.

There are two basic considerations. First, you must make sure that you can run Solaris before you try the installation and fail. Second, you need to think about how you want to organize your disks and how to integrate your machine into your network (if you have one).

In this chapter, I'll introduce these issues, including some background on how Solaris, disks, memory, and networking slot together.

Supported Hardware

The first thing you should do is ensure that your machine is actually capable of running Solaris in the first place. Solaris supports two basic computer systems—those based on the *SPARC* chip, which include all the machines available from Sun themselves, and an Intel (or x86) version which runs on most Pentium-based IBM compatible PCs. With some exceptions and caveats, any PC capable of running Windows is also capable of running Solaris.

Solingo

Scalable Processor Architecture (SPARC)—it's basically a range of processors similar to Intel's x86 range (which includes everything from the humble 8086 to the most recent Pentium 4) and the PowerPC chip used in the Apple Mac series of machines. SPARC is actually a group of interested organizations who agree and develop the SPARC standard and includes Sun Microsystems and Fujitsu to name but a few.

SPARC Platforms

It's actually easier to say which systems from Sun are not supported rather than listing all of those that are. In essence, Solaris 8 and 9 both support any Sun platform based on either the SuperSPARC and HyperSPARC CPU (sun4m) or UltraSPARC (sun4u) architectures—the old sun4c architecture is not supported. That explicitly excludes the following machines:

- ◆ 600MP systems
- ◆ SPARCstation Voyager
- ◆ SPARCstation 1/1+2/IPC/IPX/ELC/SLC

That means that at the very low end you will need a SPARCclassic or a SPARCstation 4, 5, 10, or 20. Or for a slightly better experience, use one of the machines based on an UltraSPARC processor, such as an Ultra 1 or 2 or any of the Enterprise machines, right up to and including the top-of-the-range Sun Fire 15K server.

In the new workstation range, the new Ultra 5, 10, 30, and 60 workstations, or the even-better Sun Blade 100 workstation, are also good alternatives. The new range of Ultra workstations is based on the same PCI architecture used by PCs and also uses similar IDE disks and other low-end components to make owning such a machine relatively inexpensive. The price of a Sun Blade 100 workstation is about the same as the cost of a high-end PC, although in raw performance there is probably not a lot of difference between the two platforms.

A Postcard From ...

It may seem strange—especially if you come from the PC world—to consider running Solaris on machines like the SPARCclassic, which has a CPU speed of less than 100MHz. In fact, even the top-of-the-range UltraSPARC processors have not made the 1GHz barrier, broken by PCs some time ago.

In reality, the SPARC range of processors is significantly more powerful than the Intel range of processors, MHz for MHz, and the motherboard and other design considerations that go into a SPARC-based machine make it significantly faster than a GHz PC for raw processing tasks.

In all other respects, any device which you will find fitted as standard to a SPARC machine is supported automatically by Solaris—there would be no reason for Sun not to support an element of their own hardware within their own operating system!

Third party devices will generally require a separate driver of some kind—but you shouldn't need to make use of this until after you have installed the system in the first place.

Intel Platforms

Specifying which machines are supported on the Intel platform is of course significantly more difficult. The Sun servers are a fairly small collection of machines developed by just one company. The modern PC has different motherboards, processors (if you include Intel, AMD, and other Intel compatibles), and other core components such as graphics cards, SCSI and IDE interfaces, and more.

Sun Screen _____

As mentioned elsewhere in this book, Solaris 9 Intel was dropped by Sun early in January 2002, not long after the first, relatively stable, early-access beta for the platform had been released. Solaris 8 still works and is available for the Intel platform (in fact, I use it on my own network and have for about 18 months now). The guidelines given here should apply to either Solaris 8 or 9 for Intel, whether or not Solaris 9 is ever fully released.

Although Sun has tried very hard to support as wide a range of platforms as possible, it's impossible to explicitly say whether your system will be 100 percent compatible. To help you make that decision, you *must* check out the Sun Hardware Compatibility List (HCL), which you can find at the Sun Solaris web page (http://www.sun.com/solaris).

If you are using a mainstream motherboard from one of the major manufacturers, including EpoX, Abit, Microstar, Asus, and others, or you are using an Original Equipment Manufacturer (OEM) machine provided by a company such as Dell, Compaq, Hewlett-Packard, or IBM, then it's highly likely that your machine will support Solaris. Solaris is also able to support multi-processor boards from most of these manufacturers.

For other components of your system, use the following rough guide:

- **Graphics cards:** Most of the popular graphics cards are supported, including those from ATI, NVidia, Matrox, Hercules, and others, including variations of the core chipsets (for example, the NVidia TNT2 chipset is used in a number of cards from many different manufacturers—Solaris supports the chipset, not the card).

- **Monitors:** Any *multisync monitor* should work fine, and fixed rate monitors should work okay, provided your graphics card supports the resolution offered by your monitor.

Solingo

A **multisync monitor** is one that can adjust to different horizontal and vertical frequencies in order to run at different resolutions. Most modern monitors are multisync, because they suit and work with more machines that way. Older monitors (anything older than about five years) may be fixed sync, meaning that they work either at a single resolution, or at a very reduced range of resolutions and refresh rates.

Solingo

Small Computer Systems Interconnect (SCSI), is a connection standard that allows multiple devices—hard disks, CD-ROM drives, scanners, and so on—to be connected to a single machine over a single cable. Similar to USB, although SCSI supports faster transfer rates, and Firewire (IEEE1394/i.Link), SCSI is still the interconnect standard of choice for high-speed, high-availability machines.

- **Mice:** Most PS/2 and serial mice should work, although be warned that the advanced features such as scroll wheels and additional buttons (beyond the standard two) offered by mice such as the Microsoft Intellimouse or the Logitech Wheelmouse will not be supported.

- **SCSI adaptors:** The main SCSI, SCSI-2, Fast SCSI, and SCSI-3 solutions from Adaptec, Compaq, DPT, Intel, and QLogic are supported natively. You may need drivers for some models of SCSI-3 adaptors, particularly the 39160 from Adaptec.

- **Network adaptors:** The more popular makes and chipsets from 3Com, Compaq, DEC, D-Link, Hewlett-Packard, Intel, Kingston, Linksys, and SMC are supported natively at both 10Mbit and 100Mbit speeds. For Gigabit models, support may be provided natively, but check the HCL.

If you are in any doubt at all, check the HCL for more details, and even if that doesn't include your precise configuration, you may find that your machine is still supported. If it's any consolation in this respect, my motherboard is not officially supported according to the HCL, but has been running Solaris 8 for 18 months without one single failure in that time!

Getting Ready to Install Solaris

Before you insert the CDs and start the installation process you will need to determine two basic pieces of information:

♦ Disk layout/allocation

♦ Network preferences

The former is required because you need to install the operating system into specific locations on the disk, and you also have to set up an area of swap space. Before you can make those calculations to decide how to organize your disks, you need to understand the Unix file system and swap space.

A Unix File System Backgrounder

The big difference between any Unix, including Solaris, and just about every other platform that you've ever used is that Unix does not have a concept of volumes or disks as such. In Windows you can guarantee that drive A: will be a floppy disk, and drive B:, if present, will be a second floppy disk. Drive C: will be a hard disk and drive D: may be another hard disk or a CD-ROM. In each case, you treat a different physical disk (ignoring partitions) as an individual device. If you want to copy something from the floppy to the hard drive then you know that you have to copy from A: to C:.

Solingo _____

Although you may not know it, hard disks (and indeed CD-ROMs) can be split into a number of different sections. Each section can be of literally any size and each partition can be formatted independently of all the others.

All disks have at least one partition, but you can have up to 8 partitions on a disk (more under Mac OS, although more than 8 is considered excessive!). Under Windows these partitions appear as different drive letters, and under Mac OS they all appear as different, independent volumes, even though technically they may exist on the same physical disk.

Under Mac OS you have a different volume for each disk (or partition) and you can copy files between the different volumes by dragging and dropping. Unlike Windows, there are no fixed locations. If you insert a floppy disk or CD-ROM then it just appears on the desktop as another volume. Without explicitly checking, it's sometimes difficult to specifically identify which volume is on which device. You could have booted up from any of the available partitions and you have no easily identifiable way of determining exactly which disk holds the operating system you are currently using—there is no equivalent to C:.

Under Unix, although you still have partitions, and you still will have the ability to support different disks and use CD-ROMs, floppies, and other removable media, they do not appear as separate volumes or disks to the user. Instead, all disks in Unix are *mounted* within the file system.

What do I mean by that?

Well, there is a *root* file system which generally contains the operating system and vital files required to get Solaris running. Any additional partitions are *mounted* within that file system. Here, mounted means associated, and in each case a partition or disk is associated with a directory within the root file system.

Although there is no specific requirement to split your file system across multiple partitions or even multiple disks, it does make sense when you appreciate that a failure on one file system could bring your machine down—if that one file system is your only file system, you've got a problem!

Table 3.1 lists the main file systems and their contents. You don't need separate partitions for every single one of these file systems, but it's good practice to put at least /, */usr*, and */home* onto different partitions.

Table 3.1   Standard File System Allocations

File system	Description
/ (root)	The top of the hierarchy. You cannot run a Solaris machine without this! It contains all the mount points for all the other file systems and also contains the kernel, driver files, devices, and configuration information required to get the machine running. It also holds the core commands required to administer a system.
/usr	Most of the user commands—that is, those not required to get a system running—reside on this file system, and it's usually the installation point for additional applications and extensions such as the X Windows system and Java.
/home	The location of the directories used for each user. Depending on the number of users and what they do, you might keep this small or relatively large. If you are sharing the user information, it might be placed at /export/home to indicate that it's an exported (shared) file system.

File system	Description
/var	The location of system files that change or grow. This includes log files, printer jobs, and email.
/opt	Third party software and applications such as Oracle or Netscape.
/usr/local	The default install location used by free software projects such as Perl, Python, and anything from the GNU project.

For example, if you ask *df* to give you a report of the disk space on our newly installed Solaris machine you'll end up with something like this:

```
$ df -k
Filesystem            kbytes    used    avail capacity  Mounted on
/dev/dsk/c0d0s0       246463   34444   187373   16%    /
/dev/dsk/c0d0s6      1785654  476566  1255519   28%    /usr
/proc                      0       0        0    0%    /proc
mnttab                     0       0        0    0%    /etc/mnttab
fd                         0       0        0    0%    /dev/fd
/dev/dsk/c0d0s3       246463   27371   194446   13%    /var
swap                  600800      16   600784    1%    /var/run
/dev/dsk/c0d0s5       458087      15   412264    1%    /opt
swap                  600784       0   600784    0%    /tmp
/dev/dsk/c0d0s7       192423    2001   171180    2%    /export/home
/dev/dsk/c0d0s1       492422  175808   267372   40%    /usr/openwin
```

The root file system is identified as */*; within that file system is a directory called */usr* that is actually the mount point for another file system. When you change or access a file in */usr*, Solaris automatically talks to the drive used at that mount point. These mount points can also be nested, so */var* is a separate file system and */var/run* is another separate file system.

Although this seems confusing, it actually means that you can access the information on any disk just by knowing the path—the collection of directories and an eventual filename—where the file resides. You don't have to worry about the physical disk that it might refer to.

There are other benefits to this system—you can for example redirect a file to a completely different drive without worrying about what its drive letter or volume name might be. You can also upgrade the disk space or replace a faulty drive just by creating or installing a new drive and mounting the drive at exactly the same point—you don't need to worry about giving it the same name or drive letter.

Swap Space

As part of the partitioning process, you will also need to set aside at least one partition on one of your disks (preferably at least one on the same disk as your root file system) for swap space.

In order to provide the maximum amount of physical memory available to running applications, certain applications, including those not currently in use, are swapped out to disk. In order for this process to occur you must have a swap space partition.

Opinion on how much swap space you allocate is somewhat divided. On older systems you needed about twice the amount of space as you had physical RAM because disk space, although still not as cheap as it is today, was still significantly cheaper than physical RAM. Today, the cost of either is quite low—about $300 will get you 1GB RAM, and the same amount will get you a single 160GB hard disk.

Solaris requires a minimum of 512MB of swap space—and it's likely your machine has at least this in physical RAM anyway. If you have more memory than this, you don't have to match swap space with RAM—Solaris no longer requires even the same amount of swap as RAM, let alone double that amount.

Disk Space Calculations

Based on the above information detailing the layout, you now need to decide how to lay out your file systems and partition your disks. Remember that at a minimum you need ...

◆ A root file system.

◆ A */usr* file system.

◆ A */home* or */export/home* file system.

◆ At least 512MB of swap space.

How much space you allocate to each of the above will depend on how many other partitions and file systems you intend to create. For example, if you are using the above scheme and not creating any additional file systems, you'll need a root file system of at least 512MB. If, on the other hand, you plan to create additional file systems for */var* and */opt* in addition to the */usr* and */home* file systems, then you can get away with a root file system of only 256MB, or maybe even just 128MB in size.

The exact allocations will depend entirely on how the machine will be used, how much of the operating system software and information you will be installing, and how you intend to split the file systems up. A full installation of Solaris 9, incorporating every available package and standard extension, will use a total of 2.4GB of space. For a minimum end-user-only installation you will need 1.6GB.

Here are some other nuggets of advice:

◆ Allocate extra space for each additional language you intend to install.

◆ Allocate extra space in */var* if you plan on supporting large print jobs, a high number of smaller print jobs, or email services on your machine.

- Allocate twice the amount of physical RAM on */var* if you are going to use the *savecore* option to store core dumps when your machine crashes (recommended if you are doing device driver or software development).

- Allocate extra space on */home* or */export/home* if you are going to provide user storage areas. If the users never use the machine directly, then you can get away with as little as 4K per user. For students, about 20MB each is fine; for software developers you may need to allocate as much as 1GB per user.

- Allocate extra space in */opt* if you plan on installing third party software. Oracle's database server product requires a minimum of about 450MB to install—that's before you create any databases! StarOffice requires about 150MB.

Finally, the one piece of information which applies to all calculations:

- Take whatever numbers you come up with and increase them by 30 percent, to give you some breathing space and room to grow before urgently needing more space.

I tend to create separate partitions for each of the main file systems listed in Table 3.1; you can see below the allocations I used on a brand new system, running Solaris 9 and fitted with a 4GB drive:

```
$ df -k
Filesystem            kbytes    used    avail capacity  Mounted on
/dev/dsk/c0d0s0       246463   34444   187373    16%    /
/dev/dsk/c0d0s6      1785654  476566  1255519    28%    /usr
/proc                      0       0        0     0%    /proc
mnttab                     0       0        0     0%    /etc/mnttab
fd                         0       0        0     0%    /dev/fd
/dev/dsk/c0d0s3       246463   27371   194446    13%    /var
swap                  600800      16   600784     1%    /var/run
/dev/dsk/c0d0s5       458087      15   412264     1%    /opt
swap                  600784       0   600784     0%    /tmp
/dev/dsk/c0d0s7       192423    2001   171180     2%    /export/home
/dev/dsk/c0d0s1       492422  175808   267372    40%    /usr/openwin
```

You can see that I use as little as 34MB (34444KB) on root (*/*) and 480MB (476566KB) on */usr*, although we'd use 660MB if I hadn't created a separate */usr/openwin* partition. The */proc*, */etc/mnttab*, */dev/fd*, */var/run*, and */tmp* file systems are dynamic—either they are created by the kernel at run time, or they are using memory (including swap space) to help improve performance.

During the installation, Solaris will make suggestions about how much space you need on each file system based on what you have elected to install, but it's always a good idea to plan ahead a little bit.

Networking

The final piece of information that you need to know about is your network configuration so that you can set up your machine within an existing network. If you don't have or plan to use a network, then you don't need this information.

If you are planning to use a network—that is, you want to connect your machine to your existing Ethernet network and share resources or allow your new Solaris-based machine to access the Internet through a *router*, then you need to determine the following information, either from your own records or from your system or network administrator:

Solingo

A **router** is a device on your network that routes network packets between your own network and another network—typically the Internet. It could be a box on the wall attached to your cable, Digital Subscriber Line (DSL), ISDN, or leased line (T1, T3, E1), or it could be another machine on your network that provides the functionality.

- **Hostname:** The name used to identify your single machine on the network. You can give your machine any name, as long as it's unique within your own network. You may want to choose a naming scheme, for example naming all your machines after Disney characters or Greek gods.

- **Internet Protocol (IP) address:** The unique dotted-quad number that identifies your machine. A dotted quad is basically four numbers between 0 and 255 separated by a period—for example, 192.168.1.135. If you are installing the machine into an existing network, this number must be within the range of numbers allotted for your network.

- **Subnet mask:** The mask used to locate the machines that belong to your network—for example, 255.255.255.0.

- **Domain name:** The name of the domain to which your machine will belong. For example, mcslp.com or perston.co.uk.

- **Domain Name Service (DNS) server address:** The IP addresses of the machines acting as DNS servers on your network.

If you are planning on using a DHCP server in your network, then the IP address, domain name, DNS server, and subnet mask will be supplied by the DHCP server. You'll have the opportunity to choose how your network information is configured during the installation.

If you are integrating the machine into an existing Unix network and are using NIS to share host, password, and other information, you may also want to collect the server names/IP addresses and domain name for your NIS service.

The Least You Need to Know

◆ Solaris runs on machines based on SPARC or Intel platform.

◆ You must decide how you want to organize your disks. Disks are split into logical partitions, with each space holding a file system. Different file systems have different space requirements.

◆ You must determine how much swap space you want to configure for your machine, and where it will be located.

◆ You must collect the network configuration information if you want to connect your machine to a network of some kind.

Installing Solaris

In This Chapter

◆ An overview of the installation process

◆ Starting the installation

◆ Using the Web Start Wizard

I could make this chapter very short, by saying that the way to install Solaris was to insert the boot CD into the drive on your machine and then follow the onscreen instructions. Provided you've got the information ready that I outlined in the previous chapter—that is the disk space, swap space, and network parameters—you should be able to follow the onscreen instructions.

However, things are never quite that easy, so instead in this chapter I'll walk through the entire installation process, from blank hard disk and empty machine, right through to the moment when you reboot the machine, ready to use it for the very first time.

The Solaris CD Package

You can get hold of Solaris either by ordering a Sun machine and getting the OS supplied with it, by separately ordering the software, or by taking advantage of Sun's Free Solaris program. The latter method allows you to order the CDs required to use Solaris on your machine for the cost of the CDs and the postage and packing.

You'll get a pack of CDs which includes the following:

♦ Installation CD.

♦ Device Configuration Assistant Floppy Disk (Intel versions only).

♦ Solaris Software CDs.

♦ Solaris Documentation CDs.

♦ Languages CD, with customization for a number of languages other than English.

♦ StarOffice productivity suite, Sun's answer to Microsoft Office.

♦ Software Supplement, including additional Sun driver software, applications, and documentation.

♦ Maintenance Update CDs (depending on when you purchased the OS).

♦ Software Companion CD, which includes a number of free software applications.

♦ iPlanet Internet Server applications evaluation, including Web servers, Directory servers, and E-Commerce tools (SPARC only).

♦ Forte Developer CDs, consisting of C, C++, Fortran, and TeamWare management software.

♦ Forte for Java Community Edition CD.

For the basic installation you will need only the Installation CD and Software CDs. For older Intel platforms you will also need the Device Configuration Assistant floppy disk.

Summarizing the Installation Process

The basic installation process for Solaris follows the same basic process as that of just about every other operating system:

1. Boot into the Solaris Operating system.
2. Partition the disk or disks attached to your machine to hold the different file systems.
3. Install a "mini" version of Solaris, which will then be used to boot the machine and run the Web Start Wizard to set up the core settings (networking, date/time, etc.) and then to configure and copy the Solaris packages to the new partitions and file systems.

Additional SPARC Specific Steps

There are no additional steps for a SPARC installation.

Additional Intel Specific Steps

In addition to the basic steps I've outlined above, you'll also need to:

1. Go through the Device Configuration Assistant, which helps the Solaris installer identify the important components of your system—in particular the hard drives, CD-ROM drives, and network cards.

2. Use *fdisk* to allocate the space to be used for the Solaris partitions, and also to set up and install the area that will boot the Solaris boot manager and allow the Solaris OS to start.

3. Use *kdmconfig* to configure the keyboard, display, and mouse to enable you to run the X Windows System.

Booting Up the Installer

Depending on your platform, there are different ways of starting the booting process. The SPARC system assumes that you have inserted the Installation CD into the CD-ROM drive on the machine, and then allows you to boot directly from the CD. The PC may be able to use a CD-ROM or the floppy drive to boot up the system. Once the initial booting process is over, you need to set up a small area for the Web Start Wizard.

I'll cover the exact steps individually for each platform.

SPARC Platforms

Switch on your machine and then drop into the Boot PROM by pressing the L1 and A keys on the keyboard at the same time. You should get an *ok* prompt like this:

```
ok
```

Insert the installation CD into the machine, and then type:

```
boot cdrom
```

Sun Lotion

If your Sun machine is brand new, then it may come with the Web Start Wizard already installed— this is called the JumpStart configuration. If this is the case, you can skip this stage and just switch the machine on and wait for the Web Start Wizard to start.

at the prompt. You should get output which starts with the line:

```
Boot device: /sbus/espdma@e,8400000/esp@e,88000000/sd@6,0:f File and args:
```

The rest of the output shows the operating system starting up, the devices identified in the system being configured, and then the Web Start Wizard installer should start.

If you are asked whether you want to Install or Upgrade, then it means you already have Solaris installed on your machine. If you genuinely want to perform an upgrade, check the Sun documentation for information on how to proceed—at the very least, reboot and back up your system before performing an upgrade.

If you are installing a new machine, you should be prompted to format the disk to set up the swap space required to install the mini-operating system that will do the actual installation. The preamble will look something like this:

```
The default root disk is /dev/dsk/c0t0d0
The Solaris installer needs to format
/dev/dsk/c0t0d0 to install Solaris.
WARNING: ALL INFORMATION ON THE DISK WILL BE ERASED!
Do you want to format /dev/dsk/c0t0d0? [y,n,?,q]
```

Press Y and you will be asked to set the size of the swap slice on the disk—choose a suitable size, as you won't be able to change the size later. The installer will copy across the necessary files into this swap partition and use the partition to boot the disk and start the final stages of the installation process. The easiest way is to select the default option provided by just pressing Return—the installer will have determined a suitable size for you.

Next you'll be asked to confirm the location of the swap space partition. By placing the swap space partition at the start of the disk, it will enable you to use the entire remaining portion of the disk to set up the partitions. If you don't use the start of the disk, you will be limiting the size of one of your partitions. Press Y and Return to accept the default.

Finally, you'll be asked to confirm that you want to format the disk, creating the swap partition at the start. Press Y and Return to accept this option and then wait while the installer copies across the files and then reboots and resets your system.

Your machine should boot up again using the new partition as the source and then start the Web Start Wizard.

Sun Lotion

You may need to change the parameters in your computer's BIOS to get your machine to boot from the CD-ROM instead of the hard disk. Check the manuals that came with your machine, or watch the machine as it starts up—it should tell you how to get into the BIOS.

Intel Platforms

There are two ways of starting the installer and installation process under Intel platforms, and which you use depends entirely on the age and abilities of your motherboard. If your machine supports booting from CD-ROM (most late-1997/1998 motherboards do), then insert the Solaris Installation, Intel Platform Edition CD into your CD-ROM drive. Switch on your machine and wait while the machine attempts to boot from the CD-ROM drive.

If the machine fails to boot up from CD-ROM, use the Solaris 8 Device Configuration Assistant floppy instead. Insert the floppy into the disk drive and reset the machine.

The first screen you should see once the machine has finished reading from the CD or the floppy is the Solaris Device Configuration Assistant; you can see a sample screen image in Figure 4.1.

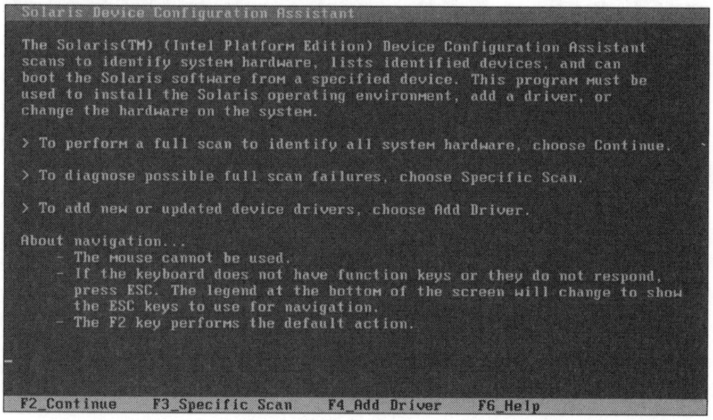

Figure 4.1

The first stage to installing Solaris on your machine.

Press F2 to continue and allow the assistant to search your machine for devices—what it's doing is looking for IDE and SCSI devices on which it can later install the operating system. Once it's finished searching for all the possible devices, you should get the screen shown in Figure 4.2, which shows a summary of the devices that have been found. If you need to you can insert additional floppy disks with Solaris device drivers to add special devices not supported by the device assistant. You only need to do this if the disk you want to install the OS onto is on a device not supported by Solaris by default.

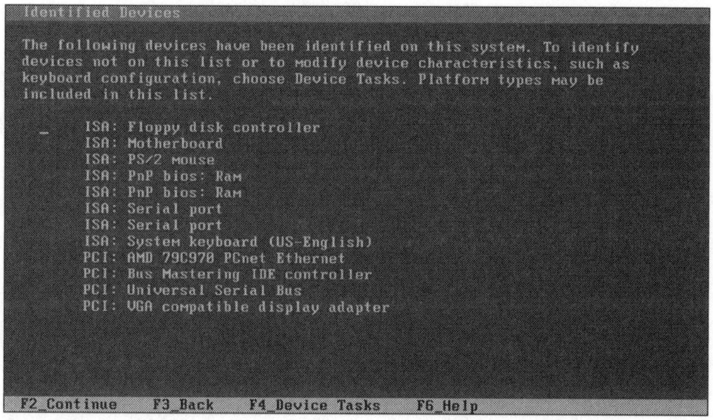

Figure 4.2

Ensuring the device list is correct.

Press F2 to continue the installation—you'll be asked to choose the location of the Solaris installer. You can install either from a physical hard disk that contains the software, over the network (if a server has been configured accordingly), or from CD-ROM. You can see the Boot Solaris screen in Figure 4.3.

Figure 4.3

Getting ready to boot Solaris.

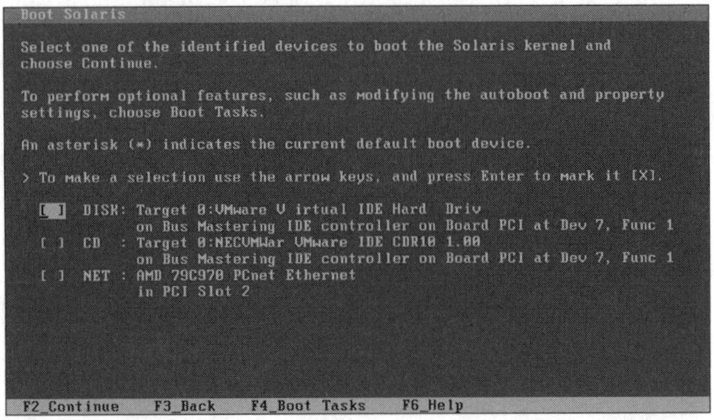

```
 Boot Solaris

 Select one of the identified devices to boot the Solaris kernel and
 choose Continue.

 To perform optional features, such as modifying the autoboot and property
 settings, choose Boot Tasks.

 An asterisk (*) indicates the current default boot device.

 > To make a selection use the arrow keys, and press Enter to mark it [X].

    [*]  DISK: Target 0:VMware Virtual IDE Hard  Driv
               on Bus Mastering IDE controller on Board PCI at Dev 7, Func 1
    [ ]  CD  : Target 0:NECVMWar VMware IDE CDR10 1.00
               on Bus Mastering IDE controller on Board PCI at Dev 7, Func 1
    [ ]  NET : AMD 79C970 PCnet Ethernet
               in PCI Slot 2




    F2_Continue    F3_Back    F4_Boot Tasks    F6_Help
```

Use the cursor keys to choose the install source (CD) and press Space to select it, then press F2 to start booting the operating system for the first time. You should be presented with the Boot Parameter screen.

Your machine should automatically start the Web Start Installation, which is responsible for setting up the default parameters of the machine, including formatting the hard disk. The first stage is to configure the devices on the system used by Solaris to refer to the different drives and hardware on your machine. This process may take some time, but you should get a "rotating" bar on the screen to show you that Solaris is still doing something.

Once the system has booted up, the first question it will ask is the language that you want to use for the installation process. Choose the language you want from the list by typing in the number and pressing Return. You will be asked to create a swap partition using *fdisk* which will be used to hold the Solaris installers. See Figure 4.4 for an example.

Figure 4.4

Using fdisk *to create a default partition on which to install the miniroot OS.*

```
 The Solaris Installer can be run in English, or any of the following languages:

   1) English                    6) Japanese
   2) German                     7) Korean
   3) Spanish                    8) Swedish
   4) French                     9) Simplified_Chinese
   5) Italian                   10) Traditional_Chinese
 Select the language you want to use to run the installer: 1
 English has been selected as the language in which to perform the install.
 Starting the Web Start 3.0 Solaris installer
 /
 Solaris installer is searching the system's hard disks for a
 location to place the Solaris installer software.

 No suitable Solaris fdisk partition was found.

 Solaris Installer needs to create a Solaris fdisk partition on your root disk,
 c0d0, that is at least 393 MB.

 WARNING: IF YOU CHANGE EXISTING FDISK PARTITION'S SIZE, ALL INFORMATION ON THE
 PARTITION WILL BE ERASED!

 May the Solaris Installer create a Solaris fdisk [y,n,?] _
```

Answer Y to the question regarding using *fdisk* on your main drive to create a temporary partition for the installer. If the disk is brand new, the system will ask you if it can create a "100% SOLARIS System partition"—this will allocate your entire disk for use by your system. Press Y and Return to use this option. If you press N you will be able to manually edit the partition table.

You will now be asked to set the size of the swap space partition for the machine. Press Return to accept the default size the system has selected—you can add more later if you need to. Now you will be asked to confirm that you want the swap space to be put as the first slice on the disk. This is vital, as it will allow you a free hand to partition the rest of the disk how you like.

As you can see from Figure 4.5, I've answered yes and selected the default size, and I'm now ready to go ahead and set up the disk.

```
Type "y" to accept the default partition, otherwise type "n" to edit the
partition table.
y
NOTE: The swap size cannot be changed during filesystem layout.

Enter a swap slice size between 382MB and 4080MB, default = 512MB [?]

The Installer prefers that the swap slice is at the beginning of the
disk. This will allow the most flexible filesystem partitioning later in the
installation.

Can the swap slice start at the beginning of the disk  [y,n,?,q] y

You have selected the following to be used by the Solaris installer:

        Disk Slice  : /dev/dsk/c0d0
        Size        : 512 MB
        Start Cyl.  : 3

WARNING: ALL INFORMATION ON THE DISK WILL BE ERASED!

Is this OK  [y,n,?,q] _
```

Figure 4.5

Selecting the default size and partitioning parameters.

Now you must wait while the installer copies across the files into this swap partition and prepares your system to be started from this partition to continue the installation process. When you see the screen in Figure 4.6, remove the CD and floppy disk from the machine and press Return to reset the machine and boot off the new temporary installation on the hard disk.

During the reboot, the machine will prompt you to select the operating system and partition to boot from (as shown in Figure 4.7). Just press Return or leave the counter to time out and let the machine boot up normally.

Once the system has finished booting, you will be placed in the Solaris Installation Program, the last part of the process before the Web Start Wizard is started. See Figure 4.8 for a sample.

Figure 4.6

Getting ready to boot the Miniroot Web Start Wizard Installer.

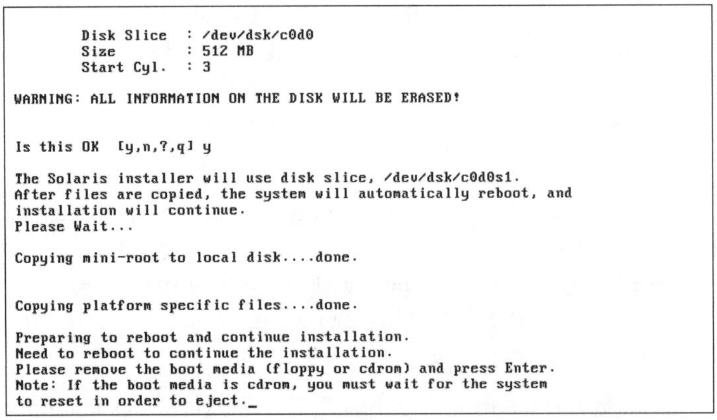

```
    Disk Slice  : /dev/dsk/c0d0
    Size        : 512 MB
    Start Cyl.  : 3

WARNING: ALL INFORMATION ON THE DISK WILL BE ERASED!


Is this OK  [y,n,?,q] y

The Solaris installer will use disk slice, /dev/dsk/c0d0s1.
After files are copied, the system will automatically reboot, and
installation will continue.
Please Wait...

Copying mini-root to local disk....done.


Copying platform specific files....done.

Preparing to reboot and continue installation.
Need to reboot to continue the installation.
Please remove the boot media (floppy or cdrom) and press Enter.
Note: If the boot media is cdrom, you must wait for the system
to reset in order to eject._
```

Figure 4.7

Booting up from the Miniroot Web Start Wizard.

```
SunOS - Intel Platform Edition              Primary Boot Subsystem, vsn 2.0



                    Current Disk Partition Information

        Part#   Status   Type      Start      Length
        ===============================================
          1     Active   X86 BOOT   1000       20400
          2              SOLARIS    22496      8366000
          3              <unused>
          4              <unused>



            Please select the partition you wish to boot:  _




6
```

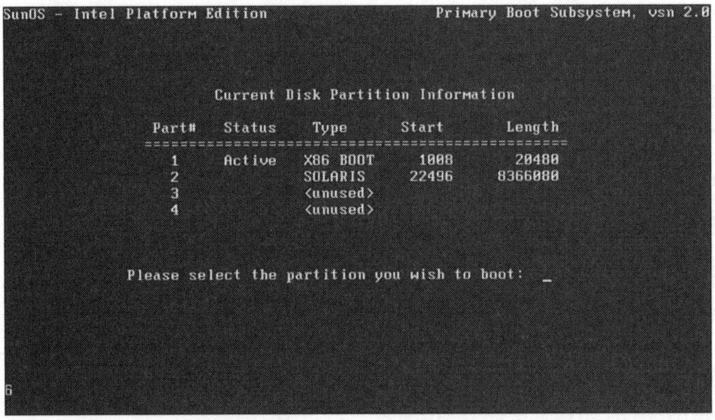

Figure 4.8

The Solaris Installation Program.

```
The Solaris Installation Program

You are now interacting with the Solaris installation program.  The
program is divided into a series of short sections.  At the end of each
section, you will see a summary of the choices you've made, and be given
the opportunity to make changes.

As you work with the program, you will complete one or more of the
following tasks:

    1 - Identify peripheral devices
    2 - Identify your system
    3 - Install Solaris software

About navigation...

    - The mouse cannot be used

    - If your keyboard does not have function keys, or they do not respond,
      press ESC; the legend at the bottom of the screen will change to show
      the ESC keys to use for navigation.



    F2_Continue    F6_Help
```

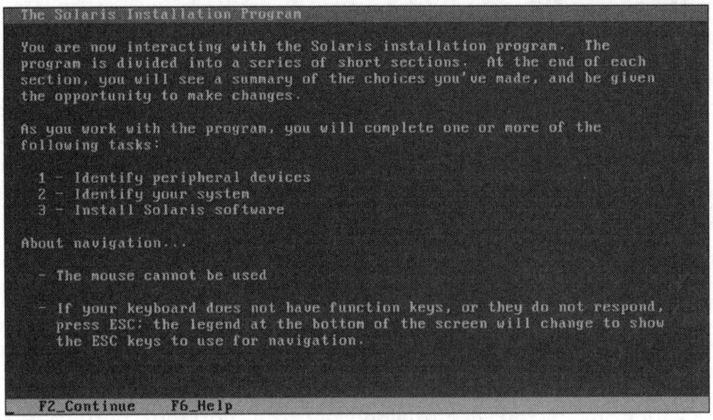

Press F2 to proceed to the next stage. The next stage of the process is to configure the keyboard, display, and mouse using the *kdmconfig* tool. The system will have tried to configure these automatically, but press F2 to confirm that the settings are correct for your machine. If they are not, use the cursor keys and space bar to select the option—Keyboard, Pointing Device (mouse), or Video Device/Monitor—that you want to modify, and then choose the correct device for your configuration.

For the Video Device/Monitor you will first be asked to select the video card, then the monitor, its physical size, and the display resolution to use. Choose the setting that most closely resembles your configuration. If in doubt, pick the Standard VGA display adaptor and the Super VGA 35.5 kHz monitor.

Once you've set the parameters, press F2 to test the settings. Assuming everything has worked okay, you should get a display like the one shown here in Figure 4.9.

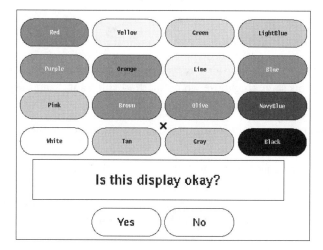

Figure 4.9

The X Windows Test screen.

Use the mouse to click on the Yes button. If things did not work, go back and check the configuration again. If everything was okay, the installation should continue, and the system identification process should start.

The Final Install Process

The penultimate part of the installation process requires you to set the basic parameters of the machine, such as its IP address and date and time. The final part is the actual selection of the packages that you want to install.

Network

The very first question you will be asked is whether you want the machine networked or not. If you answer no at this point, you will still be prompted for a hostname, which will be used by the machine to identify itself.

If you answer yes, you will be asked if you want to configure your machine using DHCP (Dynamic Host Configuration Protocol). DHCP is an automatic system that dishes out IP addresses on your network. You must have a DHCP server for this to work.

If you do not select DHCP, you will be asked to enter the hostname, the machine's IP address and the subnet mask.

Next you will be asked if you want to enable IPv6. IPv6 is a new version of the existing Internet Protocol system that gets over the current limitations in terms of IP addresses and security. Using IPv6 will affect your ability to communicate with existing devices using TCP/IP; as IPv6 is not yet the standard, you may want to continue using the standard TCP/IP system.

Name Service

Solaris can use a number of methods to determine and identify the other machines on the network. You will be asked at this stage to choose which method you want, from one of the following available choices:

- ◆ **None:** Use this if you do not know the answer, or do not want to set up the naming system at this stage.
- ◆ **DNS:** Use this option if your machine is connected to the Internet. The Domain Name System is the one used on the Internet to resolve names into IP addresses. You will be asked to enter your Internet domain name and the IP addresses of the servers you want to ask for DNS information. Ask your administrator for the details if you need them.
- ◆ **NIS/NIS+:** Use this option if you are installing a machine into an existing Unix or Solaris environment where you are sharing host, user, and group information between machines.

If you do not have the information at hand for any of these choices, don't worry; choose None and then use the chapters in Part 3, "Networking," to configure your machine once the software has been installed.

Date and Time

You need to set the time zone and the date and time on your machine. You can set the time zone either by specifying your location (the easiest method) or by specifying the offset (the number of hours ahead or behind) Greenwich Mean Time. If you choose the geographical method then the machine will also automatically adjust the time if your country employs Daylight Savings Time, European Summer Time, British Summer Time, or any other twice-yearly adjustment.

You will also need to enter the date and time. The default date and time will have been taken by the internal clock fitted to all machines. If your machine is new, or has been off for a long time, you will probably have to adjust this figure.

Root Password

The next stage is to ask you for your root password. The root user is the superuser or administrator of the machine and has access and permissions to absolutely anything on a machine. Primarily, of course, this is a good thing. You need those permissions to be able to add and edit disks, add new users, and start and stop services. On the other hand, it wouldn't be a good idea for somebody else to have the password, otherwise they would have unlimited access to your machine.

It's important to choose a root password that you will, for the moment, remember easily—if you forget the root password that you enter during installation, you will be unable to log in at all!

I find it more convenient to use an easy-to-remember password here until I've got the system up and running, when I can then change the root password to something more secure. Whatever you use at this stage, don't write it down, in case someone finds it and then changes the root password before you, locking you out of the system.

Power Management

You may be asked if you want to enable power management for your machine. If the machine is a desktop machine and is not going to provide services and facilities to other computers on your network, then enabling power management is a good idea. When power management is enabled the machine can put itself or the monitor to sleep when it's identified they are not being used, and it can switch itself off altogether when left running idle for a long period of time.

On a server, of course, you wouldn't want it to switch itself off, otherwise it would turn itself off when not being used overnight, rendering it unavailable when people need to use it the next day. If the machine you are installing is going to be a server, do not enable power management.

Confirmation

You will be asked to confirm the configuration parameters that you have just entered for the system. If they are correct, press Y and Return, otherwise, press N and go back and change the parameters before continuing.

When prompted, press Return to start the Solaris Web Start application to configure your applications. Follow the on screen prompts to enter the first CD.

Solaris Web Start

Solaris Web Start is the easiest method available for installing the necessary packages and files onto your machine. There are other methods, including using a standard configuration disk—which allows you to install the same set of packages onto a number of machines—and an interactive mode that requires you select the individual packages that you want to install.

The Web Start Wizard makes the process much easier by providing a number of "standard" collections:

- ◆ **End User** includes all the basic files and operating system components required to run Solaris, X Windows, and CDE and the core command line tools. This collection requires about 1.6GB.

- ◆ **Developer** includes everything in End User plus the additional headers and libraries required for developing software. This collection doesn't include a C/C++ compiler—use the Forte disks to install suitable compilers. You'll need about 1.9GB for this installation.

- ◆ **Entire Distribution** includes everything on both software CDs. There are in fact two setups, one includes only the drivers required for your machine, and the other includes all the drivers supported by Sun. These two collections require 2.3GB and 2.4GB respectively.

To select the packages that you want to install, follow the on-screen prompts which will guide you through the selection process. You'll be prompted to insert the second software CD, and any additional CDs such as the AnswerBook to install additional packages onto your machine.

If you choose to perform a custom installation, you will also be asked to configure the partitions that you planned based on the information in Chapter 3, "Preparing for Installation."

The Long Wait

Once the system has decided what it needs to install, you will just have to leave the machine to go through its motions of copying the files over to the new file system.

Once it's finished, you will be asked to remove any media, and then reboot the system. When the machine comes up again, turn to Chapter 5, "Post-Installation Tips," to see how to continue.

The Least You Need to Know

◆ Installation takes place in two stages, a "miniroot" installation to get the base operating system and installer on the disk, and secondary Web Start installation which performs the actual configuration and installation.

◆ The SPARC installation should be relatively painless, as Solaris already knows how to deal with the hardware.

◆ Intel installations use additional steps to identify the hardware and configure the devices and display system on the machine.

Post-Installation Tips

In This Chapter

- ◆ A word about logins
- ◆ A quick system tour for users
- ◆ A quick system tour for administrators

So far I've concentrated only on getting the software installed onto the machine and getting the machine into the state where you can actually start using it. Hopefully, if you've been following the book from the beginning, you'll already be in a state where you need to get started and actually doing some work.

If you followed the advice in the intro and are a user of the Solaris operating system, then you should have skipped the earlier chapters and started with this one—in which case, skip right on to the sections "A Quick Tour of the System (for Users)," and "A Quick Tour of the System (for Administrators)."

If you've followed the earlier chapters and performed an installation, then you are an administrator and you therefore need to read the whole of this chapter, first to understand the basics of the operating system, and then to understand the major components of the system with respect to administration and management.

Log In? What Do You Mean, Log In?

The first time you switch your machine on or sit in front of a machine running Solaris you will be asked to *log in*. Your login is a combination of a user name and a password, and you should have been given this information by your systems administrator (that's you, if you've just installed the system!).

The user name will generally be between 6 and 8 characters, although it can be shorter. It's probably made up of your first and last names, usually the first letter of one and the full portion of the other—that is mbrown or martinb or even brownm. Your login is case dependent, but it's best to enter your user name in lower case.

Solingo

When you log, or register, yourself into the computer to start using it, you **log in**. When you disconnect from the machine, you *log out*. Just think of yourself as clocking in or out of a factory.

Your password on the other hand is case sensitive, so make sure you enter your password exactly as you were given it. You may well be asked to enter a new password the first time you log in—if this is the case, enter a new password and when prompted enter the password again. By entering the password twice the system verifies that you really did want to type the password and can type it the same way twice.

If you are not asked to enter a new password the first time you log in, your first job should be to change your password to something you can remember. To do this, type *passwd* at a command prompt:

```
$ passwd
```

If you were presented with a graphical login screen, then log in with your user name and password, and when prompted select Common Desktop Environment (CDE) as your desired environment. You should be presented with a screen looking like Figure 5.1.

You will need to open a terminal window to get a shell prompt and use *passwd* to change your password. To do this:

1. Right click (that is, use the right, rather than left, mouse button) on the desktop.

2. Choose Tools from the menu that appears.

3. Within the sub menu, choose Terminal.

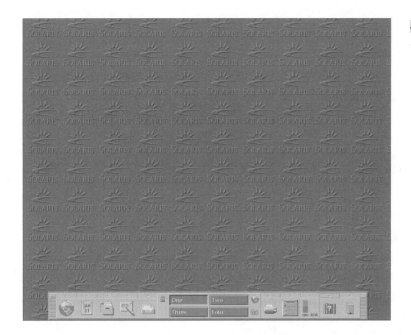

Figure 5.1
The CDE desktop.

A Quick Tour of the System (for Users)

As a user, most of your interaction with the system will be through the shell or a windowing system called CDE. In order to help you understand how to use a Unix machine, you need to understand some of the basics, including finding out who you are, where you are, and how you can find out more information about the system you are using.

The Shell

If you've logged in to the console or over a network and have been presented with a text interface, then you will have been placed into a shell. I won't go into the technicalities here, but the shell is just the way you communicate with the machine and give it commands and run other applications.

To run a command at the shell, type in the command at the prompt. For example, you can get a list of files using the *ls* command:

```
$ ls
```

Press Return when you have finished entering the command, the command will execute. Simple!

XWindows

If you were presented with a graphical login screen, then you are using a machine running X Windows. X Windows is a Graphical User Interface (GUI) providing a similar sort of interface to that provided by Windows or Mac OS.

I won't go into the details here—X Windows provides much the same functionality as that offered by other GUIs on other operating systems and is a generally simple way of accessing and using the system. You'll be looking at X Windows and the environments available for it (CDE and Gnome) in more detail in Chapter 16, "Using CDE."

Logging Out

To log out of a machine—something you should do if you are not going to use the machine for some time, especially if you are using a public machine—you just need to terminate the shell or X Windows system.

To log out of a text interface, where all you have is a shell, just type *exit* at the prompt:

```
$ exit
```

You should be disconnected, and if you are on a console or terminal the *login*: prompt should reappear, waiting for the next person.

If you are using CDE, click the Exit button on the navigation panel at the bottom of the screen.

Who, What, Where?

First of all, now that you've logged in, it's time to find out who you are, what machine you are using, and where you are. Along the way, you'll be looking at some of the major elements of the Solaris operating system and covering some of the basics that you need to understand before going any further.

First of all, let's see who you are by typing *who am i* at the command line:

```
$ who am i
mc          pts/6      Jan 30 14:26    (:0.0)
```

In this case, you're logged in using X Windows/CDE and you typed this into a terminal window. The first item on that line is your login, "mc." The next item is the terminal you're using; the *pts* is a series of pseudo terminals used to communicate with terminals in X Windows. The 6 tells you that you're using the sixth pseudo terminal device. The date given is the date at which you logged on, or in this case, the date you started the terminal. The last item, in parentheses, is your location. If you'd logged in remotely over *telnet*, this would include the hostname of the machine you had connected from. In this case, it's ":0.0", which refers to the address of the device being used for my X Windows session—":0.0" is the video card built into the machine.

Now let's find out where you are on the system. The *pwd* command prints the current working directory, and assuming you haven't moved, it should tell you the location of our home directory, where you can create files that only you can access:

```
$ pwd
/export/home/mc
```

Now, finally, let's find out the name of the machine you are using and what operating system it's running:

```
$ uname -a
SunOS sol9penguin 5.9 Beta i86pc i386 i86pc
```

The *uname* command gets information about the current system. You can see from the output above that you are using a version of SunOS, the machine is called "sol9penguin," the operating system version is "5.9 Beta" and you are running on the Intel i386 platform.

Online Help

Unix comes with its own built-in manual which is accessed through the *man* command and which works in much the same way as the online help available in Windows or Mac OS. To get full details on how to use a command or the format of a file, just supply the name of the command to man. For example, to get help about the *ls* command you would use:

```
$ man ls
```

The *man* pages are actually split into a number of distinct sections; you can see a list of the different sections in Table 5.1. Because the different sections may contain a *man* page of the same name—for example, section 1 includes

Solingo

Telnet is a protocol used to communicate with a remote machine. Because Unix is a multi-user system, they needed a way in which a remote user could open a shell and access the machine through that shell over the network. That solution is telnet, and you can use telnet to use and administer a machine from any other machine on the network, whether it's another machine running Solaris or one running Windows, Mac OS, or a variety of other platforms.

Solingo

Man pages have nothing to do with calling your computer he or she or any sort of comment on the masculinity of the modern computing environment. A *man* (short for manual) page is just the term used to express the online help for a specific element of the system. You'll be using *man* pages throughout the book to point to more specific and detailed information on a given subject.

information on the command *passwd*, and section 4 contains information about the file format for the */etc/passwd* file. The different pages are referenced directly by specifying the page name and its section number in parentheses. For example, *passwd(1)* refers to the documentation in section 1 and *passwd(4)* to the documentation in section 4.

Table 5.1   Manual Page Sections

Section	Short name	Description
1	User Commands	Describes the commands and utilities available to all users when using Solaris. This includes details on all the different shells, shell commands, applications, developer tools, and third party applications. Each page includes full details on the syntax and usage of the commands, diagnostic information, examples, and cross-references to related commands and pages from other sections.
1M	Administration Commands	Describes all the commands used to manage and administer the machine. Only of any use to system administrators.
2	System Calls	Describes the functions and Application Programming Interface (API) for communicating with the operating system services and systems. Solaris is written in C, and the *man* pages in this section assume you are familiar with C.
3	Library Interfaces	Documents the additional libraries and headers that provide additional functionality to the system. Section 3 is actually further subdivided into a number of subsections, each of which defines a specific set of extensions. For example, 3NSL contains information on the network services and library functions for communicating over a network. For a full list of the different sections see the *intro(3) man* page.
4	File Formats	Documents the different file formats of all the various files used by the system. Primarily this is used to describe the format of configuration files such as */etc/passwd* or */etc/nsswitch.conf*, although it can be used for any file format.

Section	Short name	Description
5	Standards, Environments, and Macros	Describes the miscellaneous subjects, environment information, macro packages (used for some system options and reporting, and configuring certain tools, as well as being used to format and describe the *man* page format), character sets, and other standards.
6	Demos	Describes the demos and games provided free with the Solaris software.
7	Device and Network Interfaces	Documents the different device and network interfaces used on the system, including the definitions and formats of file systems, networking protocols, and other elements.
8	Administration Commands (defunct)	Section 8 used to hold the information on system administration commands. The section is now empty and all documents have been moved to section 1M.
9	DDI and DKI Drivers	Documents the interface for communicating directly with the kernel, particularly when developing a new driver for a piece of hardware.

To access the *man* page from a specific section, use the *-s* command line option to specify which section to use. For example:

```
$ man -s 4 passwd
```

accesses the *passwd* page from section 4.

One final feature of man is that you can search the entire *man* page archive for pages matching a particular string. To do this, use *-k* on the command line. For example, to search for all the pages which might have something to do with *passwd* use:

```
$ man -k passwd
d_passwd        d_passwd (4)      - dial-up password file
getpw           getpw (3c)        - get passwd entry from UID
kpasswd         kpasswd (1)       - change a user's Kerberos password
nispasswd       nispasswd (1)     - change NIS+ password information
nispasswdd      rpc.nispasswdd (1m) - NIS+ password update daemon
passwd          passwd (1)        - change login password and password attributes
passwd          passwd (4)        - password file
pwconv          pwconv (1m)       - installs and updates /etc/shadow with
                                    ➥information from /etc/passwd
rpc.nispasswdd  rpc.nispasswdd (1m) - NIS+ password update daemon
rpc.yppasswdd   rpc.yppasswdd (1m)  - server for modifying NIS password file
```

```
yppasswd       yppasswd (1)      - change your network password in the NIS database
yppasswdd      rpc.yppasswdd (1m) - server for modifying NIS password file
```

The other main location for information is the Solaris AnswerBook. AnswerBook is an online system that allows you to view formatted system documentation through a web browser. To access it, just start the AnswerBook system within CDE or type *answerbook2* into a command tool or xterm window. The big benefit of AnswerBook over the standard *man* pages is that it includes administrator and user guides as well as raw reference information. You can also perform full text searches on the data when looking for a particular item.

Sun Lotion

To enable the keyword search, you need to have run the *catman* command with the *-w* command line option. If you are the system administrator, do this now and then make a note to do it again whenever you install new software. If you are not the administrator, ask your friendly, ever-helpful administrator to do it for you if *man -k* doesn't return any results or produces an error.

Where Next?

If you are not an administrator, skip right on over to Chapter 16 for more information on how to use your machine, start applications, and make use of the shell and other facilities provided by the machine.

If you are an administrator, read on.

A Quick Tour of the System (for Administrators)

If you are the administrator of a system rather than simply a user, then things are slightly more complex. You need to know a bit more about your system, a bit more about how Unix works, and how you can find out this information to make your job as a system administrator somewhat easier.

The role of an administrator is fairly straightforward—your job includes, but is certainly not limited to …

♦ Administering users of the system, creating new users, and ensuring that existing users have access to the resources they need.

♦ Monitoring the system to ensure that the machine is running as efficiently as possible.

♦ Installing and managing applications, and ensuring that the machine is kept up-to-date and patched.

♦ Installing and configuring new devices and systems.

♦ Setting up security systems and ensuring that the security of your machine is not broken.

♦ Ensuring your machine's stability, including providing suitable services and monitoring a system to ensure it's not about to fail.

Although some of these are fairly broad definitions, it's true to say that for most situations the actual administration of a machine will take up a relatively small amount of time. Unix is designed, more or less, as a fit-and-forget operating system. You shouldn't have to spend too much time making sure things are working, and there are automated systems and tools that will make that job even easier.

On the other hand, your responsibilities shouldn't be ignored—fitting and forgetting the system is bound for failure if it later runs out of disk space or a drive fails and you need to replace it.

The Superuser

In order to perform any sort of administration on the machine you must be logged in as the user *root*. The root user is otherwise known as the superuser, and I really mean super user. When you are superuser there is *absolutely nothing you cannot do*.

The superuser is exactly that—it provides you with unlimited and unrestricted access and control over the system. As superuser you can configure users, change the system configuration, access any file on the disk, whether or not you should have permissions to it, start the machine up, shut it down, disconnect people …

Are you getting the idea?

Because the superuser is such a powerful person, and before I go on to talk about how to actually become the superuser, I want to make a few things clear:

- ◆ Do not, *ever*, use superuser as your main login for a system. Even if you are the only user of your machine, create yourself a dummy user that you can use to do 99 percent of your work and keep superuser for systems administration tasks. It only takes one slip of keyboard to completely ruin your system, and your chances of doing this are much higher if you only ever use the root account.

- ◆ Do not, *ever*, leave your machine logged in as root, especially if you walk away from the machine for any period of time. In 30 seconds, someone could use your session to change a user's password, email themselves an important document, or give themselves unlimited access to your machine. Whenever you log in as root, do what you need to do and then log out.

- ◆ Change the root password regularly and be religious about doing so. If someone finds out your root password, it won't matter what other security systems you have in place.

- ◆ Do not, *ever*, forget that while you are root that you can do whatever you want. I mean it. I won't be there to pick up the pieces when you accidentally delete all your files the day before your four-year project is due. The superuser account should be used for administration and nothing else.

CAUTION

Sun Screen

If you haven't already got the gist of what I've been saying in the previous section, the superuser is a dangerous beast and you shouldn't wield that power properly until you know and understand what being superuser really means.

Superuser really does mean super user and there's absolutely nothing that a superuser can't do, from accessing files and systems to deleting files and users. Without concentrating it's possible to completely disable your machine and in the worst cases delete every file on the system before you even noticed that you'd asked the machine to do so.

To actually become superuser, either log in as root when prompted to do so or use the substitute user command *su*. Unless you or the system administrator have configured the machine otherwise, you will only be able to log in as root on the machine's console. To use *su*, just specify *root* on the command line:

```
$ su root
```

Solingo

Ask a lot of system administrators what **su** does and they will probably tell you that it allows you to change to root. While this isn't strictly lying, it's not strictly true either. The *su* command stands for substitute user, and you can use it to change to any other user on the system, providing you know what their password is.

You'll be prompted for the root password. If you don't know what it is, you probably haven't been told it for a reason! If you want, use *su* to log in as root just as if you had logged in on the console using a single hyphen:

```
$ su -
```

or more explicitly:

```
$ su - root
```

Configuration Files

Solaris stores the majority of its configuration information in the */etc* directory. Unix uses standard text files to store most of the information used to configure the system and many of the files have a specific file format that is followed to ensure that the information is easy to read, update, and process by the computer.

For example, the */etc/passwd* file holds information about the users that may log in to a system and the file has a single line for each user, with that line split into a number of fields, delimited by a colon.

Configuring and administering Unix is therefore something that can, and frequently is, performed using a text interface, often remotely over a network and sometimes even from a different location and different country. Remember that Unix predates the GUIs that you have come to know and love for a number of years.

Processes and Services

Unix is a multitasking operating system and so it's capable of running a number of different processes and background services at the same time. The quickest way to determine what processes are currently running on your machine is *ps*. You'll look in more detail at the *ps* command and how it can be used in Chapter 25, "Monitoring Performance." For the moment, use the command *ps -efl* to get a complete listing of what's going on inside your machine:

```
$ ps -efl
 F S    UID   PID  PPID  C PRI NI    ADDR      SZ    WCHAN    STIME TTY      TIME CMD
19 T    root    0     0  0   0 SY fec27d70      0           12:48:32 ?       0:02 sched
 8 S    root    1     0  0  41 20 de75d808    271 de94ee0e 12:48:32 ?       0:00
➥/etc/init -
19 S    root    2     0  0   0 SY de75d108      0 fec48be8 12:48:32 ?       0:00 pageout
19 S    root    3     0  0   0 SY de75ca08      0 fece1ce8 12:48:32 ?       0:48 fsflush
 8 S    root  370     1  0  40 20 de75c308    394 de946ca8 12:49:18 ?       0:00
➥/usr/lib/saf/sac -t 300
 8 S    root  375   370  0  41 20 de75bc08    393 dee026ce 12:49:19 ?       0:00
➥/usr/lib/saf/ttymon
 8 S    root  262     1  0  47 20 de75b508    729 de5ed37a 12:49:04 ?       0:00
➥/usr/lib/lpsched
...
 8 S    root  425   367  0  51 20 df077c28    758 deee6802 14:44:51 ?       0:01
➥/usr/local/sbin/sshd2
 8 S    root  436   427  0  41 20 df077528    571 df077594 14:44:58 pts/3   0:01 -bash
 8 S    root  448   436  0  53 20 df076e28    419 df076e94 14:48:40 pts/3   0:00
➥/bin/ksh /usr/sadm/lib/smc/bin/smc
 8 O      mc  557   401  1  61 20 df076728    215           20:29:45 pts/2  0:00 ps -efl
 8 S    root  460   448  0  40 20 df061830  20489 df190aee 14:48:44 pts/3   9:49
➥/usr/java/bin/java -Djava.security.
 8 S    root  471     1  0  41 20 df061130  15337 df24d64e 14:49:41 ?       4:59
➥/usr/java/bin/java -Dviper.fifo.pat
```

I've trimmed the output above, because it's not really that interesting. Just be aware that your machine is doing a lot more than it appears while you are using it.

Administration Tools

It's not possible in a book like this to list all of the commands and utilities that you will be using to administer your system. It's also not possible to say that you will use a completely different set of tools and commands as the superuser than when you are a user. The superuser is just another type of user with better privileges—you will always be using a combination of "user" tools and "superuser" tools to administer the system.

That said, there are two primary tools which we'll be covering and using in this guide, over and above the standard command line utilities. The *admintool* is the original GUI administration tool for the Solaris operating system and was provided back with the first versions of Solaris. Its limited to setting up some of the core elements such as users, groups, hosts, and printers and that's it, but it's a practical tool that is sometimes more powerful and easy to use than the other available tools.

To start the administration tool, you must be in X Windows. To actually start the tool, type *admintool* into a command prompt as root. If you've used *su* to become root within a terminal window then you'll need to do two other steps. First, before you *su* to root, type:

```
$ xhost +hostname
```

where *hostname* is the name of your machine. This opens up X Windows security to allow other users to display a Window within your session. Second, after you have become root, but before running *admintool*, type:

```
set DISPLAY=:0.0
export DISPLAY
```

This configures your session to display any new X Windows clients to the X Windows server running on the console. You can see a sample of the *admintool* in Figure 5.2.

Figure 5.2

The graphical admintool.

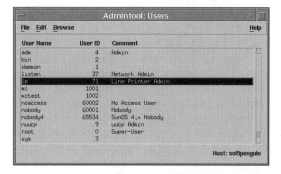

The Solaris Management Console (SMC) is actually a Java-based application that provides you with a GUI interface for setting up and monitoring your system. It provides everything from basic user and group administration right up to disk management and performance monitoring tools. To start SMC, change to root and then enter *smc* at the command prompt. If you get an error about a missing DISPLAY variable or not being allowed to connect to a given host, use the details above to set up your environment first.

You can see the SMC in action in Figure 5.3. The window is split into three main sections. The panel on the left is a navigation panel and this allows you to choose which part of the system you want to configure. The bottom panel is the help panel, and the main right-hand panel is where most of the work will be done.

In addition to the GUI interface, the SMC also provides a text-based interface which enables you to administer a system remotely through telnet, or directly on the console when X Windows is unavailable.

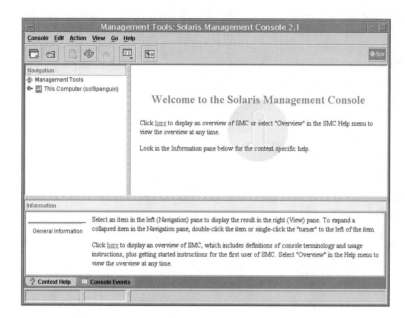

Figure 5.3

The Java-based Solaris Management Console.

More About Your System

Your first job on any new system is to make sure you know about the machine's configuration, both at a hardware level and at a software level. Although it may not be obvious when you first start using the machine, a lot of information about your machine is available if only you know where to look and what commands to run. I'll cover the major areas in this section.

Obviously if you've just set up and installed Solaris onto your machine, you'll probably have a pretty good idea about how it's configured. However, if you are new to the machine, or new to both Solaris and the machine, there's no harm in doing a little bit of digging to find out the configuration of the machine and how Solaris has translated that configuration.

Solaris (and other Unix variants) treat every physical device in more or less the same way. For each physical device, a driver is loaded by the kernel and in most cases that driver creates a corresponding device entry in the */dev* directory. All communication with that device is handled by sending information to or from that device file. For example, the system reads input from the keyboard through */dev/kbd* and from the mouse using */dev/mouse*.

The use of files to communicate with devices introduces an interesting paradox in that you can communicate with the hard disk drive used to boot up your machine through a file on that hard disk.

The *prtconf* tool should be your first command—it will describe the current state of the hardware on your machine, including the basic platform, physical RAM specification, a list of identified devices (IDE and SCSI drives and PCI/SBUS/ISA expansion cards), and also information on the number of CPUs. For example, the output below was generated on a single-processor Intel machine running Solaris 9:

```
$ prtconf
System Configuration:  Sun Microsystems  i86pc
Memory size: 128 Megabytes
System Peripherals (Software Nodes):

i86pc
    +boot (driver not attached)
        memory (driver not attached)
    aliases (driver not attached)
    chosen (driver not attached)
    i86pc-memory (driver not attached)
    i86pc-mmu (driver not attached)
    openprom (driver not attached)
    options, instance #0
    packages (driver not attached)
    delayed-writes (driver not attached)
    itu-props (driver not attached)
    isa, instance #0
        motherboard (driver not attached)
        asy, instance #0
        asy, instance #1
        fdc, instance #0
        i8042, instance #0
            keyboard, instance #0
            mouse, instance #0
        PNP0C02 (driver not attached)
        PNP0C02 (driver not attached)
        PNP0C02 (driver not attached)
        bios (driver not attached)
        bios (driver not attached)
    pci, instance #0
        pci8086,7192 (driver not attached)
        pci8086,7110 (driver not attached)
        pci-ide, instance #0
            ide, instance #0
                cmdk, instance #0
```

```
        ide, instance #1
            sd, instance #0
    pci8086,7112, instance #0
    pci8086,7113 (driver not attached)
    display, instance #0
    pci1022,2000, instance #0
used-resources (driver not attached)
objmgr, instance #0
cpus (driver not attached)
    cpu, instance #0 (driver not attached)
pseudo, instance #0
```

The *sysdef* command displays the current system configuration, including attached devices and associated drivers, the list of currently loaded kernel drivers and modules, and in-depth kernel and system configuration information. The information reported is not immediately helpful unless you understand the significance of each element, but most administrators should be able to identify the major components and information reported back. Unfortunately I don't have the space to include a sample log here—it would run to about 15 pages!

Lastly, the *dmesg* command reports the information that was written in the log buffer while the machine was starting up, and also any important information reported while the system was running. The *syslog* system, which I discuss later in this chapter, has now usurped *dmesg* as the primary location for important log information, but *dmesg* remains as the main location for vital startup details.

The information in this log is more useful if you want to match up those device file entries with the physical hardware to which it refers. For example, the output from *dmesg* reproduced below comes from a multi-processor Intel machine running Solaris 8. In this log you can identify the individual CPUs as they are enabled, and individual drives and sizes and their corresponding device. Note that for space I've trimmed the date, time, and hostname information from the start of each line.

```
genunix: [ID 540533 kern.notice] SunOS Release 5.8 Version Generic_108529-03
➦32-bit
genunix: [ID 784649 kern.notice] Copyright 1983-2000 Sun Microsystems, Inc.
➦All rights reserved.
unix: [ID 168242 kern.info] mem = 523900K (0x1ff9f000)
unix: [ID 930857 kern.info] avail mem = 513257472
rootnex: [ID 466748 kern.info] root nexus = i86pc
rootnex: [ID 349649 kern.info] pci0 at root: space 0 offset 0
genunix: [ID 936769 kern.info] pci0 is /pci@0,0
pcplusmp: [ID 637496 kern.info] pcplusmp: ide (ata) instance 1 vector 0xe
➦ioapic 0x2 intin 0xe is bound to cpu 1
last message repeated 1 time
```

```
ata: [ID 714954 kern.info] ata_init_drive_pciide: dma disabled
ata: [ID 640982 kern.info]    ATAPI device at targ 0, lun 0 lastlun 0x0
ata: [ID 521533 kern.info]    model MATSHITA CR-586, stat 50, err 0
ata: [ID 241969 kern.info]        cfg 0x85c0, cyl 0, hd 0, sec/trk 0
ata: [ID 674665 kern.info]        mult1 0x0, mult2 0x0, dwcap 0x0, cap 0xf00
ata: [ID 350272 kern.info]        piomode 0x200, dmamode 0x200, advpiomode 0x3
ata: [ID 245087 kern.info]        minpio 120, minpioflow 120
ata: [ID 435839 kern.info]        valid 0x2, dwdma 0x407, majver 0x0
...
scsi: [ID 193665 kern.info] sd1 at adp0: target 0 lun 0
genunix: [ID 936769 kern.info] sd1 is /pci@0,0/pci9004,8078@c/sd@0,0
scsi: [ID 365881 kern.info]    <DEFAULT cyl 14321 alt 2 hd 3 sec 417>
scsi: [ID 193665 kern.info] sd3 at adp0: target 2 lun 0
genunix: [ID 936769 kern.info] sd3 is /pci@0,0/pci9004,8078@c/sd@2,0
scsi: [ID 365881 kern.info]    <DEFAULT cyl 11194 alt 2 hd 5 sec 320>
...
unix: [ID 832595 kern.info] cpu 0 initialization complete - online
unix: [ID 721127 kern.info] cpu 1 initialization complete - online
```

Again, I've truncated the output because of the sheer size of the information reproduced, but you can see how the different devices are scanned and identified.

Note that the information generated by *dmesg* is actually written into the */var/adm/ messages* file when the file is available—since that may not always be the case it's a good idea to get used to using *dmesg* to reproduce the most recent information.

Logs

One of the most important roles of a system administrator is to monitor the systems and ensure that they are running correctly. The easiest way to do this is to monitor the logs.

Solaris actually uses a combination of different systems to log events on the system. The primary logging system is called *syslog*. The *syslog* system is a configurable logging system in many ways similar to the Windows NT/2000 event log. Different messages and errors are reported to *syslog*, which in turn makes decisions about where the error should be reported. Urgent errors—for example a lack of disk space—are reported directly to the console and should appear on the monitor. They are also written to the */var/adm/messages* file. Other errors and messages which are not considered urgent or critical are written in to the */var/log/syslog* file.

Table 5.2 includes a quick overview of some of the different logs produced, where they are stored, and how to access them.

Table 5.2   Logs Generated by Solaris

Log	Description
/var/adm/messages	Critical errors and warnings—also echoed to the console.
/var/log/syslog	Noncritical errors and information reported by *syslog*.
/var/log/authlog	Authorization requests (and failures) when using *su* to change the user.
/var/adm/lastlog	A binary file holding information about the last time a user connected to a machine.
/var/adm/wtmpx	A binary file containing a log of the time and duration that a user was logged in to a machine. Access the information using *last*.
/var/cron/log	A list of the processes executed automatically via the *cron* system.
/var/lp/logs/requests	A list of the requests and jobs sent to the printing system.

Where Next?

If you are new to any kind of Unix then you should really first move on to Chapter 16 and the other chapters in Part 4, "Using Solaris." This will give you a basic grounding in Unix, the command line, and the environment and help you to get to know Unix from a user's perspective. Once you've finished, move on to Chapter 6, "Managing Users and Groups."

If you are familiar with Unix or Solaris and just want to know how to start setting up users and other systems, move right on to Chapter 6.

Sun Lotion

The *last* command has one trick up its sleeve—it keeps a record of each time a machine is shut down or rebooted. If you use *last reboot* on the command line the machine will report the last time the machine was rebooted.

The Least You Need to Know

◆ To start using a machine you must log in using the user name and password provided to you by your administrator.

◆ You can change your password using the *passwd* command.

◆ Unix has its own online manual accessible through the *man* command and the AnswerBook system.

◆ The superuser has special privileges to be able to administer and use the system.

◆ There are a number of administration tools, with the two primary tools supported through X Windows being *admintool* and the Solaris Management Console.

◆ You can find out information about the system's configuration by using the *prtconf*, *sysdef*, and *dmesg* commands.

Part 2

Basic System Administration

Although Solaris can be a *fit-and-forget* operating system, it's unlikely that you will never need to perform some sort of administration on the machine at some point in the future. Administration involves many elements, including setting up users; setting up disks, printers and other devices; and starting and stopping the system and its services.

Managing Users and Groups

In This Chapter

- ◆ Understanding user and group security
- ◆ Managing users
- ◆ Managing groups

Users and groups are the cornerstone of the Unix and therefore Solaris security model. You need a user name to log in to the machine. Once you have logged in, your user name and the groups to which you belong control the files, applications, and actions you are able to perform.

In this chapter, I take a closer look at how users and groups affect the security and access to a Solaris machine, how this information can be used to your advantage, and how to create, edit, and manage the users and groups on a machine.

The User/Group Security Model

Unix is a multi-user operating system. The multiuser capability works on two levels:

- ◆ A number of different users can connect to the machine at the same time and run their own applications.
- ◆ Each user has his own login, his own file storage area, and his own set of preferences for the applications and the systems he uses.

When users log in to a Solaris machine they enter their login and password, and once verified they are logged into the machine and placed into their home directory. Their home directory is the location where they store all of their files and preferences. For example, my home directory on my machine is */home/mc.*

Because it's likely that there will be other people that you may want to share files with, all users also belong to one or more groups. For example, a user using a machine within the sales department at a company may want to share his files with other people in the sales department.

Finally, a third classification called simply *other* controls how everybody else—that is, everybody other than yourself and other members of your group—can access the files and resources on the system.

These three classes—user, group, and other—give you a fine level of control over how resources are accessed within the system. If you want to restrict access to a specific group of people then you create a new group, add those users to it and set the permissions to provide access only to members of that group. If you want to give anybody access, then you set the permissions for the other class.

How Security on Files Works

Since you already know that virtually all information within Unix is available in some way through the file system, the easiest way to demonstrate the system in action is to look at the permissions on files and directories. If you do a long listing within any directory, the first column of output tells you the permissions for the file or directory, and two further columns show the user and group ownership for the file or directory.

```
$ ls -l
total 186060
-rw-r--r--   1 mc       staff    2367114 Jan 24 12:36 25fig01.tif
drwx------   2 mc       staff        512 Dec  9  2000 Desktop/
-rw-rw-rw-   1 mc       staff          0 Jan  6 16:48 GL50Tryout.bin
-rw-r--r--   1 mc       staff        321 Oct 12 16:09 SystemVersion.plist
-rwxr-xr-x   1 mc       staff       1736 Oct 18 09:31 cklnks.pl*
----rw----   1 mc       sales       2000 Oct 19 15:22 news
```

The first column (with entries like *-rw-r--r--*) shows the permission information. The first character in this column tells you what the type of entry is—*d* for a directory and - for a file. There are other letters here, but we won't worry about that for the moment.

The rest of the column consists of three letters for the three different possible users: owner, group, and other. The first three define the permissions for the different classes of user owner of the file, the next three group, and the last three other. The owner of the file is the user listed in the third column, in this case "mc," and the group owner of the file is the group listed in the fourth column, "staff."

Sun Lotion _____

Because Unix uses files both for storing information and for communicating with devices and even with other machines and applications, the file type specification as the first letter of the permissions list is more significant than you might think. Other file types include *c* for a character device, *b* for a block device, and *l* for a link.

There's even a *D* for a door—but it's not as exciting as it sounds, and you won't find another world or dimension on the other side of the door. Doors are part of a caching system used to improve the performance of websites.

For example, for the first file, *25fig01.tif*, the permissions for the owner (mc) are *rw-* and for the group owner and everybody else *r--*. The three letters relate to the ability to read, write, or execute (r, w, or x) a file. Actually, it's slightly more complicated than that:

◆ **Read (r) access** allows the corresponding class to read the contents of the file. If a directory, then read access allows you to get a list of the contents.

◆ **Write (w) access** allows the corresponding class to write and modify the contents of the file. If a directory, then write access allows you to delete a file in the directory.

◆ **Execute (x) access** allows you to execute a file (if it's an application or script). If a directory, execute access allows you to access a file in the directory if you know its name.

Sun Lotion _____

Note that the access permissions of a directory do not affect the files which it contains—having read access to a directory does not automatically give you read access to all the files in that directory.

Conversely, having write access to a file only means that you can modify the contents. Deleting the file is actually a modification of the directory in which the file is stored—if you can't modify the directory (that is, don't have write permissions to it) then you cannot delete the file.

It's important to remember that these modes apply only to a given class. That is, a file with read permissions on the directory for the user and group will only allow the user and group owner specified for the directory entry to get a list of files. Everybody else is barred access.

Using this information, we can determine the accessibility of each of the files in our listing:

◆ *25fig01.tif* can be read by the owner (mc), members of the group *staff*, and anybody else (effectively everybody), but can only be edited or modified by the owner.

- Desktop is a directory and can only be accessed by the owner (mc).
- *GL50Tryout.bin* can be read from or modified by everybody.
- *SystemVersion.plist* can be read by anybody, but written to only by the owner (mc).
- *cklnks.pl* can be read from or executed by everybody, but only modified by the owner (mc).
- news can only be read or modified by members of the sales group.

Permissions are set using a command called *chmod* (for change mode) and group and ownership information are set using the *chown* (for change owner) and *chgrp* (for change group) commands. Permissions are set either by specifying the letters for access or by specifying an octal mode. I'll look more closely at this process in Chapter 19, "Enforcing Permissions and Security."

Sun Lotion

One of the common needs of any system is the ability to easily exchange files between users. The quickest method of doing this is to use the */tmp* directory, a special area used by the system to store temporary files of all kinds. The */tmp* directory is not the best solution though—it tends to be of limited size and by default is emptied during startup, making it useless on a system that is rebooted frequently—and certainly a problem if you have a crash.

Instead, the best method is to create a directory into which you place individual directories for each user. Within each user's directory, create an Incoming directory and an Outgoing directory. The files in Incoming are those supplied by other people. If you set the permissions on the directory to be writable and executable by everybody then anybody can add files to this directory, but nobody can get a list of the files it contains. The Outgoing directory is used to let anybody copy a file and should be readable by everybody, but writable only by owner.

Getting Security Right

As you can see from our file example, the permission system employed by Unix is incredibly powerful—you can explicitly grant access to specific users, groups of users, and everybody else, and it's possible to grant access to everybody except a specific user or group, or any other combinations thereof.

It's critical therefore to get the user and group management right—and that's why I'm looking at it now rather than as part of the security discussion. Create a user and get his group ownership incorrect and you could prevent him from accessing a vital system. Get the permissions wrong, and you could open the system up for abuse or accidental damage.

User Management

In order to gain access to a system you must be a user and have a login and password. All users of a system have the following elements:

- **Login or User Name:** The name used to identify them to the system and the name displayed by the system to show the ownership of different resources.

- **Password:** This is used to grant access to the system.

- **User ID:** A unique ID given to each user. Solaris stores the user IDs rather than names, as IDs are more efficient.

- **Primary Group:** All users are a member of at least one group, even if all users are a member of the same single group.

- **Full name:** Used mostly for reference, but also applied by default to each email you send.

- **Home directory:** The location where the user stores his or her preferences and typically their own files.

- **Shell:** The path to the shell which is started when the user connects to the system.

When you create a user, you'll need to set up this information in order to grant a user access to the system.

What Is a User?

Your first instinct is to answer that question by saying "A user is someone who is using the computer." In essence you are not in any way incorrect. However, Unix (and ergo Solaris) is slightly different from other operating systems in that users are defined to identify different parts of the operating system and their significance *as well* as being used to identify a human using the machine.

These "computer people" users can execute processes and applications on the system, and they have their own set of files and directories which they can access. Because they are configured as individual users, the system can decide who to share the files and directories with, without sharing information normally owned and accessible by the superuser.

For example, the *lp* user is used by the system to control and manage the printer system. Any user can communicate with and place files into the directories used by *lp* in order to print a file. Although *lp* is a system user, access to the print system does not grant any user automatic access to the other system areas.

Solingo

The /etc/passwd file contains information about the users configured on the system. The file contains the user name, ID, and other information about a user and is used to identify a user when he logs into the system. It's also used in reverse to put names to the user IDs which are stored when a file is created.

The only piece of information about a user not stored in /etc/passwd is the user's password (despite the implication). One of the reasons for this is that although a user's password is stored in an encrypted form that is difficult to decrypt, it's still possible to use a brute force mechanism to determine a user's password. The brute force method uses a program that tries every combination of letters and numbers until it finds the one that matches a user's password.

If standard users don't have access to the encrypted passwords, this method won't work. Instead, the encrypted passwords are placed into a different file, readable only by the superuser, called /etc/shadow.

In all other respects though, a user is exactly what your first answer was—a human (or cat, dog, or other pet, depending on how well it's been trained) that wants to use your computer. Unless you have specific concerns that can't easily be addressed by the other aspects of the Unix system, you should create one user for each person who needs access to the machine.

Adding Users

There are a number of different ways in which you can add users to the system. The most obvious solution would seem to be to edit the */etc/passwd* file directly. However, this is fraught with problems—not least of which is the fact that you will also need to manually edit the */etc/shadow* file to create them a password and allow them access.

A better solution is to use with the *admintool* administration application or the Solaris Management Console (SMC). Both offer a much simpler way of creating and managing users.

To use the *admintool* you must be in X Windows. Once in, start a command tool or terminal and type *admintool*. You should get a window like the one shown here in Figure 6.1, showing a list of the current users configured on the system.

Sun Lotion _____

The user IDs under any Unix are the important part. Any operation which requires storing user information—such as storing or accessing a file—uses the user ID rather than the user name. It's user ID that is actually the unique identifier on the system. When you get a file list, the system looks in */etc/passwd* for each user ID stored with the file information in order to display each user name.

You *must* therefore ensure that the */etc/passwd* file can be read by all users, but only be accessible for writing by the superuser, otherwise the user names will not be reported.

Incidentally, the use of IDs over names provides one small advantage—you can change a user's login without changing the user ID and without changing the user ID of all the files and resources on the system that you want to grant the user access to.

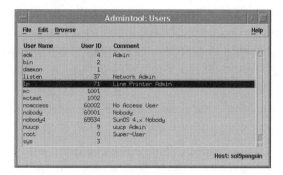

Figure 6.1

Using the admintool *to view the current list.*

To add a user, select Add from the Edit menu. You see the window shown in Figure 6.2.

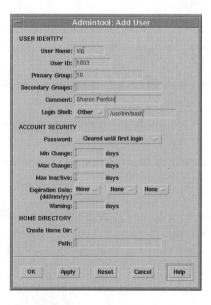

Figure 6.2

Adding a user with admintool.

You've already covered most of the options available for configuration in this window, although there are a few other points I need to mention.

In the password area you can configure the initial state of the password. The four different states are …

 ◆ **Cleared until first login:** The password is not set, and the first time the user connects they will be asked to enter and confirm their password.

 ◆ **Account is locked:** The account is created but cannot be used until the administrator sets a password for the account.

 ◆ **No password:** The account has no password and cannot be used, files and programs can use the account.

 ◆ **Normal password:** You will be prompted to enter the user's initial password.

You can also optionally configure the password to expire automatically after a set period. If you are concerned about security (and you should be!), setting these options is a good idea because they help to limit how long a single password is valid for, and therefore force staff to update and refresh their passwords. Even if someone discovers a password, it may be that the password has already been refreshed by the time they get to use it.

To set up the auto-expiry you can configure the expiry period, either in terms of the period of days between changes or specific dates according to the following rules:

 ◆ **Min Change:** This is the minimum number of days that a password must be active. At least this number of days must have elapsed before the password can be changed. You can use this to prevent users from regularly changing their password. If set to a value one less than the *Max change* figure it also prevents modifications until the next time a change is due.

 ◆ **Max Change:** This is the maximum period that can elapse before a user must set a new password. If the user reaches this period during login then they will be prompted to enter a new password during the login process.

 ◆ **Max Inactive:** This is the maximum number of days that a login can remain unused before it must have its password changed.

 ◆ **Expiration Date:** If supplied, this is the absolute date at which a user's password will expire.

 ◆ **Warning:** The number of days before their password expires that a user will be warned that a password change is required.

The final element is the user's home directory. If the *Create Home Dir* box is checked, then *admintool* will create the new directory for the user and copy across the appropriate files from the */etc/default* directory. The path should be the full location of the directory that you want to create.

Sun Screen

I hope that it should go without saying that distributing passwords is a highly sensitive process. Don't for a second contemplate emailing someone a password; visit them directly and tell them the password or write it on a piece of paper that you later destroy. Although these seem like espionage-like tactics, the truth is that most hacking and computer break-ins happen from within a company and from people overhearing or finding passwords where they shouldn't have been in the first place.

If you want to store passwords—and occasionally this is vital for systems passwords in case of sickness or death of the system administrator—put the current passwords on a piece of paper and put it in an envelope. Seal the envelope and then sign your name across the seal—that will enable you to tell if someone has opened the envelope. Now put the envelope in the safe (with your backup tapes), give it to your boss, or take it home.

Within the Solaris Management Console, open the tab for This Computer (or the computer you want to set up users for), then expand the System Configuration and Users elements. You should reach the screen shown here in Figure 6.3.

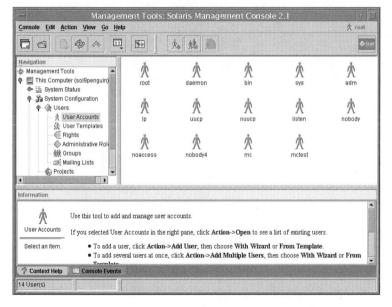

Figure 6.3

Configuring users with the Solaris Management Console.

To add the user, select the Action Menu and choose Add User and then Using Wizard. You should be presented with the window shown here in Figure 6.4.

Figure 6.4

Setting up the user name and real name information for a user using the SMC Add User Wizard.

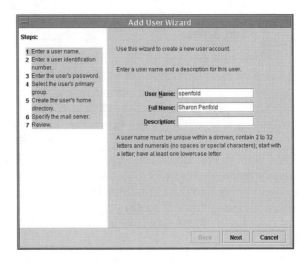

The process with the SMC is by default much more interactive, with the SMC using separate windows to ask you a series of questions for each stage. I've included screenshots of most of the stages involved in Figures 6.5, 6.6, 6.7, 6.8, and 6.9.

Figure 6.5

Setting the User ID number using the SMC Add User Wizard.

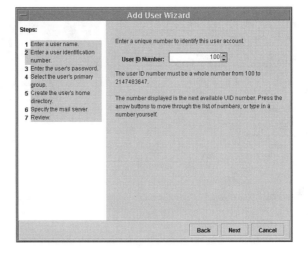

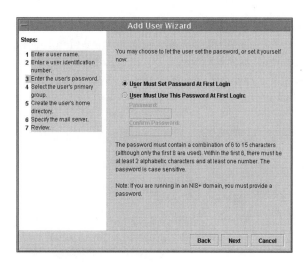

Figure 6.6

Setting the password preferences using the SMC Add User Wizard.

With the wizard you are limited as to the information you can initially configure for a user. To set some of the other information you'll need to use the group area of the SMC tool and set individual properties for each user.

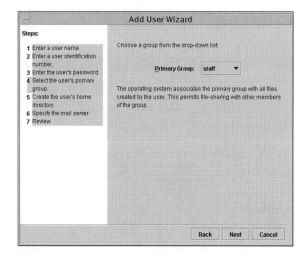

Figure 6.7

Setting the primary group using the SMC Add User Wizard.

The benefit of the SMC is that you can also use the same tool to configure other servers, and you can set up individual user templates that contain preconfigured information about the location of home directories, user ID ranges, and default groups to use when setting up different types of users. For example, you could have a user template set up for each of your departments and then use that to create each individual user.

Figure 6.8

Setting the user's home directory using the SMC Add User Wizard.

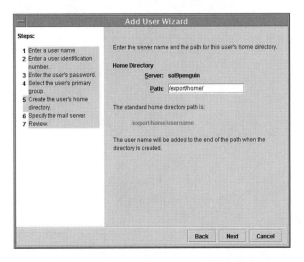

Figure 6.9

Reviewing the information for a user before creation using the SMC Add User wizard.

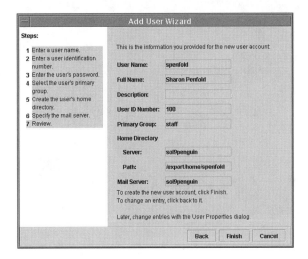

Changing Users

The most obvious change that you will ever make to a user is to change their password. All users can change their own password using the *passwd* command. The superuser can also change anybody else's password by supplying the name of the user to *passwd*. For example, to change the password for the user *mc* you'd use:

```
$ passwd mc
```

A Postcard From ...

When you enter a password for a user—or when the password is changed with the *passwd* command—the actual password that is typed in is encrypted using a function called *crypt* which comes as part of the system. *Crypt* uses an algorithm that encrypts the string so that the user's password cannot be determined by looking at the contents of the */etc/shadow* file. The algorithm used encrypts the password very quickly, but does it in such a way that it would take a tremendous amount of processor power to decrypt.

Although this seems like a daft method, it works if you stop worrying about decryption. Unlike a document, we do not need to view the password again when it's entered, even to validate a user. Instead, when a user enters the password the string they enter is also encrypted—to validate the password, we just have to compare the two encrypted versions, i.e., the one in */etc/shadow* and the one entered.

This is just one of the ways in which Unix helps to keep your machine secure.

To make any other changes, just go into the AdminTool or SMC to make the changes directly.

Deleting Users

There is more to deleting a user than simply removing their entry from the */etc/passwd* file. What about all the files the user has created on the system? What about their email?

There's an easy answer to these latter two questions. The actual deletion process in both the *admintool* and SMC is simply a case of selecting the user and choosing Delete. In both cases you will be asked if you want to delete the user's home directory.

Doing this operation *first* is generally a bad idea. What I do is:

1. Disable the user's account, either by editing the account using the *admintool* or SMC, or by setting the password of the account to something that couldn't possibly be guessed—I don't even keep a record of it myself, as superuser I can change it back if I need to.

2. If the system is being used to store the user's email, I archive the email off the system (to tape or CD) and then delete it manually.

3. I check the contents of the user's home directory. Anything that shouldn't be there or that is personal is immediately deleted, and then the directory contents are archived off to tape or CD before being manually deleted.

4. Finally, I use *find* (see Chapter 18, "Navigating and Managing Files") to search for files owned by that user. I'll check through that list, deleting anything that I know we no longer need. Anything that needs to be kept is copied to an area accessible only by root in case someone needs it. If it's a general file being used or edited by other people (as part of a development or web project, for example) then I change the ownership of the file to the supervisor for that group, or to another user who will be taking responsibility for the files in question.

5. Now I delete the user using *admintool* or the SMC.

Although this method is more long-winded, it ensures that no files remain on the system which were owned by this user—important because a new user may end up with the same user ID, and therefore have access to these files. It also means that you always have a copy of the files the user created, either on disk, tape, or CD, that you can recover in an emergency.

Group Management

Groups allow you to subdivide users into a number of sets which you can then use to help control what information they access and how you provide information and services to them. Groups are possibly the simplest part of the system to administer. The actual group definitions are held in the */etc/group* file.

Sun Screen

As with users, there are a set number of standard groups which are configured by default in Solaris. You shouldn't delete or modify these groups—doing so could render your machine completely useless to genuine users on the system.

What Is a Group?

A group is just a collection of users. A user's primary group (as configured when the user is set up) is the group used when a new file is created. Any other groups to which the user belongs define which other files and directories the user can access.

Adding Groups

To add a group with the *admintool*, change to the group list (by selecting Browse > Groups) and then choose Edit > Add. You'll be prompted with the window shown in Figure 6.10.

Figure 6.10

Creating a new group with the admintool.

Just enter the group name, a unique group ID, and a list of users, separated by commas, into the fields and click OK.

In the SMC, change to the This Computer > System Configuration > Users > Groups panel and choose Action > Add Group from the menu. You should get a window like the one shown in Figure 6.11. In this case you enter the group name and ID and then use the group list on the left to add members to the new group by copying their name in the list on the right. You can also use the sort and filter buttons to restrict the list to a more manageable size if you have a lot of users. Once complete, click OK.

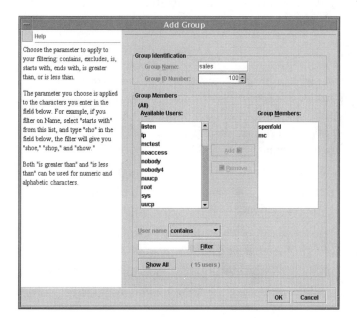

Figure 6.11

Adding a new group using the SMC.

Adding/Changing the Users in a Group

Using the *admintool*, double-click on the group and then modify the list of users shown in the Members List field. Not the friendliest of interfaces, but it works. Using the SMC, double-click on an existing group and use the same interface as shown in Figure 6.11 to edit the members of a particular group.

The groups database is actually the only one in which I advocate using a standard editor to modify the contents, as there is no danger of seriously corrupting information that cannot be fixed, or of creating a group without a password. Be careful, however; it's still not pleasant—each group definition must be confined to a single line, and the individual users on each line should be separated by a comma (not a space!).

Unless you cannot get access to a graphical interface, my favorite interface is the SMC, which makes the information, especially on busy systems with lots of users, significantly easier.

Deleting Groups

There is not quite so much danger in deleting a group as there is in deleting a user. The worst that will happen when deleting a group is that you might remove access to a directory that an existing set of users would not otherwise have access to. The solution to this problem is to use *find*, as we did with users, to find all the directories and/or files that you intend to remove and assign them to another group.

As with deleting users, to delete a group just select the group and select Delete from the Edit or Action menu for *admintool* and SMC users accordingly.

Distributing Users

One of the problems associated with user management through the */etc/passwd* and */etc/group* files is that the information is local to the machine on which the */etc* files reside. For a single machine this is not a problem, but it does become an issue as you start to work with other machines in the network, especially if you are supporting an environment that allows users to use different machines.

For example, let's say you have a small network of 12 machines used for training. Any user could potentially sit at any machine during the course of the training program. By using the default local files method you'll experience a few annoying problems:

◆ You need to edit the information across 12 machines in order to provide everybody with access, and we have to ensure that all the information you enter is the same.

◆ If a user connects to a machine and then changes his password, he will change his password only for the machine he is using. Move to a different machine and he will need to use his old password.

◆ The user would need to have access to the same set of files no matter which machine he was connected to.

The last item could be solved by sharing the directory from one machine to all the others using NFS—that way any user would automatically have access to the same shared directory on each machine.

The user issue is more difficult—you need a way of reliably sharing the user information across more than one machine and allowing users on any machine within the network to modify their password.

Luckily, Solaris has a number of such solutions available to use. Which one you use depends entirely on whether you need to integrate into other systems, and whether you want to use the system for storing more than just user names and passwords.

CAUTION

Sun Screen _____

I once had to repair the damage done by sharing the /etc directory to clients through the NFS system to support a shared database for users. Unfortunately, because the /etc directory was also used for all the configuration information, it led to some interesting results. Not the least of which was the fact that the real data used by the machine during startup was in a local copy of /etc, which was usurped when the NFS /etc was mounted.

In short, don't do it. Please.

NIS/NIS+

Years ago the Yellow Pages system for Unix was introduced. The idea was that a central server held copies of the configuration files—users, groups, hosts, and so on—within the /etc directory and made them available over the network to clients. When a user logs in, the login system verifies the user name and password against the server database and validates the user. When a hostname is entered, the hostname resolver looks in the server tables, rather than the system's local /etc files for the result.

The Yellow Pages name was dropped, because of a conflict with British Telecom which already had the Yellow Pages name trademarked for use on telephone directories. The system was rebadged NIS (short for Network Information System), and a slightly upgraded version of the self-same system exists in Solaris today. NIS and NIS+ are the most popular systems available for sharing this information, and I'll cover the NIS/NIS+ systems in Chapter 14, "Configuring NIS."

LDAP

The Lightweight Directory Access Protocol (LDAP) is a tree-based system that allows you to store information in a structured format. Unlike NIS, which was designed to handle some very specific pieces of information, LDAP was designed as a general directory storage system and allows you to store not only the basic user name and password information, but also contact details (address, email address, phone numbers) and information about devices and services offered over the network.

LDAP is now seen as the directory service of choice for large networks—it has the benefit of being a public standard and LDAP servers can be used to validate logins through more than just the Unix login system. They can also validate web access, and the information can be shared amongst Unix, Windows, and other platforms. Using LDAP it's quite possible to support a single sign on (SSO) facility, so your users never enter their password more than once, no matter what resources and systems they access across your network.

LDAP is beyond the scope of this book, but check out the AnswerBook documentation for more information on how it can be used within Solaris.

XFN

The X/Open Federated Naming (XFN) system was devised by the X/Open group as an open standard for sharing information within a given organization. It's supported by Sun, IBM, HP, and others as a way of sharing information between machines about users and resources.

XFN and the Federated Naming Service (FNS) are not really replacements for NIS/NIS+. Instead they use the information provided by NIS/NIS+, but in a more structured and open way that allows the information to be used and accessed in a more open form.

XFN is new to Solaris 9 and unfortunately beyond the scope of this book. For more information, see the Sun documentation on the system. In particular, the Federated Naming Service Programming Guide gives a good background to the system and how it works.

The Least You Need to Know

- Users and groups are used to provide access to the system and also control the security and access to files and resources on a system.
- A user is a single entity that has the permission to access the computer and own files on that computer.
- User information is stored in */etc/passwd*, with password information stored in */etc/shadow*.
- Group information is stored in */etc/group*.
- We can configure user and group information either manually or through the *admintool* or Solaris Management Console.
- Three systems, NIS/NIS+, LDAP, and XFN are available for sharing login information across more than one machine.

Understanding Disk Management

In This Chapter

◆ Looking at disk devices

◆ Setting up partitions

◆ Creating and managing file systems

◆ Using removable media

Sooner or later you are going to need to add or recreate a disk on your machine. I'm a firm believer that the data you store expands to fill up the space available. Five years ago I was happy with a machine with a 2GB disk. Today I have about 0.5TB (terabyte, 1024 gigabytes!). Am I really storing anything substantially more useful? I can't honestly answer that—but I do know that the two drives I bought at the start of the year are already half the size of the newer, bigger drives now available and if I got those drives, I'd be running out of space on them, too.

Under Solaris, adding disk space is relatively easy—once you've added the disk physically to your system all you need to do is divide it up into some logical sections, create a new a file system on each section and then mount each file system to make the space available. I'll be covering all three of those processes, plus one or two other tricks along the way.

Exploring Disk Devices

Devices under Solaris are available through the */dev* directory. The directory actually holds a list of "logical" device names—for example, names which us mere mortals may be able to understand more easily. The real devices names are stored in */devices*.

Disk devices, other than the floppy disk and special aliases for each CD-ROM/DVD-ROM drive attached to a machine, are stored in */dev/dsk*. Each file in that directory refers to an individual partition (or slice) of each available disk. For an IDE disk the file will look like this:

```
c0d0s0
```

Where the number c defines the controller number, d defines the disk number on that controller and s defines the slice (or partition) on that disk. For example, the above refers to the first slice on the first disk connected to the first controller. In case of an IDE device like this, it actually refers to the first partition on the master disk of the primary hard disk controller. The first partition on the slave disk would be */dev/dsk/c0d1s0* and the first drive on the second IDE controller would be */dev/dsk/c1d0s0*.

For SCSI drives, an additional specification, the "target," is added to allow support for SCSI-attached units that contain multiple disks, but appear as only one SCSI ID. The basic format in this case becomes:

```
c0t0d0s0
```

Sun Screen

With a few exceptions, all of the examples and commands in this chapter require root or superuser access to the machine. Solaris will prevent any user but superuser from manipulating either physical devices or the major components of the file system. Be careful!

The above refers to controller 0, target 0, disk 0, and slice 0. If you are using standard SCSI disks, then all your target specifications will be 0. The drive number is also directly equivalent to the SCSI ID. That is, c0t0d6s0 refers to the first slice on the drive with SCSI ID 6 connected to the first controller.

The controller number in either IDE or SCSI disks will depend on what controllers you have attached to your machine, and is obviously incremented for each controller you have attached to the machine. If you have a PC, the chances are the IDE controllers will be listed first, and any SCSI controllers, even those on the motherboard, will be listed later. For example, in my main Solaris server—a PC—I have the standard dual IDE channels, which appear as controllers 0 and 1, a motherboard SCSI interface, controller 2, and a PCI SCSI card which appears as controller 3.

All of the entries in */dev/dsk* are the block special devices. Block special devices are those used when communicating with the disk in blocks—generally when talking to them as a file system. However, if you want to do any low-level work on them then you need to access the partition as a "raw" device. Luckily, all that means is that you use the alias in */dev/rdsk*. You'll need to use the raw disk alias when creating the file system and when checking and repairing the file system with *fsck*.

Adding Drives

If you have newly added a drive to a machine and it has not appeared in /dev, don't be surprised. The reason is that Solaris doesn't automatically check for new devices each time you switch it on. Instead, you must tell the kernel to rebuild the device list during startup. You can do this either by using *b -r* when prompted under Solaris x86, or by using *boot -r* at the PROM prompt on a SPARC machine.

Alternatively, if you've just started the machine up you can reboot using *reboot − -r* to reboot and then configure the devices. If you are not in a position to reboot, try using the *devfsadm* command which will recreate the devices and device links for you.

Creating Partitions

Before you can start using a new hard disk device it must be partitioned. A partition is just a slice or area of the disk which you want to set aside for use as a particular file system or with some database systems the partition may be used directly. Although it's tempting to use the entire disk all the time, there are file systems where you don't need all the space of an entire drive—especially with disk sizes today starting at 10 to 20GB.

There are two different pieces of partitioning software. The *format* command is suitable for both Intel and SPARC systems for partitioning a drive, but for Intel systems only it is unable to set up the Intel style partitions required by the Intel hardware. In these situations you must also use *fdisk* to create the Intel partition map and then use *format* to create the Solaris partitions.

Using fdisk (Intel)

You only need to use *fdisk* if you are setting up a new hard drive on an Intel system. If you are using a SPARC system, skip this step and go on to "Using format."

You need to use *fdisk* to create the primary partition table and if necessary the master boot record (MBR) in order for Intel machines to understand the format of the disk and access its contents. In most situations, you will use *fdisk* to create a partition that spans the entire range of the disk.

CAUTION

Sun Screen _____

The partitions created by *fdisk* relate to a low-level organization of the disk. Multiple partitions are employed to allow different operating systems to coexist on the same disk.

The partitions created by *fdisk* are *not* the same as the partitions you will be creating with *format*, which are partitions you use to hold a particular file system. It's best to think of the Solaris partition as a "slice" hence the use of "s" to indicate the slice number in the disk device name.

To set up the partitions with *fdisk* for a disk, you must supply the raw device name for the disk you want to partition. In our examples we'll use the slave hard disk on the master IDE controller:

```
# fdisk /dev/rdsk/c0d1p0
```

If there is no existing partition table, you will be asked if you want to create one configured as a 100% Solaris partition:

```
No fdisk table exists. The default partition for the disk is:

  a 100% "SOLARIS System" partition

Type "y" to accept the default partition, otherwise type "n" to edit the
partition table.
```

Type *y* to accept, and you're done.

If you wanted to create a partition table that would allow you to share a portion of the disk, type *n* and then follow the on screen prompts to set up each partition.

Using format

The format command is supported under both the Intel and SPARC platforms and is used to divide a disk up into the individual slices which will eventually have a file system created on them. To use this command, type *format* at the command line:

```
# format
Searching for disks...done


AVAILABLE DISK SELECTIONS:
       0. c0d0 <DEFAULT cyl 8319 alt 2 hd 16 sec 63>
          /pci@0,0/pci-ide@7,1/ide@0/cmdk@0,0
```

```
    1. c0d1 <DEFAULT cyl 8123 alt 2 hd 16 sec 63>
       /pci@0,0/pci-ide@7,1/ide@0/cmdk@1,0
Specify disk (enter its number):
```

You will be prompted to select one of the identified disks on the system. If your drive doesn't appear, make sure that you reconfigured the devices on your machine during boot.

You're configuring the IDE disk you just added, so you press 1—once you've selected the disk you want to partition (and pressed Return), you'll be presented with a menu like this:

```
selecting c0d1
Controller working list found
[disk formatted, defect list found]


FORMAT MENU:
        disk       - select a disk
        type       - select (define) a disk type
        partition  - select (define) a partition table
        current    - describe the current disk
        format     - format and analyze the disk
        fdisk      - run the fdisk program
        repair     - repair a defective sector
        show       - translate a disk address
        label      - write label to the disk
        analyze    - surface analysis
        defect     - defect list management
        backup     - search for backup labels
        verify     - read and display labels
        save       - save new disk/partition definitions
        volname    - set 8-character volume name
        !<cmd>     - execute <cmd>, then return
        quit
```

Don't worry—you don't need most of these commands to do what you want to do here. Instead, Press P to change to the partition menu (format allows you to shorten the different commands, as you've done here):

```
PARTITION MENU:
        0      - change '0' partition
        1      - change '1' partition
        2      - change '2' partition
        3      - change '3' partition
        4      - change '4' partition
        5      - change '5' partition
        6      - change '6' partition
        7      - change '7' partition
        select - select a predefined table
```

```
modify - modify a predefined partition table
name   - name the current table
print  - display the current table
label  - write partition map and label to the disk
!<cmd> - execute <cmd>, then return
quit
```

Now press P to display the current partition table:

```
Current partition table (original):
Total disk cylinders available: 8123 + 2 (reserved cylinders)

Part      Tag    Flag     Cylinders        Size            Blocks
  0 unassigned    wm     0                 0        (0/0/0)           0
  1 unassigned    wm     0                 0        (0/0/0)           0
  2     backup    wu     0 - 8122       3.90GB      (8123/0/0) 8187984
  3 unassigned    wm     0                 0        (0/0/0)           0
  4 unassigned    wm     0                 0        (0/0/0)           0
  5 unassigned    wm     0                 0        (0/0/0)           0
  6 unassigned    wm     0                 0        (0/0/0)           0
  7 unassigned    wm     0                 0        (0/0/0)           0
  8       boot    wu     0 -    0       0.49MB      (1/0/0)        1008
  9 alternates    wm     1 -    2       0.98MB      (2/0/0)        2016
```

The partitions are numbered from 0 to 7—you cannot change partition 8 which is the boot area used by the system if this was a boot disk. Partition 2 is special—it *always* refers to the entire expanse of the usable portion of the disk and it can be used during backups. Although you can change the configuration of this, I don't recommend it.

To set up a new partition, type the number of the partition that you want to change. Let's set up an area in partition 1 of 1GB in size:

```
partition> 1
Part      Tag    Flag     Cylinders        Size            Blocks
  1 unassigned    wm     0                 0        (0/0/0)           0

Enter partition id tag[unassigned]:
```

The partition tag is an identifier used by Solaris to determine what the partition will be used for. Common values are *unassigned* for an area not being used, *swap* to refer to an area to be used as swap space—in fact only partitions marked as *swap* can be used as swap—and *alternates* to refer to a generic partition used for holding a file system mounted somewhere other than / or */usr*.

Next you'll be asked to specify the permissions for the partition:

```
Enter partition permission flags[wm]: ?
```

Valid values are *wm* (read/write, mountable), *wu* (read/write unmountable), *rm* (read-only, mountable) and *ru* (read-only, unmountable). You'll probably want *wm*.

The remaining questions ask you to specify the physical range of the slice on the disk:

```
Enter new starting cyl[1]:
Enter partition size[0b, 0c, 1e, 0.00mb, 0.00gb]:
```

The starting cylinder is the first cylinder number to be used to store information—slices are allocated only in terms of whole cylinders. You'll need to enter a value one higher than the previous partition. The size is just the approximate size (rounded up, or down, to the nearest whole cylinder). You can see from the options that you can specify the size in terms of blocks, cylinders, the real final cylinder number, megabytes, and gigabytes. Enter the figures, and you're done.

You need to ask to see the partition table again, and you can see the new 1GB partition:

```
Total disk cylinders available: 8123 + 2 (reserved cylinders)
```

Part	Tag	Flag	Cylinders	Size		Blocks
0	unassigned	wm	0	0	(0/0/0)	0
1	alternates	wm	1 - 2081	1.00GB	(2081/0/0)	2097648
2	backup	wu	0 - 8122	3.90GB	(8123/0/0)	8187984
3	unassigned	wm	0	0	(0/0/0)	0
4	unassigned	wm	0	0	(0/0/0)	0
5	unassigned	wm	0	0	(0/0/0)	0
6	unassigned	wm	0	0	(0/0/0)	0
7	unassigned	wm	0	0	(0/0/0)	0
8	boot	wu	0 - 0	0.49MB	(1/0/0)	1008
9	alternates	wm	1 - 2	0.98MB	(2/0/0)	2016

For reference, here's the partition table for the boot disk of a Solaris server:

```
Total disk cylinders available: 14321 + 2 (reserved cylinders)
```

Part	Tag	Flag	Cylinders	Size		Blocks
0	root	wm	840 - 1678	512.49MB	(839/0/0)	1049589
1	swap	wu	1 - 839	512.49MB	(839/0/0)	1049589
2	backup	wm	0 - 14321	8.54GB	(14322/0/0)	17916822
3	usr	wm	1679 - 5031	2.00GB	(3353/0/0)	4194603
4	unassigned	wm	5032 - 5870	512.49MB	(839/0/0)	1049589
5	unassigned	wm	5871 - 10548	2.79GB	(4678/0/0)	5852178
6	var	wm	10549 - 10968	256.55MB	(420/0/0)	525420
7	home	wm	10969 - 14321	2.00GB	(3353/0/0)	4194603
8	boot	wu	0 - 0	0.61MB	(1/0/0)	1251
9	unassigned	wm	0	0	(0/0/0)	0

As soon as you've finished creating your partition table and you are happy with it, quit from the partition menu using Q. You now need to label the disk to write this partition table into the Volume Table of Contents (VTOC). To do this, just type *label* at the main menu:

```
format> label
Ready to label disk, continue? y
```

That's it! Quit out of format by pressing Q again and your disk is ready to have file systems created on it.

Creating File Systems

Once you have partitioned a disk, you must create a file system on it so that you can use it. Without a file system, Solaris is unable to determine where, physically, on the disk a particular file is and how to identify and refer to that file in the rest of the system.

What Is a File System?

A file system is a logical container of files, used by an operating system to map the physical locations of a file as it is stored on the disk to a more familiar file and directory structure. File systems are quite complex items, but all you need to know at this stage is ...

♦ File systems map physical disk space and locations with a logical reference.

♦ Most file systems use a special structure to hold the information about a given file and its physical location. Under Solaris, the standard terminology for this structure is the *inode*.

♦ The inode also contains information such as the file's real name, permissions and ownership information, and modification times.

It's important to appreciate that relationship between the inode and the rest of the file system. If you run out of inodes then you will be unable to create any new files or directories. Running out of inodes doesn't prevent you from adding more information to an existing file, though.

Conversely, the storage space on a disk is just as important—if you run out of space then you will be unable to create any more files *or* update any existing files, whether you have any spare inodes or not. For this reason, Solaris automatically sets a "minimum free" figure on each file system it creates. The default is 10 percent, and it exists solely to prevent a typical user from using up all the space on the drive. The superuser can make use of this space in an emergency—such as when you've run out of space and need to archive or compress files.

A Postcard From ...
If you want to explicitly limit the space and inodes for individual users then you can use the quota system. This sets limits for both values for different users on a file system by file system basis. In a college or university environment this is an ideal way to prevent users from filling up their machine with MP3s and other high-volume data, but be wary of limiting inode numbers, as students writing software will need a larger number of files than typical users. In a commercial environment, quotas are an excellent way to limit usage to a specific size and charge different amounts based on the amount of data people need to store.
If you think quotas would be useful to you, check the *edquota* and *quotaon* manual pages for more information.

For information on the file system structure used within Solaris, see Chapter 24, "Fixing and Tuning File Systems." You'll need to understand the structure a bit more to make decisions during a file system repair.

File System Types

There are a number of standard file system types, all designed to work with different types of media, including both traditional physical formats like hard disks and CD-ROM, and also memory- and network-based file systems. The default type for a standard disk used for storing files is UFS—the root, /usr, and other partitions used to store files for the system all use the UFS format.

Network-based file systems include the Network File System (NFS), which allows Unix machines to share directories with each other.

Pseudo file systems are typically used to speed up or cache information from slower formats, either using another file system (such as UFS) or memory. For example, the CACHEFS file system is used to cache files from an NFS file system on the local hard disk.

Table 7.1 shows a list of the major supported formats.

Table 7.1   Major File System Types

Format	Description
Cache File System (CacheFS)	A pseudo file system used to store files on the local hard drive from a network drive.
High Sierra File System (hsfs)	The format used by CD-ROM media.

continues

Table 7.1   Major File System Types   (continued)

Format	Description
Loopback File System (lofs)	A pseudo file system used to provide alternative mount points for a given directory or file system.
PC File System (pcfs)	The format used by floppy disks formatted to be compatible with, or formatted by, a Windows/DOS PC.
Process File System (procfs)	A special pseudo file system used by Solaris to manage and communicate with processes.
Temporary File System (tmpfs)	A pseudo file system used to store files in the computer's swap space.
Universal Disk Format (UDF)	The format used by CD-R/CD-RW media when written in packet-writing mode, and that used by the DVD standard (including DVD-ROM and DVD-Video).
Unix File System (ufs)	The format used for hard disk file systems.

Using newfs to Create a File System

The *newfs* command creates a new file system. Despite the complexity of the actual process that goes on behind the scenes, the *newfs* command is very straightforward to use. All you need to do is supply the name of the raw partition to create the new file system on—I'll use the 1GB partition (*/dev/dsk/c0d1s1*) I created earlier when demonstrating the *format* command:

```
# newfs /dev/dsk/c0d1s0
newfs: construct a new file system /dev/rdsk/c0d1s1: (y/n)? y
/dev/rdsk/c0d1s1:      2096640 sectors in 2080 cylinders of 16 tracks, 63
➡sectors
        1023.8MB in 65 cyl groups (32 c/g, 15.75MB/g, 3904 i/g)
super-block backups (for fsck -F ufs -o b=#) at:
 32, 32352, 64672, 96992, 129312, 161632, 193952, 226272, 258592,
 290912, 323232, 355552, 387872, 420192, 452512, 484832, 516128,
 548448, 580768, 613088, 645408, 677728, 710048, 742368, 774688,
 807008, 839328, 871648, 903968, 936288, 968608, 1000928, 1032224,
 1064544, 1096864, 1129184, 1161504, 1193824, 1226144, 1258464,
 1290784, 1323104, 1355424, 1387744, 1420064, 1452384, 1484704,
 1517024, 1548320, 1580640, 1612960, 1645280, 1677600, 1709920,
 1742240, 1774560, 1806880, 1839200, 1871520, 1903840, 1936160,
 1968480, 2000800, 2033120, 2064416,
```

You'll be asked to confirm the operation, and if you are remotely in any doubt, press N and then double check that you've selected the right disk and partition—selecting the wrong one will overwrite any information on the disk, and you'll need to recover the information from backups (see Chapter 22, "Backing Up and Restoring File Systems.")

The information that *newfs* generates is quite useful—first of all it generates information about the size and make up of the disk. You should be creating a file system that is about 1GB in size—and you are. The long list of numbers are the locations of the backup superblocks—see Chapter 24 for more information on these numbers, as they are sometimes required when fixing a file system.

Note that you'll need to repeat the process for any other partitions that you've created on the disk—the *newfs* command only creates a single file system on a single partition.

Mounting and Monitoring File Systems

If you followed the description of the Unix file system in Chapter 3, "Preparing for Installation," you'll remember that Unix (and therefore Solaris) uses a single file system, starting at the root file system (/), to hold all the files and pointers to other file systems and hard disks. Therefore, when mounting and unmounting file systems you have to specify both the device that you want to mount and the directory within the file system where that device should be mounted.

Mounting a File System

You mount a file system by using the *mount* command. The command in its basic form accepts the device to be mounted—which must have a valid file system on it—and the name of the directory where you want that device attached to the entire file system for a machine. For example:

```
# mount /dev/dsk/c0d1s1 /usr/local
```

The above command mounts the file system on the partition you created earlier in this chapter, mounting it at */usr/local*—the standard location for free software to be installed.

You can also specify a number of options to the file system by using the *-o* command line option, and you can mount a file system as read-only—preventing anybody from making changes—by using the *-r* command line option. See the *man* page about mount for more information.

Note that whenever you mount a file system on a directory, any contents of the directory will be unavailable—the new file system completely replaces what is accessible at the mount point. To gain access to the directory contents, you'll need to unmount the file system.

Mounting File Systems Automatically During Boot

If you want to mount a file system each time the machine is switched on, you must add the details of the device and the mount point that you want to mount the file system at in the */etc/vfstab* file. The file is scanned during the boot process and all the file systems listed in the file are checked and mounted, as shown in the following example:

```
#device            device          mount     FS    fsck mount   mount
#to mount          to fsck         point     type  pass at boot options
#
#/dev/dsk/c1d0s2 /dev/rdsk/c1d0s2 /usr       ufs    1   yes      -
fd                 -              /dev/fd    fd     -   no       -
/proc              -              /proc      proc   -   no       -
/dev/dsk/c0d0s4    -              -          swap   -   no       -
/dev/dsk/c0d0s0  /dev/rdsk/c0d0s0 /          ufs    1   no       -
/dev/dsk/c0d0s6  /dev/rdsk/c0d0s6 /usr       ufs    1   no       -
/dev/dsk/c0d0s3  /dev/rdsk/c0d0s3 /var       ufs    1   no       -
/dev/dsk/c0d0s7  /dev/rdsk/c0d0s7 /export/home ufs  2   yes      -
/dev/dsk/c0d0s5  /dev/rdsk/c0d0s5 /opt       ufs    2   yes      -
/dev/dsk/c0d0s1  /dev/rdsk/c0d0s1 /usr/openwin ufs  2   yes      -
swap               -              /tmp       tmpfs  -   yes      -
```

Incidentally, in the majority of system files, the hash, gate, or pound character (#) is used to indicate that everything after that character, up to the end of the line, is a comment and can be safely ignored. You can insert this character into a line to have the machine ignore the contents, or you can use it, as shown here in the */etc/vfstab* file, to describe the contents of the file.

Table 7.2 describes the different fields in the */etc/vfstab* file.

Table 7.2   Fields Supported by the /etc/vfstab File

Field	Description
Device to mount	The logical block device name of the partition to be mounted.
Device to fsck	The raw device name of the partition to the mounted. This is used by the *fsck* command during startup to check and if necessary repair the file system.
Mount point	The directory where the file system should be mounted.
FS Type	The file system type.
fsck pass	The order in which *fsck* should check the file system. A value of *0* or - will skip the checks. File systems with *1* will be checked first—use this for vital system volumes. Additional noncritical volumes should be checked next, so use a value of *2*.

Field	Description
Mount At Boot	If *yes*, file system is mounted during boot-up, if *no*, file system is not mounted.
Mount options	Any suitable mount options for the file system should be listed here.

For example, to add your file system put the following line at the end of the */etc/vfstab* file:

```
/dev/dsk/c0d1s1  /dev/rdsk/c0d1s1 /usr/local ufs 2 yes -
```

Unmounting a File System

To unmount a file system you use *umount* command, specifying either the device or the mount point. For example, to unmount the */export/home* file system use:

```
# umount /export/home
```

You will only be able to unmount file systems that are not currently in use. In use includes any open files or applications and even a user with a shell whose current directory is within the file system you are trying to unmount. Obviously an operation such as trying to unmount the root file system is bound to fail.

Other times a file system won't unmount for less obvious reasons. If it's an emergency, or you can see no other reason why a particular file system is in use, use the *fuser* command to list all process IDs using a particular file system:

Sun Lotion

One of my most common mistakes is to try unmounting the disk which is currently in use by me—usually because I've used *su* to become root. If you are told that the device is busy, check that you are not using the directory in either your current session or another session open on the machine (for example another Terminal window or telnet session).

```
# fuser -c /usr
/usr/local:    20561m   20560m   20559m   20558m   20557m   20556m
20555m   20554m   20553m   20552m   20551m   20550m   20393m
20116m   16004m   15784m   15356m   14381tm   14371tm   13839tm
13396tm   7685tm   632tom   629tom   628ctm   627tom
626m   603ctom   596tm   575tm   543m   496tm   487m
374c
```

The letters after each ID show how each process is using the a file on the file system, as described in Table 7.3

Table 7.3 Letter Codes for Determining Process/File Usage

Letter	Description
c	Indicates that the process is using the file as its current directory.
m	Indicates that the process is using a file mapped.
n	Indicates that the process is holding a non-blocking mandatory lock on the file.
o	Indicates that the process is using the file as an open file.
r	Indicates that the process is using the file as its root directory.
t	Indicates that the process is using the file as its text file.
y	Indicates that the process is using the file as its controlling terminal.

If you use the *-k* option instead, *fuser* will use *kill* to kill each process for you.

Checking Disk Space

The *df* command reports the "disk free" for all the currently mounted file systems:

```
# df
/                   (/dev/dsk/c0d0s0   ):  424016 blocks   120843 files
/usr                (/dev/dsk/c0d0s6   ): 2618176 blocks   411513 files
/proc               (/proc             ):       0 blocks     1883 files
/etc/mnttab         (mnttab            ):       0 blocks        0 files
/dev/fd             (fd                ):       0 blocks        0 files
/var                (/dev/dsk/c0d0s3   ):  438090 blocks   121682 files
/var/run            (swap              ): 1290904 blocks    20004 files
/opt                (/dev/dsk/c0d0s5   ):  916144 blocks   230326 files
/tmp                (swap              ): 1290904 blocks    20004 files
/export/home        (/dev/dsk/c0d0s7   ):  380838 blocks    98102 files
/usr/openwin        (/dev/dsk/c0d0s1   ):  633228 blocks   235780 files
/export/share       (twinsol:/export/share): 1511376 blocks  1065132 files
/export/contrib     (twinsol:/export/contrib): 1941546 blocks   419567 files
/usr/local          (twinsol:/usr/local): 4962830 blocks   526395 files
```

The output above shows the number of free blocks (typically 512 bytes each) and the number of free files. The output is not particularly useful since you really need the information in kilobytes. To get this, use the *-k* command line option:

```
$ df -k
Filesystem          kbytes    used    avail capacity  Mounted on
/dev/dsk/c0d0s0     246463   34455   187362    16%    /
/dev/dsk/c0d0s6    1785654  476566  1255519    28%    /usr
/proc                    0       0        0     0%    /proc
```

```
mnttab                    0       0       0    0%    /etc/mnttab
fd                        0       0       0    0%    /dev/fd
/dev/dsk/c0d0s3      246463   27418  194399   13%    /var

swap                645464      20  645444    1%    /var/run
/dev/dsk/c0d0s5     458087      15  412264    1%    /opt
swap                645444       0  645444    0%    /tmp
/dev/dsk/c0d0s7     192423    2004  171177    2%    /export/home
/dev/dsk/c0d0s1     492422  175808  267372   40%    /usr/openwin
```

The *df* command tells you how much space is available and a total of the disk space used, but it won't tell you who or which directories are using the most space. To get an idea of which directories are using the most space use the *du* command, optionally supplying the name of the directory you want to check (the default is the current directory):

```
# du
```

The only problem is that it will begin to list the sizes of every directory beneath the one you specify, when what you probably wanted was a quick idea of the top-level directories. It'll also show disk blocks, not kilobytes. Use the *-s* option to ask for a summary of the disk space used for each directory or file you specify and *-k* to show the usage in kilobytes:

```
# du -sk /usr/*
du -sk /usr/*
1          /usr/5bin
1          /usr/X
1          /usr/adm
148217     /usr/answerbook
132        /usr/aset
14423      /usr/bin
1851       /usr/ccs
```

To find out how much space each user is using up on a particular file system (whether or not you are using quotas), use *quot*:

```
# quot /export/home
/dev/rdsk/c0d0s7:
 1972   mc
   28   root
    4   spenfold
```

Working with Removable Media

Because Solaris does not refer to individual disks in the same way as other operating systems, you may be wondering how to deal with and access floppy disks, CD-ROMs, and other removable media formats. You actually access them in the same way as you would any other type of file system on a Solaris machine—by accessing the directory point at which they are mounted.

In terms of mounting them, the easiest way to do this is use the volume manager. The manager, *vold*, is enabled by default and it monitors the removable devices on your machine, automatically mounting the disk using the appropriate file system type and other information when a disk is inserted. For example, I've just inserted the Solaris 8 installation CD into my Solaris machine and if I type *mount*, the bottom two lines tell me that it's mounted two file systems from the CD:

```
/cdrom/sol_8_1000_ia/s2 on /vol/dev/dsk/c1t0d0/sol_8_1000_ia/s2 read
only/nosuid/maplcase/noglobal/rr/traildot/dev=1740003 on Fri Feb  1 12:07:09 2002
/cdrom/sol_8_1000_ia/s0 on /vol/dev/dsk/c1t0d0/sol_8_1000_ia/s0 read
only/nosuid/intr/largefiles/onerror=panic/dev=1740001 on Fri Feb  1 12:07:09 2002
```

I can now access the CD by changing to the directory listed in the first part of each line.

Floppy disks appear in much the same way. Other removable media will need to be mounted manually using the techniques you saw earlier.

To get your CD back you need to ask Solaris to eject the CD:

```
# eject cdrom
```

The file systems will be automatically unmounted and the disk ejected.

The Least You Need to Know

- ◆ You access the information stored on a disk using a file system.
- ◆ To set up a new hard disk you must first organize the disk into a number of slices (or partitions) using *format* (and *fdisk*, under Intel).
- ◆ To create the file system you need to use *newfs* on each partition.
- ◆ You mount a partition and make it available for use by using *mount*.
- ◆ You unmount a partition and remove it from use by using *umount*.
- ◆ You can monitor the available disk space using *df*, the disk space used in different directories using *du*, and the disk used by individual users using *quot*.

## Chapter 8

Starting and Stopping Services

In This Chapter

◆ Starting up and shutting down

◆ Boot, reboot, and shutdown

◆ Manual Service Management

Solaris is an operating system that is designed to be switched on and left on, but that doesn't mean that you never have to reboot the system. There are numerous times when you need to change the running state of the machine, from reducing it into "single user" mode to perform system administration tasks right through to rebooting and shutting a machine down completely.

In this chapter I explain what happens when you start a machine up, what happens during a shutdown, and how to control these operations. I'll also explain what happens when you switch the machine on and ask it to shut down.

In the final part of the chapter, I'll discuss how to modify the startup and shutdown process and how to manually start and stop the services used to support different facilities on your machine.

What Happens During Startup and Shutdown?

Behind the scenes of the boot up process that you saw earlier are a series of systems that help control what happens when you start up or shut down a machine.

Booting Up

There are quite a few stages between switching on your machine and the point at which your machine becomes usable.

On a Sun SPARC machine the basic sequence is:

1. **Boot PROM loads.** This is the ROM loaded by the computer when it is switched on. The Boot PROM loads the code necessary to let the computer identify disks and network devices and then find a bootable component—usually a disk. The Boot PROM on a SPARC machine can be used to do other things too, but most users will never need to use them.

2. **Boot loader starts.** The PROM and its boot loader looks for the *ufsboot* program (loaded from disk, or other the network) and executes it. The role of *ufsboot* is to load the kernel.

3. **The kernel loads.** The kernel is the core of the Unix operating system and is responsible for communicating between the hardware devices and the rest of the system. All programs communicate with and interact with the kernel in some way, even if it's only loading the program and any libraries it needs. The kernel calls the *init* process.

4. *init* **starts processes.** The *init* process is used to start all the other processes required to actually run the system. It runs the programs that check the machine and its disks, load services and daemons, and loads the daemon that allows you to log in to and use the machine.

On Intel machines the basic process is the same, but the terms are slightly different:

1. **BIOS loads.** The BIOS loads and provides the core interface between the hardware and user and allows you to configure the machine and boot device. It's also responsible for actually booting an operating system from a suitable device (network or disk).

2. **Boot loader is started.** The boot loader software, *pboot* is loaded. This is a precursor to the full kernel and allows you to select the device to boot the kernel from and change any boot parameters for the kernel.

3. **The kernel loads.** The kernel is loaded and executed and starts to load its modules and other services before finally calling the *init* process.

4. *init* **starts processes.** The *init* process is used to start all the other processes required to actually run the system. It runs the programs that check the machine and its disks, load services and daemons, and loads the daemon that allows you to log in to and use the machine.

Sun Lotion _____

Most of the operating system configuration is handled by the files in /etc and the daemons and services which use and rely on these files. However, some of the features and facilities need to be controlled at such a low level that they are determined by the kernel. You can change these parameters by modifying the contents of the /etc/system file.

In this file you can define global parameters such as the number of supported users and processes and you can also control which kernel modules are loaded and where they are loaded from. The kernel itself is actually very small, and most of the functionality that we identify as being kernel-related is actually located within a module loaded by the kernel either during boot time or afterwards by using the *modload* command. Kernel modules include the drivers for communicating with the keyboard, mouse, and disk drives as well as the modules that define how to read the information from different file system types.

The *init* process is really the center of attention from this moment on—the kernel sits in the background, servicing the requests of the rest of the system, communicating with the hardware and executing programs when asked to do so. The *init* program decides what to run by using a file called *inittab*, which specifies a number of "runlevels" for the machine.

Runlevels

When you start up a Unix machine, it starts up using a specific runlevel. This has nothing to do with its movement ability or its speed, however; it affects what the machine is able to do and what services it provides. For example, there is a runlevel designed for multiuser access, another used for multiuser access with NFS, and another for single user access, which is used for system administration tasks.

The configuration of these different runlevels is controlled by a file called */etc/inittab* which is read by the *init* process—one of the core elements of the Unix operating system and as you've already seen the final element of the booting process. Before I show you how to change the runlevel (and therefore the machine's running state), it's worth taking a look at which runlevels are available. The following listing shows a sample */etc/inittab* file:

```
ap::sysinit:/sbin/autopush -f /etc/iu.ap
ap::sysinit:/sbin/soconfig -f /etc/sock2path
fs::sysinit:/sbin/rcS sysinit          >/dev/msglog 2<>/dev/msglog
                                      ➥</dev/console
is:3:initdefault:
p3:s1234:powerfail:/usr/sbin/shutdown -y -i5 -g0 >/dev/msglog 2<>/dev/msglog
sS:s:wait:/sbin/rcS                    >/dev/msglog 2<>/dev/msglog
                                      ➥</dev/console
```

```
s0:0:wait:/sbin/rc0                    >/dev/msglog 2<>/dev/msglog
                                       ➥</dev/console

s1:1:respawn:/sbin/rc1                 >/dev/msglog 2<>/dev/msglog
                                       ➥</dev/console

s2:23:wait:/sbin/rc2                   >/dev/msglog 2<>/dev/msglog
                                       ➥</dev/console

s3:3:wait:/sbin/rc3                    >/dev/msglog 2<>/dev/msglog
                                       ➥</dev/console

s5:5:wait:/sbin/rc5                    >/dev/msglog 2<>/dev/msglog
                                       ➥</dev/console

s6:6:wait:/sbin/rc6                    >/dev/msglog 2<>/dev/msglog
                                       ➥</dev/console

fw:0:wait:/sbin/uadmin 2 0             >/dev/msglog 2<>/dev/msglog
                                       ➥</dev/console

of:5:wait:/sbin/uadmin 2 6             >/dev/msglog 2<>/dev/msglog
                                       ➥</dev/console

rb:6:wait:/sbin/uadmin 2 1             >/dev/msglog 2<>/dev/msglog
                                       ➥</dev/console
sc:234:respawn:/usr/lib/saf/sac -t 300
co:234:respawn:/usr/lib/saf/ttymon -g -h -p "'uname -n' console login: " -T
sun-color -d /dev/console -l console -m ldterm,ttcompat
```

I won't go into the specific details of the file contents—chances are you will never need to modify the contents, but it is important to understand what the effects are.

Each line in the file specifies a different setting, but not always an individual runlevel. The line is split into several fields, each separated by a colon. In order, these are ID, rstate, action, and process. The ID is a unique identifier for the runlevel, and rstate specifies which runlevels trigger the line to be evaluated. For example, s2 (system state 2) is triggered when the system is changed to runlevel 2 or 3, whereas *rb* (short for reboot) is triggered only when you change to runlevel 6.

The next field defines what to do when the state is executed. There are a number of available settings, including wait, which starts the *process* specified and waits for its termination before continuing to evaluate *inittab* and *respawn*, which forces *init* to immediately restart the specified *process* if it dies. This option is used on items critical to the system such as the login prompt—without which the machine would be rendered fairly useless!

The last field is the command that is executed. For example, standard runlevels such as 2 and 3 execute the */sbin/rc2* and */sbin/rc3* commands respectively—we'll look at these in more detail later in this chapter. Others run something more mundane—for example runlevel 6 calls *uadmin*, which is used to shutdown, reboot, or switch off a machine. For runlevel 6, the effect is to shut down and reboot the system.

Right at the start of the file is the most important line of all—it sets the default runlevel for the machine:

```
is:3:initdefault:
```

The default runlevel is 3—multiuser mode with NFS support. You can modify this value to another runlevel, but it's unlikely that you will need to do this.

> ### Sun Screen
>
> Don't *ever* modify the default runlevel unless you know what you are doing, and make double and triple sure that you check the runlevel before you reboot the machine or change the runlevel through *init*.
>
> I once had to fix a server where an unsuspecting and unknowing user had changed the default runlevel to reboot the machine, rather than using one of the more usual methods, and ended up with a machine that continually started up and rebooted itself!

A full description of the effects of each of the default runlevels is shown here in Table 8.1.

Table 8.1   Supported Runlevels

Runlevel	init State	Supported Operations
0	Power Down	The system is shut down. All users are forced off the system and any running services are stopped in an orderly manner. On a SPARC machine you will be returned to the OpenBoot prompt. On an Intel system you will be prompted to press any key to reset the machine or manually power the machine down.
S or s	Single User mode	The system is prepared for administration or maintenance. The most basic services are disabled and only the superuser can use and administer the machine using the console.
1	Administrative	Administrative state with multi-user access. Similar to single user mode, where all services except the basics are stopped, but it allows other people to access the machine. Can be useful if you need to perform a number of administration tasks simultaneously.
2	Multiuser	The normal operational mode, all services *except* NFS serving are available, and users can connect and log in to the machine as normal. Client NFS operations are unaffected. All the file systems (including NFS) in */etc/vfstab* are mounted.

continues

Table 8.1   Supported Runlevels   (continued)

Runlevel	init State	Supported Operations
3	Multiuser with NFS	The same as runlevel 2, but NFS client and server services are supported.
4	Alternative Multiuser	Unsupported in the default system. Can be customized for your own use.
5	Power Down	Similar to 0, except that it will power down the machine (SPARC or Intel) if that option is supported in the motherboard.
6	Reboot	The system is shut down and then restarted, bringing it back to the standard runlevel (typically 3).

All the runlevels are special in their own unique way, but the single-user mode is probably the most important of the runlevels that you should know about. Single-user mode is used for administration tasks that affect other users or require them to be off the system. These tasks include, but are not limited to, repairing, installing, or removing disks and partitions, installing patches and new software, and backing up and restoring a machine during an emergency.

In single-user mode, you can only use the machine through the console—either the keyboard/display or a terminal/computer attached to the serial port. This makes it useless for remote administration (and even if this was supported, networking is disabled, too!). You can also only use the machine if you have superuser/root access.

If you start up in single-user mode, then only the root (/) and *usr* file systems will be mounted—any others that you require will need to be mounted manually. Because nobody else is on the system, you have a free hand to make changes and add or remove patches, software, and disk partitions without risking upsetting what another user is doing.

You will occasionally need to change into single-user mode to perform some of the operations in this book—I'll let you know when this is required.

Changing Runlevels

To add to the confusion, there are also essentially two actual states for the runlevel, the level that you are currently in, and the level you are changing to. There are a number of different ways in which you can change the runlevel, which I've listed in Table 8.2.

Table 8.2   Ways of Changing the Runlevel

Command	Runlevels	Description
/usr/sbin/halt	0	Immediately shuts down the system.
/usr/sbin/poweroff	5	Shuts down the system and switches the power off (if supported).
/sbin/init	Any	Changes the runlevel, including reboot, power off, and shutdown.
/usr/sbin/reboot	6	Shuts down and then reboots the system.
/etc/shutdown	0,1,5,6,s	Shuts down the system either to single-user mode, to power off, or shuts down and reboots.
/usr/sbin/shutdown	0,1,5,6,s	Shuts down the system either to single-user mode, to power off, or shuts down and reboots.
/etc/telinit	Any	Changes the runlevel, including reboot, poweroff, and shutdown.
uadmin	0,5,6	Allows you to shut down, power off, or reboot.

For example, you can reboot a system using any of the following:

```
% init 6
% reboot
% shutdown -r
```

The *-r* option to *shutdown* tells it to shut down the system and then reboot the system.

To shut down to single-user level you can use any of the following:

```
% init s
% init S
% shutdown
% shutdown -i S
```

The *-i* option to *shutdown* tells it which runlevel to change to—in this case, I've specified the single user *S* runlevel.

To shut down and switch off a machine you could use any of the following:

```
% init 5
% shutdown -i 5
% poweroff
```

Which one you use typically depends on which one you are either most familiar with or most comfortable with, or what you are doing. For a client machine, for example, the *init* command is probably the easiest to use, as it just goes ahead and changes the runlevel of the machine to what you specify.

On a multiuser machine, the *shutdown* command should be used. Unlike all the other commands, *shutdown* can broadcast a message to all the users currently connected to the machine and it can delay the shutdown process (a so-called *grace period*) to give users time to save their work and log out before the machine shuts down completely.

You set the grace period by using the -g option and specifying the number of seconds to wait before starting the real shutdown process. To supply a message, you just include the message details at the end of the command. For example, you might give users a warning and 5-minute grace period of an impending shutdown for maintenance using:

```
% shutdown -i s -g 300 Shutting down for scheduled maintenance.
```

The *shutdown* program will broadcast the message and show the warning time to each user connected to the machine—unfortunately it only does this for those connected via telnet/ssh. Those accessing a shared disk are not warned. The following output shows a sample warning:

```
Shutdown started.    Tue Jan 22 15:07:47 GMT 2002

Broadcast Message from root (pts/3) on sol9penguin Tue Jan 22 15:07:48...
The system sol9penguin will be shut down in 5 minutes
Shutting down for scheduled maintenance.
```

One other benefit of *shutdown* is that because it gives a grace period, you can quit out of the shutdown process before the actual shutdown begins. Being able to delay the shutdown, or even cancel it completely, can be useful if you suddenly realize that you've forgotten to do something!

What Happens When You Change Runlevels?

When you change the runlevel, the program defined in */etc/inittab* is executed. For all the runlevels this has the effect of executing the scripts within the */etc/rcN.d* directory, where *N* is the runlevel you have chosen. Within each directory are a number of "run control" (rc) scripts. Each rc script is used to perform a different operation from setting up the network to starting a database or other service. For example, runlevel 2 starts a program called */sbin/rc2* which in turn executes the scripts within the directory */etc/rc2.d*.

The following output lists the *etc/rc2.d* directory, showing all the different rc scripts:

```
K06mipagent*          S72slpd*
K07dmi*               S73cachefs.daemon*
K07snmpdx*            S73nfs.client*
K16apache*            S74autofs*
K21dhcp*              S74syslog*
K27boot.server*       S74xntpd*
K28kdc*               S75cron*
K28kdc.master*        S75savecore*
K28nfs.server*        S76nscd*
README                S80PRESERVE*
S01MOUNTFSYS*         S80kdmconfig*
S05RMTMPFILES*        S80lp*
S10lu*                S80spc*
S20sysetup*           S85power*
S21perf*              S88sendmail*
S30sysid.net*         S88utmpd*
S40llc2*              S90wbem*
S47pppd*              S92volmgt*
S69inet*              S93cacheos.finish*
S70uucp*              S94ncalogd*
S71ldap.client*       S95ncad*
S71rpc*               S95svm.sync*
S71sysid.sys*         S99audit*
S72autoinstall*       S99dtlogin*
S72inetsvc*
```

You'll notice that each script is prefixed by a single uppercase letter (either K or S) and a number. The numbers are used to control the execution order of the scripts. The *sendmail* rc script, for example, is not executed until the networking script has been executed. If there was no way to control the order then it's likely the sendmail script would fail because the networking script may not have been executed first.

A Postcard From ...

Although it doesn't seem like it at the time, when you switch on and boot up a machine, you are really just changing to the default runlevel. If you remember the contents of */etc/inittab* from earlier in this chapter, you'll notice that the default runlevel is 3, and that a number of entries in */etc/inittab* apply to this runlevel. In each case, for each program in */etc/inittab* to which runlevel 3 applies, each program is executed and the scripts in one of the */etc/rcN.d* directories are executed.

For runlevel 3 this includes all the startup scripts in runlevel 2 and runlevel 3, which is why you'll find that */etc/rc3.d* seems relatively devoid of rc scripts—the reason is that it only needs the scripts that set up (or shut down) the NFS system.

The letter prefix is more important. Each rc script typically has two modes of execution, *start* and *stop*. If you call a script and specify *start* on the command line, for example,

```
% sendmail start
```

then the sendmail service will start, and if you use

```
% sendmail stop
```

then the sendmail service will be terminated.

Every script with a *K* prefix is executed with the *stop* argument, and everything with an *S* is executed with the *start* argument.

This is how the different services available in a particular runlevel are controlled. When you change to runlevel 2, for example, each script in */etc/rc2.d* is executed: the *K* scripts stopping services, such as the NFS server, and the *S* scripts starting services, such as sendmail.

If you change from runlevel 2 to runlevel 3 then all the *K* and *S* scripts are run accordingly in the */etc/rc3.d* directory. If you look at that directory, you'll notice that a lot more of the scripts are K, rather than S scripts.

We can change these options around. For example, if we wanted to permanently disable *sendmail* we could delete the scripts, but it's much better to simply rename *S88sendmail* to *K88sendmail* to ensure that the service is shut down during a runlevel change, even if sendmail had been started manually.

The files in the */etc/rcN.d* directories are actually symbolic links to the real scripts in */etc/init.d*. This allows you to change the script contents without having to copy the new script into each directory. It also means that you can easily modify the services in different levels without worrying about the script location each time—it should always be available in */etc/init.d*.

Solingo

The Unix file system enables you to create links between two files in the same way that Windows has shortcuts and Mac OS has aliases. A link is exactly that—it's just a simple pointer to another file.

Unix supports two types. The hard link is a duplicate directory entry that allows the same physical file to be accessed by two different names.

Symbolic links are closer to shortcuts and aliases. A symbolic link is just a pointer to another file that could be on a different file system. The content of a symbolic link is the path (the directory and name of a file)—when you access a symbolic link, the system opens the real file to which it points.

Note that when you delete a link you only delete the link, not the file.

Manual Service Management

Because the *etc/init.d* directory contains the scripts that start up the different services, you can use those scripts to manually manage services just by calling them with the corresponding *start* or *stop* options.

For example, if you want to temporarily disable *sendmail* you can just use:

```
% /etc/init.d/sendmail stop
```

By using this method you avoid having to look for the sendmail process and manually killing it. To start the service back again afterwards you just use:

```
% /etc/init.d/sendmail start
```

Easy!!

Special Boot Options

When you are presented with the boot loader screen on an Intel machine or with the Boot PROM prompt on a SPARC machine, you can tell the kernel to perform some special operations, such as starting up into single-user mode or rebuilding the device tables. You can also specify these options to the *reboot* command when rebooting a system.

From a boot prompt (the "ok" prompt) you do this by specifying a number of options, similar to command line options, to the boot command. The full list of options supported is shown in Table 8.3.

Sun Lotion

The Intel boot loader gives you a grace period to enter any kernel options, but a SPARC system will often boot and load the kernel so quickly that you don't have a chance to enter any options.

You can go back to the Boot PROM prompt on a SPARC system by pressing the L1 and A keys on the keyboard at the same time. L1 is the top right key on the extra function pad on the right hand side of a Sun-compatible keyboard. If you are connected to the machine over a serial port, use Control-X to terminate the boot process, and then you can enter the options.

Table 8.3 Boot Options to the Kernel

Option	Description
-a	Ask the user for configuration information such as the location of the system file (*/etc/system*), where to mount the root operating system, and the name of the kernel you want to load. This can be useful if your */etc/system* file is corrupt (use */dev/null* as the system file location to use the default options) or to load a kernel that you know works.
-f	Causes Autoclient systems to flush and reinitialize the client system's local cache.
-r	Reconfigures the */dev* and */devices* directories by probing all the attached hardware devices. You'll need to use this whenever you add a new device to a system or if you change the configuration (master/slave, SCSI ID number, or similar) of a hardware device. The kernel will rebuild the */dev* and */devices* directory with all the names and references required to use the devices.
-s	Boot into single-user mode (runlevel *s*). Useful if you are having system problems and need to boot into single-user mode to fix the problems.
-v	Boot with verbose messages. This is the output normally sent to the *syslog* service.
-x	Do not boot in clustered mode—only applicable to a machine running clustering software in a clustered configuration.

Solingo _____

The /dev/null device is a special device that contains nothing and if supplied with any information simply discards it. You can use this as a source for creating a new file, for supplying no information when a file is absolutely required, or to receive information that you know you definitely don't want—for example, errors from a command that you know produces errors you're not interested in.

To specify these options during the boot process use:

b -sr

when prompted on an Intel machine, or

> boot -sr

on a SPARC machine.

To set these options when using the *reboot* command, you should first use -- (double hyphen) to end the *reboot* options and then specify the boot parameters. For example:

```
% reboot -- -sr
```

It's a good idea to remember the *-s* option used to start up in single-user mode, as in an emergency it may be the only way of starting your machine.

The Least You Need to Know

◆ All Unix machines have a runlevel used to determine what services a machine provides.

◆ The default runlevel is 3 (multiuser mode with NFS client/server support).

◆ You can change the runlevel using *init*, *reboot*, or *shutdown*.

◆ You can reboot a machine by using *init 6*, *reboot*, or *shutdown -r*.

◆ You can shut down a machine into single-user mode using *shutdown* or *init S*.

◆ You can power down a machine using *init 5* or *shutdown -i 5*.

Setting Up a Printer

In This Chapter

- Introducing the printer system
- Adding printers
- Monitoring and managing the print service

The paperless office isn't here yet and despite attempts at making the dream of a paperless office a reality, it seems that we are still a number of years away from reading and writing everything using a computer. We therefore need a way to get our ideas and information out on paper.

Solaris provides the ability to print both to printers attached directly to the machine and to those printers available on the network, either directly or by communicating with other computers on the network which are sharing their printers.

In this chapter I show you how to add a printer to your system, share your printer with other computers, and manage the jobs and printer queues.

The Printer System

Before I leap into the setting up and management of a printer it's a good idea to look at how the printer service works. Like most other parts of the Unix system where some form of service is provided, there is a background task devoted to actually supporting requests. Within Solaris a single daemon, *lpsched*, is responsible for handling the printing system. It receives requests and sends the requests on to a specific printer to be printed.

A Postcard From ...

Years ago, before laser printers and inkjets were commonplace, printers were either "golf ball" or "dot matrix" based. Dot matrix printers were the most prolific because they were the cheapest. A small set of pins in a matrix were fired against a printer ribbon as the head moved across the page. The "golf ball" printer has nothing to do with the amount of time it spent out on the fairway; instead it referred to the print head, which was about the size and shape of a golf ball and had on it the individual characters that could be printed. As the print head moved across the page, the ball would be rotated and pivoted so as to allow each character to press against a ribbon and then on to the page.

Golf ball printers were preferred for business communication as the page looked as if it was printed. Dot matrix was generally only used where either the volume of information produced was so high or where the eventual reader didn't matter, for example, an internal report. Both were line printers—they produced their output by printing out one line of information at a time. Inkjet printers are still examples of line printers, but the quality and abilities have improved. Laser printers are page printers, as they image and print entire pages at the same time.

The *lp* portion of all the printer service commands relates to the old line printer systems.

The overall printing system is quite extensive and includes the following facilities:

- **Multiple queues:** You can set up as many different printers as you need, and each printer can be a different type, or just a different configuration for the same printer.

- **Printer classes:** Printers can be logically grouped into classes. For example, you may create a group of laser printers. When a job is sent to the laser printer class, it's printed on the first available printer; so even if two out of three printers in the class are busy, the job will still be printed.

- **Remote printing:** Jobs can be sent to remote printers, either those connected to another machine or to network printers that allow network printing.

- **Printer sharing:** Any Solaris machine can accept and therefore share any printers that are configured for the system.

- **Print Jobs:** Jobs can be moved between printers.

- **Queue management:** Individual printers and the entire print system can be paused and resumed or stopped altogether.

Adding a Printer

The easiest way to add a printer is using the *admintool*. Although it can be done on the command line, it's not the easiest method for printer administration. I won't be covering the manual method in this guide, but check out the *man* page for *lpadmin* if you need to set up a printer in this way.

You can configure two types of printers:

◆ **Local printer:** A local printer is one that is physically attached to the machine through a serial, parallel, or USB connection.

◆ **Remote printer:** A remote printer is one that is available on your network, either one that directly provides a network service or one that is shared through another Unix machine.

To add a printer, open the *admintool* and use the Browse menu to switch to the list of configured printers. To add a new printer, select the Edit menu and choose which type of printer you want to create, either Local Printer or Access to Printer for a networked printer.

For a local printer there are a number of settings which you must configure. You can see the basic layout of the configuration page in Figure 9.1.

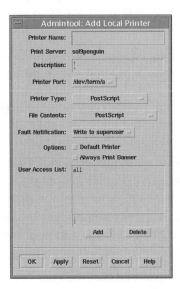

Figure 9.1

Adding a local printer with admintool.

Here are some tips on the data you should be entering:

- **Printer Name:** This is the name of the printer as it will be identified on *this* machine. The printer name can be made up of upper or lowercase characters, numbers, hyphens, and underscores. All other characters are illegal. The name can be up to 14 characters long.

- **Description:** A description of the printer and/or its location.

- **Printer Port:** This is the physical port used to communicate with the printer. Common values are */dev/term/a* or */dev/term/b* for the two serial ports, or */dev/lp1* for the first parallel port on your machine.

- **Printer Type:** This sets the printer driver to use when sending jobs to the printer. Solaris supports a number of standards, including PostScript, support for nearly all HP printers (inkjet and LaserJet) and a number of others.

- **File Contents:** Use the popup to select which types of jobs will be accepted by the printer. For example, a printer that only accepts PostScript jobs can be set to ignore anything but PostScript jobs. Conversely, you probably wouldn't want to be able to send PostScript to a printer that doesn't support it.

- **Fault Notification:** This specifies how an error with the printer will be notified. The Write to Superuser option will send a message directly to an administrator's terminal (if he or she is logged in) while Email to Superuser will send an email to the administrator. Selecting None will disable fault notification.

- **Default Printer:** This configures this printer as the default printer for the entire system.

- **Always Print Banner:** If you are setting up a machine that will be used in an environment where lots of people print jobs to the same printer, it's a good idea to enable this feature. Before each job is printed, it will print a single page banner showing the user who submitted the job and the job number. It becomes easier then to identify an individual printout.

- **User Access List:** This is an inclusive list of the users who will be allowed to print to the printer. You can restrict access to individual users, and if anything other than All is specified then only the listed users will be able to print to the printer.

When setting up a remote printer, the list of options is much simpler. The fault notification, printer type, and accepted types are controlled by the remote printer, rather than the local queue we create.

To set up a remote printer, select the Edit menu and choose Access to Printer. You will be presented with a window like the one shown in Figure 9.2.

Figure 9.2

Adding a remote printer with admintool.

The different options you need to configure are:

♦ **Printer Name:** The name of the printer that will be used to identify the printer, both on the local machine and as the name of the queue on the remote server.

♦ **Print Server:** The hostname of the server providing access to this printer.

♦ **Description:** A description of the printer and/or its location.

♦ **Default printer:** Whether to create the printer as the default printer on this machine.

Sun Lotion

Actually, the command line *lpadmin* tool is the quickest way to set up remote printers. It's also the only way to set up a remote printer if you want the name of the printer on the local machine and the name of the printer on the remote machine to be different.

To set up a remote printer with *lpadmin* use *lpadmin -p printer -s host!remlp*, where *printer* is the local name you want to give the printer, *host* is the name of the remote machine to print to and *remlp* is the name of the remote printer queue. Be careful when using *!* within *bash* and *csh*; use *\!* instead.

When creating a local printer it is automatically set up so that it can be shared with other clients on the network, but you must tell those remote systems to allow your machine to send requests on to that queue. For example, if *sol9penguin* wants to print via the *lp* queue on *twinsol*, you need to:

1. Set up the printer on *sol9penguin*.

2. Tell the print system on *twinsol* to allow users on *sol9penguin* to submit jobs.

To do this, you need to use the command line *lpadmin* tool. The format, however, is quite simple. The command must be entered on the remote system (*twinsol* in this example) and it will only work for other Solaris systems (check the documentation for other platforms):

```
# lpadmin -p printer -u [allow|deny]:host!user
```

The *printer* is the name of the printer queue that you want to allow remote access to. The *[allow|deny]* defines whether you want to allow or deny a specific host or user to access the printer. For example, you can basically allow everybody, but deny a few users, or allow everybody or deny everybody, and so on. Basically users and/or hosts have to have been given explicit access, or if access is given to everybody, you can selectively exclude specific users.

The *host* should be the name of the machine and *user* should be a comma-separated list of users given access. You can also use the special word "all" in either location; for example, *twinsol!all* provides access to all users on host *twinsol*, and *all!mc* provides access to the user *mc* from any system. Finally, the simple specification of *all* allows anybody from any host to use that queue.

For example, to provide access to everybody on the *lp* print queue use:

```
# lpadmin -p lp -u allow:all
```

However you have set up your printer, it's a good idea to test the printer queue you have just created to make sure it's working. The *lp* command will print a file, but for testing purposes it's probably easier just to change to a relatively empty directory and do:

```
$ ls|lp
```

to print out the directory listing. Hopefully something will appear on the printer pretty quickly. If it doesn't, time to check the printer status.

Monitoring the Print Service

The easiest way to check the print service is to use the *lpstat* command. The lp system keeps fairly good tabs on what its printers are doing, including monitoring paper out states. If you are trying to communicate with a remote printer, it'll try and tell you the status of the remote printer, too.

In its basic form, *lpstat* will report the list of jobs currently being printed, if there are any waiting. A more useful report is provided by using the *-t* command line option, which prints out all the available information for all the configured printers, including information about the default printer, ports, or remote printer queues used and their current status. For example:

```
$ lpstat -t
scheduler is running
system default destination: lp
system for sol9lp: twinsol (as printer lp)
system for _default: laserjet (as printer lp)
system for lp: laserjet
device for lpp: /dev/printers/0
```

```
sol9lp accepting requests since Jan 31 14:21 2002
_default accepting requests since Jan 31 14:21 2002
lp accepting requests since Jan 31 14:21 2002
lpp accepting requests since Fri Mar 15 11:33:57 GMT 2002
printer sol9lp unknown state. enabled since Jan 31 14:21 2002. available.
printer _default unknown state. enabled since Jan 31 14:21 2002. available.
JetDirect lpd: no jobs queued on this port
printer lp unknown state. enabled since Jan 31 14:21 2002. available.
sol9lp-2               root@sol9penguin    129    Jan 31 14:21
sol9lp-3               root@sol9penguin    129    Jan 31 14:21
sol9lp-6               root@sol9penguin    129    Jan 31 14:21
```

You can see here from the entries starting "system" that the *lp* queue points to a remote queue (lp) on the *laserjet* host, while *sol9lp* points to a queue on *twinsol*. You can also see the device (the first parallel port) used for the *lpp* printer, and that the printer is accepting and waiting for print jobs. You can also see three outstanding jobs, submitted by *root* to the *sol9lp* queue.

Print Service Management

There are times when you need to move a job from one printer to another (because it's important and the existing printer has died or run out of paper), cancel the job altogether, or change the state of a given printer queue.

Canceling Jobs

To cancel a job, you must know the request number of the job. Printer jobs are numbered sequentially, with each job number being prefixed by the printer name. For example, the sixth job on the printer *sol9lp* would have the job number *sol9lp-6*. This is given when the job is first submitted, or in the output from *lpstat*. To kill the job you use the *cancel* command, so to cancel the request ID *sol9lp-6* use:

```
# cancel sol9lp-6
```

As superuser, you can also cancel all the jobs for an individual user by using the *-u* option and then specifying the user name:

```
# cancel -u mc
```

The above cancels all the jobs by that user on all printers. To cancel only the jobs on a specific printer you can add a list of printers to the command line:

```
# cancel -u mc sol9lp
```

In this case, you've asked to cancel all the jobs on the print queue *sol9lp* for the user *mc*.

Moving Jobs

Occasionally, you may want to move specific jobs from one printer to another—perhaps because you need them quicker, or because the existing printer is no longer available. You can move jobs using the *lpmove* command. You should supply a list of jobs and then the destination, as in:

```
# lpmove sol9lp-2 sol9lp-3 lp
```

This will move the two jobs from the *sol9lp* queue to the *lp* queue. Alternatively, you can move all the jobs from one queue to another by supplying the source and destination queue names:

```
# lpmove sol9lp lp
```

Changing the Default Printer

To change the default printer, use *lpadmin* with the *-d* option. For example, to change the default printer to *sol9lp*, use:

```
# lpadmin -d sol9lp
```

Deleting a Printer

To delete a printer, the easiest method is to use *lpadmin* with the *-x* command line option. For example, to delete the printer *lp*, use:

```
# lpadmin -x lp
```

The queue for the printer should be empty before you delete it.

Pausing and Resuming Printing

You can pause and later resume printing on a given queue. The *disable* command stops printing on a given queue but does not prevent jobs from being submitted to the queue—this is logically equivalent to pressing the offline button on your printer (if you have one). To use it, just supply the name of the print queue on the command line:

```
# disable lp
```

To start printing jobs again, use *enable*:

```
# enable lp
```

Any jobs that were partway through printing when the queue was disabled will be restarted from the beginning.

Stopping and Starting Print Queues

If you want to stop people from submitting jobs to a queue, but still allow the queue to continue printing, then use *reject*:

```
# reject lp
```

To tell the system to start accepting requests again, use *accept*:

```
# accept lp
```

Sun Lotion

The *enable* command is actually an internal command for the *bash* shell, and you'll get an error if you try calling enable within *bash*. Instead, explicitly refer to the *enable* command by using /usr/bin/enable.

Starting and stopping the queue can be useful if there is a serious problem on the printer but you don't want to stop people from actually printing anything. I've used it in the past as the best way to change toner cartridges and when moving or reconfiguring the printer. It's also often the only way of pausing printing on some of the newer printers that don't have an online/offline button.

The Least You Need to Know

◆ Solaris allows you to set up both local (physically attached) and remote printers.

◆ The easiest way to set up a printer is with the *admintool*, although you can use the *lpadmin* command if you need to.

◆ You can monitor the printer status using *lpstat*.

◆ You can cancel jobs using *cancel*.

◆ You can move jobs from one print queue to another using *lpmove*.

◆ You can pause printing on a queue using *disable* and start printing again using *enable*.

◆ You can reject new print requests on a queue using *reject* and allow them again using *accept*.

Managing Software

In This Chapter

- ◆ Installing and managing packages
- ◆ Applying patches
- ◆ Installing software from source code

It's unlikely that you'll ever just install the operating system and forget it. You'll want to add more features to the operating system, install new applications, and quite probably download a few pieces of useful free software to help with programming, Internet services, and administration.

To make the process of installing software and additional operating system components easier, Solaris provides a system called packages. You can install and remove packages and even check packages that have been installed to ensure your system has not become corrupted. Longer term you'll also need to install patches—these are small collections of files that update files to fix bugs and potential security problems.

Not everything you might want to install is available as a convenient package. Occasionally you'll need to be a little more interactive with your installations, especially if you are downloading and using free software. This is often supplied as source code which will need to be compiled with a C compiler before the application or drivers can actually be used.

In this chapter I'll explain these three main methods of installing, managing, and manipulating the software on your system.

Handling Packages

If you've had a chance to play around with Solaris and dig around looking for files and toys to play with, you will probably have noticed that there are a huge number of files that make up the operating system.

Sun Lotion _____

You'll need to be superuser, either by logging in as root or by using the *su* command to perform any of the operations in this chapter.

Remember, when I discussed how to install Solaris (in Chapter 4, "Installing Solaris"), I talked about packages. A single package holds a combination of binary files, text files, directory information, and other components such as install and uninstall scripts. Each package is self-contained—it contains all of the files, instructions, file permissions, and other information in order to install the software or information contained within it onto a machine.

The package system is built right into the operating system—in fact, even the operating system components are installed using packages as part of the installation process, and if you later decide to include something from the CDs at a later stage you'll be installing from one of the many installer packages.

If you've ever installed software onto any machine before, you know that occasionally the software you are installing needs some other piece of software or component before it can be installed correctly. For example, some games require additional 3-D drivers, the DirectX drivers, or if you're installing a package from source code you need some other library or application.

As part of the collection of information included with a package, the package software also knows what other packages are required in order for the application to work correctly. Furthermore, during installation the package system will check and verify that you have the correct packages to enable the software to be installed. This eliminates at least some of the headache involving package installation, although you still need to find and install the other packages that are required!

The packages themselves can either be a file into which all the files, package information, and scripts are archived and extracted during the install process, or it can be a directory. The former method is used to distribute a package, especially over a network and particularly the Internet. The latter directory structure is used on CDs and other media as it's quicker (you don't need to extract the data first) and often more convenient.

Table 10.1 provides a quick rundown of the tools you'll be using to manage the packages on your Solaris system.

Table 10.1   Command Line Tools for Managing Packages

Command	Description
pkgproto	Creates a prototype file to hold the list of files contained in a package. Used when creating a package.
pkgmk	Creates a package directory.
pkgadd	Installs a package from a package file.
pkgtrans	Converts a package directory into a file.
pkgrm	Removes (uninstalls) a package.
pkgchk	Verifies the installed packages and files.
pkginfo	Prints information about a package or packages.

In addition to all the command line tools, you can also use the main *admintool* or its alias *swmtool* to manage your packages. I'll start with the command line tools, as you'll need to know these when logging in remotely or if you haven't yet installed the X Windows system.

Checking the Manifest

Before you jump in and start messing around installing packages and fiddling about, you should first find out what's already installed on your system. As I mentioned earlier, everything in the Solaris operating system belongs to a package. During the software installation phase when you first set up the machine, you are in fact installing packages onto the new machine.

You can get a list of all the installed packages by using the *pkginfo* command:

```
$ pkginfo
system       AMImega      MEGA Family SCSI Host Bus Adapter
system       CADP160      Adaptec Ultra160 SCSI Host Adapter Driver
system       CPQncr       Compaq Family SCSI HBA
system       CPQsmii      Compaq SMART-2/E Family of Array Controller
system       HPFC         Agilent Fibre Channel HBA Driver
system       NCRos86r     NCR Platform Support, OS Functionality (Root)
application  NSCPcom      Netscape Communicator
system       SK98sol      SysKonnect SK-NET Gigabit Ethernet Adapter SK-98xx
...
system       SUNWzlib     The Zip compression library
system       SUNWzsh      Z shell (zsh)
system       SYMhisl      Symbios 8XX Hi-Performance SCSI HBA
```

As usual, I've cropped the output here. A full installation of Solaris 9 on the Intel platform incorporates about 359 packages that if listed here would take up some 10 pages of the book!

The output is split into three columns: package type, package ID, and a description. The package type just displays whether the package is an application or system package. Application packages are not critical to the operation of your system and are typically third party additions to the base system. System packages are those which relate directly to the operating system, such as the kernel, administration tools, and device drivers.

The package ID is a unique reference used to identify the package. The ID is used throughout the entire system to refer to the package and its contents. The ID is composed of an uppercase element which indicates the supplier of the package and a lowercase element, the name of the package itself. The description is the long name given to the package when it was created.

You can also get information about a specific package by using the *-l* command line option:

```
$ pkginfo -l SUNWzsh
   PKGINST:  SUNWzsh
      NAME:  Z shell (zsh)
  CATEGORY:  system
      ARCH:  i386
   VERSION:  11.9.0,REV=2001.06.22.12.42
   BASEDIR:  /
    VENDOR:  Sun Microsystems, Inc.
      DESC:  Z shell (zsh)
    PSTAMP:  sfw81-x20010622124449
  INSTDATE:  Dec 30 2001 10:32
   HOTLINE:  Please contact your local service provider
    STATUS:  completely installed
     FILES:      3 installed pathnames
                 2 shared pathnames
                 2 directories
                 1 executables
               815 blocks used (approx)
```

You can see here all the information about the package, including its name, architecture, version number, installation date, and the summary information for the files and storage used by the package.

Because packages refer to files, you can also do the opposite and find out information about a particular file, including which packages rely on the file for their operation, by using the *pkgchk* command:

```
$ pkgchk -l -p /usr/bin/zsh
Pathname: /usr/bin/zsh
Type: regular file
Expected mode: 0555
Expected owner: root
Expected group: bin
```

```
Expected file size (bytes): 381112
Expected sum(1) of contents: 21127
Expected last modification: Jan 05 23:08:16 2000
Referenced by the following packages:
        SUNWzsh
Current status: installed
```

Unsurprisingly, the *usr/bin/zsh* shell is referenced by the SUNWzsh package. The output also shows the expected size, owner, group owner, and mode of the file. The package system also records the checksum of the file as produced by the *sum* command. This reads the file and produces a checksum that corresponds exactly to the file in its installed state. If the file gets corrupted or inadvertently modified, you can use the checksum to determine whether the content is correct—even if the length is the same, any difference produces a different checksum. I'll discuss ways of verifying and fixing some of this information in the "Verifying a Package" section of this chapter.

Adding Packages to Your Collection

To add a package, you use the *pkgadd* command. As I mentioned earlier, there are two formats for the package, either as standalone files or as directories, typically on a CD. The file format keeps everything required in a single file. Typically the filename includes some useful information, such as the platform and suggested OS version. For example, the GNU C compiler package is provided from Sun Freeware in a file called gcc-3.0-sol8-intel.pkg. You can tell from this:

◆ That the file is a package by the .pkg extension.

◆ That it's for the Intel, not SPARC platform (from intel).

◆ That it's for Solaris 8 (from sol8).

◆ That it contains gcc, version 3.0 (from gcc-3.0).

Some packages will be compressed (the package format does not include compression by default); see the section on decompression later in this chapter for information on how to decompress a file.

To install the package use the *pkgadd* command with the -d option. This tells *pkgadd* to install from the package supplied on the command line. For example, you can install this package using:

```
$ pkgadd -d gcc-3.0-sol8-intel.pkg
```

For packages on a CD or other medium that are contained in directories, all you actually see is the package ID—one directory for each package. For example, here's a fragment from the Solaris 9 CDs:

```
AMImega/      SUNW5udc/     SUNWcdhcm/    SUNWcudim/    SUNWdhcm/     SUNWeorte/
CADP160/      SUNW5xfnt/    SUNWcdhe/     SUNWcudst/    SUNWdhcsb/    SUNWepdas/
CPQncr/       SUNW5xmft/    SUNWcdhev/    SUNWcudt/     SUNWdhcsr/    SUNWesbas/
CPQsmii/      SUNW5xplt/    SUNWcdhez/    SUNWcudte/    SUNWdhcsu/    SUNWesdst/
...
```

Obviously you can't really deduce anything from purely the package name—you'd need to know exactly what package you are required to install to continue. To install a specific package from this directory, you must specify the current directory as the package location, and then specify the package ID you want to install. For example, I just happen to know that the NSCPcom package includes the Netscape browser, so you could install it from this directory using:

```
$ pkgadd -d . NSCPcom
```

The other alternative is to omit the package ID. This forces *pkgadd* to provide a list of all the packages, including their descriptions, platforms, and version numbers from which you can select the packages you want to install:

```
$ pkgadd -d .
The following packages are available:
   1  AMImega        MEGA Family SCSI Host Bus Adapter
                     (i386) 1.1.0,REV=2001.04.13.12.59
   2  CADP160        Adaptec Ultra160 SCSI Host Adapter Driver
                     (i386) 1.21,REV=2001.04.13.12.59
   3  CPQncr         Compaq Family SCSI HBA
                     (i386) 1.1.0,REV=2001.04.13.12.59
   4  CPQsmii        Compaq SMART-2/E Family of Array Controller
                     (i386) 1.1.0,REV=2001.04.13.12.59
   5  HPFC           Agilent Fibre Channel HBA Driver       .
                     (i386) 1.1.0,REV=2001.04.16.14.39
   6  JSatsvr        Japanese Input System ATOK12 root files
                     (i386) 1.0,REV=2001.02.15.16.32
   7  JSatsvu        Japanese Input System ATOK12 usr files
                     (i386) 1.0,REV=2001.04.26.15.51
   8  JSatsvw        Japanese Input System ATOK12 X11 support files
                     (i386) 1.0,REV=2001.02.01.10.57
   9  NCRos86r       NCR Platform Support, OS Functionality (Root)
                     (i386) 11.9.0,REV=2001.05.25.19.04
  10  NSCP5com       Traditional Chinese (BIG5) Netscape Communicator
                     (i386) 20.4.76,REV=2001.04.11.13.46

... 1060 more menu choices to follow;
<RETURN> for more choices, <CTRL-D> to stop display:
```

Better still, if you can, use *admintool* which displays the information in a convenient format on screen where you can pick and choose the package you want.

Sun Lotion _____

If you make the mistake of simply typing *pkgadd* and get confronted by the error *pkgadd: ERROR: no packages were found in </var/spool/pkg>*, don't panic. The default location to look for a directory of packages is in the /var/spool/pkg directory, but as a standard there's never anything installed there. Just try typing the command you really wanted to enter in again.

If you make the mistake of selecting the wrong package, don't worry either—you'll be asked to confirm whether you want to install the package before continuing.

Whichever way you start the process, the result is the same—an installation script starts that will ask you some questions, including confirming that you want to install the package. You will always get a list of the possible values and be told what the default option will be if you just press Return. Most of the time you can get away with pressing Return to all the questions.

For example, let's look at the process for installing the GNU C compiler from the package you looked at earlier:

```
$ pkgadd -d gcc-3.0-sol8-intel.pkg
The following packages are available:
  1  SMCgcc3     gcc
                  (i386) 3.0
Select package(s) you wish to process (or 'all' to process
all packages). (default: all) [?,??,q]:
```

Sometimes you'll get more than one package listed here for what is essentially a single package file. You'll also get a list here if you've just specified the directory, but not the specific package that you want to load. If you type Q and press Return, you will have exited from the installer. Press Return to install the package:

```
Processing package instance <SMCgcc3> from </export/contrib/incoming/
➥gcc-3.0-sol8-intel.pkg>

Gcc
(i386) 3.0
Free Software Foundation
Using </usr/local> as the package base directory.
## Processing package information.
## Processing system information.
## Verifying disk space requirements.
## Checking for conflicts with packages already installed.
## Checking for setuid/setgid programs.
```

```
Installing gcc as <SMCgcc3>
## Installing part 1 of 1.
/usr/local/bin/c++
/usr/local/bin/c++filt

...
```

Now the files that make up the package start being installed onto the system. It will take a while for some packages to complete this task as they contain hundreds and sometimes thousands of files. It will take even longer if you are installing from CD!

Eventually you'll get:

```
/usr/local/man/man1/gcov.1
[ verifying class <none> ]
/usr/local/bin/g++ <linked pathname>
/usr/local/bin/i386-pc-solaris2.8-c++ <linked pathname>
/usr/local/bin/i386-pc-solaris2.8-g++ <linked pathname>
/usr/local/bin/i386-pc-solaris2.8-gcc <linked pathname>

Installation of <SMCgcc3> was successful.
And the installation has completed.
```

Although each package installation is different, they all have the ability to perform a number of tests, checks, and other operations as part of the installation procedure. Be prepared to answer (and in some cases act upon) any of the following issues:

- ◆ **Check for existing files:** The installation will warn you if the files that are being installed already exist for some reason.

- ◆ **Check for existing packages:** This is the dependencies system mentioned earlier on. Most of the time you'll need to be aware of what it asks so that you can install any additional packages required.

- ◆ **Check for existing partial installations:** Sometimes an installation will start and then terminate halfway through because of a crash or a fault in the installation process.

- ◆ **Allow setuid/setgid files to be installed:** setuid/setgid files can be a security hazard so you will be asked to confirm that you want a package containing such files to be installed.

- ◆ **Allow setuid/setgid scripts to be run:** Some installations need to run scripts as other users to complete the installation. There is a potential security risk here, but since you need to be logged in as root you should have permissions to do what you need.

- ◆ **Installation dependencies:** This is the list of other packages that should be installed for the software to work properly. Some packages require that the other packages already be installed; others just provide a warning and let you install the other packages later.

- ◆ **Removal dependencies:** Some packages require that you remove another package before continuing.

◆ **Correct runlevel:** Some software can only be installed in a specific runlevel (specifically single user or multi-user [2 or 3]). You'll need to change runlevels to guarantee that the software will be installed correctly.

◆ **Sufficient disk space:** You cannot install software if you don't have enough disk space. All packages will fail if there is not enough disk space to hold the files you are trying to install.

From the command line you can elect to install interactively or noninteractively. In interactive mode (the default) you'll be asked to confirm any items that the installer is unsure of. In noninteractive mode (activated by using the -*n* command line option), any questions which arise and require a response will cause the installation to terminate.

Removing Packages

Removing a package is as easy as using the *pkgrm* tool and specifying the package ID. For example, to remove the GNU C compiler you just installed use:

```
$ pkgrm SMCgcc3
The following package is currently
installed:
   SMCgcc3          gcc
                    (i386) 3.0


Do you want to remove this package? Y


## Removing installed package instance
➥<SMCgcc3>
## Verifying package dependencies.
## Processing package information.
## Removing pathnames in class <none>
...
## Updating system information.

Removal of <SMCgcc3> was successful.
```

Sun Screen

Be very careful with *pkgrm*, as electing to remove the wrong package could render your machine either mildly sick or completely dead. You will be prompted before removing any package, but always double check that you are removing the correct package. Remember, you don't want to get burned!

As you can see, you get prompted to ensure that you don't inadvertently delete the wrong package. Assuming you answer yes, the package is deleted.

Verifying Package Information

It's inevitable that on occasion you will do something that changes the permissions or contents of a file by mistake. Realization of this mistake does not always come until some time after you made the mistake, but help is at hand. The *pkgchk* command will check all of the files installed as part of a package and compare:

♦ The file permissions

♦ The owner

♦ The group owner

♦ The file size

♦ The checksum

♦ The modification time

The permissions are important, especially if you want to maintain security on your machine, and the owner and group owner are part of that security. The file size is important because it's a quick but entirely reliable check on whether the file has changed. For some files, a change in the size would indicate tampering or corruption of some sort. This can be at the very least a potential problem when running applications and at worst a security risk.

File sizes though are not perfect. The size of the file can be the same even if the contents are different. Just think about "hello" and "adios"—they are both five characters long, but made up of different characters. The checksum gets around this. Rather than relying on the file size, a checksum is a number that will be relatively unique to a file and its contents. Changing a single character in a file will result in a different checksum value.

If you run *pkgchk* it will report any discrepancies between the value expected and the current value:

```
$ pkgchk
ERROR: /boot/solaris/bootargs.rc
    modtime <06/19/01 07:09:40 PM> expected <12/30/01 03:08:00 PM> actual
    file size <83> expected <0> actual
    file cksum <5909> expected <0> actual
ERROR: /boot/solaris/bootenv.rc
    modtime <06/19/01 07:09:40 PM> expected <12/30/01 10:33:10 AM> actual
    file size <568> expected <811> actual
    file cksum <52155> expected <6815> actual
...
```

Checksum and size warnings should be taken with a reasonable pinch of salt. Because packages are used to track all the files on the system, it's inevitable that some of the files will get modified. Even the configuration files such as /etc/passwd and /etc/aliases are recorded in the package system, but they have to be modified to add new users and email aliases. However, size and checksum warnings on commands and library files should be taken more seriously.

Since permissions and ownership information is easy to change (and probably doesn't indicate tampering) you can also get *pkgchk* to fix permissions information as it checks the files. You do this by specifying the *-f* command line option:

```
$ pkgchk -f
```

Sun Lotion

Just as you should at a station or airport, you should check your packages with *pkgchk* regularly. Often the report produced by *pkgchk* will highlight potential problems and errors that you might not identify until some later stage, probably when it's too late to fix the problem.

I generally run *pkgchk* once a month, just to be sure nothing untoward is happening on the system. On critical systems I run *pkgchk* each week. In both cases, I also compare the output using *sdiff* with a report that I know is okay in terms of size and checksum errors. This filters out these generally irrelevant errors and instead just highlights the real problems. If I think the changes fit in with any modifications I've made recently, I update the compare file so it's ready for the next run.

Using a Visual Package Manager

If you prefer a visual tool for managing your packages, then check the Packages portion of *admintool* or run *swmtool* from the command line. You get a window like that in Figure 10.1. The window shows a list of all the packages currently installed on the system, nicely organized by their vendor and package group.

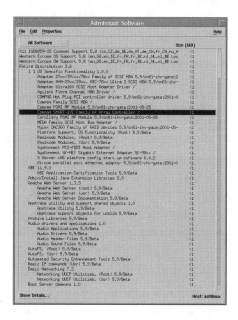

Figure 10.1

The swmtool/admintool *package management system.*

To get more information on a package, select a package from the list and click on the Show Details button. You get a window like the one in Figure 10.2.

Figure 10.2

*Getting the package infor-
mation for a specific package.*

To delete a package, select an item from the list and then choose Delete from the Edit menu. You'll be asked to confirm the operation before continuing.

To add some software, choose Add from the Edit menu and you'll be prompted for the directory to find the files. The default is the first slice of the first CD-ROM drive, but you can specify a directory for a downloaded package. Once the source has been set and the packages scanned, you get a window like the one shown in Figure 10.3.

Figure 10.3

*Selecting the packages to
install from a CD or other
source disc.*

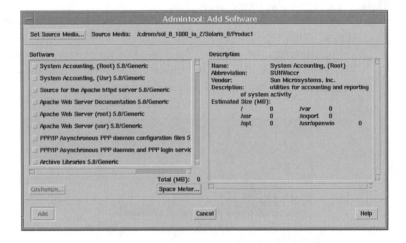

From here you can select the packages to be installed (by using the checkbox on the left of the package name) and monitor the amount of space required for each package. Once you've selected what you want to be installed, click the Add button and the installation will start. By default, what will actually happen is that the installation will be started in a terminal window and you'll need to follow the earlier instructions to complete the installation properly.

Alternatively, you can switch to an almost automatic mode that answers the queries for you—this is particularly useful if you've got a large number of packages to install. To do this, open the Package Administration window (from the Properties menu) and use the pop-ups to select the response given to the different questions normally posed by the installer. You can see the window in Figure 10.4.

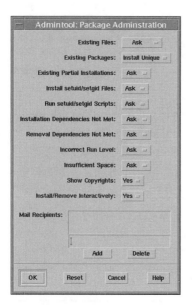

Figure 10.4

Configuration options for installing packages within the visual package manager.

Patching Things Up

Patches are small fragments of software that patch up bugs, security problems, and other difficulties experienced with some software. Unlike a package, patches only include the files required to fix the problem in a particular area. For example, a bug fix patch might include only one file, even though the package it is patching consists of hundreds of files.

Although a patch is there to fix a problem, it's not, as the name suggests, a temporary fix. Try not to think of a patch as a Band-Aid over a cut on your finger, but instead as replacing a broken component.

Solingo

The *showrev* command shows revision information for the machine and the software installed. Without any arguments it produces a list of the machine information and basic operating system revision. If you are new to a machine, it should be one of the commands you run to find out more about the machine and its configuration.

Unsurprisingly, Sun has a simple system for installing patches that is aware of the package system, the method with which files and packages are installed, and with the system. You can find out the current patch and revision level by using the *showrev* command:

```
$ showrev -p
Patch: 109804-01 Obsoletes:  Requires:  Incompatibles:  Packages: SUNWxcu4,
➥SUNWcsu
Patch: 109012-01 Obsoletes:  Requires: 108998-01, 108990-01, 108992-02, 108994-01,
➥108529-01 Incompatibles:  Packages: SUNWxcu4, SUN
```

```
Wcsu
Patch: 109239-01 Obsoletes:  Requires: 109237-01, 108992-03 Incompatibles:
➡Packages: SUNWxcu4, SUNWipc
Patch: 110959-01 Obsoletes:  Requires:  Incompatibles:  Packages: SUNWxsvc
...
```

To install a patch, you'll need to download it and then extract the files. Check the documentation before you install the patch. Some patches can be installed while a system is running multiuser mode, others need to be installed in single user mode.

Sun Lotion

To change to single user mode, use the command *shutdown -i S*, which will change the system into single user state immediately, or add *-g* and a figure to give the grace period in seconds. Remember as well that you'll need to do this on the machine—the moment the system switches to single user mode any network connections will be shut down.

Included with every official patch from Sun is a command called *patchadd* that installs the patch and updates the files and the package management system so that everything is in sync again. This means that should you later remove a package, it'll correctly remove the patched files and then show that both the package and any patches applied to it have been removed.

Installing from Source

Not all software is supplied (or available) in the form of a nice convenient package. If you want to make use of the huge array of free software and shareware available, then you will need to know at least the basics on how to extract, configure, and build an application from its source code.

Why source code? Well, due to the hundreds of thousands of minor differences between the different Unix flavors, providing a single pre-compiled binary version of an application is not practical. Unlike Windows or Mac OS—which are fairly controlled environments— even on all the different types of hardware the systems support, the same basic software, libraries, and interfaces are available.

With Unix, commands with the same name may do different things, and commands with different names may do the same thing. Now imagine how much more complicated it will be behind the scenes. The differences are often minor between different versions, even of the same operating system, and an application that may work on one version of Solaris may not work on another.

For that reason many packages are released as source code which can then be compiled on your machine, taking into account any differences before producing the final binary.

Using source code in this fashion is not entirely without its problems; minor differences at the source code level can also complicate matters. For example, the header file for the string manipulation library can be *string.h* or *strings.h* (the latter is plural, in case you missed it) and the contents and functions supported by the libraries can also be different.

To make the process easier, people have developed complex and sometimes convoluted mechanisms for determining and accounting for the differences, from providing separate source code trees for different platforms to providing a single script that automatically determines all the information required. In both cases you end up with a *Makefile* which can be processed by *make* in order to build the source package. You can even use the same tool to install the application.

In this section, you're going to look at the entire process, from start to finish, of decompressing, unpacking, configuring, and building an application from its source code. For pointers on where to download free software, see Appendix A, "Resource Guide."

Sun Lotion

Compiling from source code requires a C compiler and possibly some other tools such as *make* and *ranlib*. The latter are available in the SUNWbtool compiler tools package. The Forte for C compiler that comes with the Solaris should do for a C compiler. However, many of the source packages require GNU tools, including *autoconf*, *automake*, or GNUs own *make* tool. You can download these from Sun Freeware. See Appendix A for more information.

Decompression

Packages are generally supplied in an archived format using a tool like *tar*, *zip*, or very occasionally *cpio*. The zip format both compresses and collects files, directories, and their structures into a single file. The tar and cpio formats simply collect files into a single package. Nobody likes downloading a file for hours on end, so to make the files smaller the archives are compressed. Since the contents of the files are generally text you can achieve quite high compression ratios, shrinking a 1MB file down to about 200KB and sometimes even less.

There are two main formats, compress and gzip, both of which are supplied as standard with Solaris. A third package, bzip2, is becoming increasingly popular, as it can achieve compression ratios as low as 20:1, shrinking that 1MB file down to about 50KB.

To determine which type your file is, either examine the filename or use the *file* command. The final component of the filename should give an indication of its compression type. You can use the information in Table 10.2 to determine the different types. The table shows both the full filename and the shortened version which may have been used.

Table 10.2 Unix Compound File Extensions

Full Name	Long Name	Abbreviations
.cpio.Z	CPIO Archive, Compressed	.cpZ
.cpio.gz	CPIO Archive, Gzipped	.cgz
.cpio.bz2	CPIO Archive, Bzipped	.cbz
.tar.Z	Tarred, Compressed	.tZ, .trZ
.tar.gz	Tarred, Gzipped	.tgz
.tar.bz2	Tarred, Bzipped	.tbz, .tb2
.pkg.Z	Solaris Package, Compressed	.pkZ
.pkg.gz	Solaris Package, Gzipped	.pgz
.pkg.bz2	Solaris Package, Bzipped	.pbz, .pb2

The *file* command ignores file extensions entirely and instead looks at the actual content of a file to determine its type. To use the command, just supply the name of the file or a file specification on the command line:

```
$ file *
jakarta-tomcat-4.0.1.tar.Z:      compress'd data 16 bits
jnios-1.7:                       directory
jnios-1.7.tar.gz:                gzip compressed data, deflated,
                                 ➥original filename,
`jnios-1.7.tar', last modified: Fri Feb  4 18:42:09 2000, os: Win/32
jspbook.zip:                     Zip archive data, at least v1.0
                                 ➥to extract
name.gif:                        GIF image data, version 89a, 287
                                 ➥x 50,
netscape-6.0-sol.tar.bz2:        bzip2 compressed data, block size
                                 ➥= 900k
netscape-i686-pc-linux-gnu-installer.tar:   GNU tar archive
ntp-4.0.99k-15.i386.rpm:         RPM v3 bin i386 ntp-4.0.99k-15
```

You can see from the above that you have a collection of Gzip, compress, bzip2, and other files, all of which have been successfully identified. It even shows you the size of a GIF image!

In each case, you uncompress a file by using the decompression tools. These are *uncompress*, *gunzip*, or *bunzip2* in each case. To use them, just supply the name of the file you want to decompress on the command line:

```
$ gunzip webapp-module-1.0-tc40-linux-glibc2.2.tar.gz
```

The process should replace the original file with its decompressed version which will have the same name, but with the final compression format removed. For example, file.tar.gz will become simply file.tar.

All the commands will fail if the name of the compressed file does not have the correct extension. You can rename the file or you can use the cat mode, which decompresses the file and sends the output to the standard output (usually the terminal). You can then redirect this into a file. All the commands use the same command line option for this, *-c:*

```
$ gunzip -c file.tar.gz >file.tar
```

You can also use this mode if you want to decompress the file without removing the compressed original, and there's also another trick which you'll look at shortly using this very same technique.

In each case, all you end up with is one single file—you still need to extract the individual files from the archive file.

Archiving

There are three main archiving formats, *tar*, *cpio*, and *zip*. As you already know, *zip* is also a compression tool. It's probably the easiest to use, because you can unzip a zip file with one single command:

```
$ unzip jspbook.zip
Archive:  jspbook.zip
   creating: src/
   creating: src/com/
...
   inflating: asf-xml-license.txt
   inflating: asf-jakarta-license.txt
   inflating: release_notes.html
   inflating: Readme-License.txt
```

I've skipped an awful lot of content here because it's really not that interesting, but you get the general idea. Note that it creates all of the directories for you automatically.

The *tar* tool is the most popular. It's short for Tape Archiver and we'll be seeing it again when you look at backup solutions. As well as working with tape devices, *tar* also works with files. To extract the contents, give the *tar* command the *x* option, and to extract from a file rather than a device you use *f*. For example:

```
$ tar xf myfile.tar
```

You can also combine the *uncompress*, *gunzip*, or *bunzip2* with *tar* to decompress and extract from an archive in one stage:

```
$ uncompress -c myfile.tar.Z|tar xf -
$ gunzip -c myfile.tar.gz|tar xf -
$ bunzip2 -c myfile.tar.bz2|tar xf -
```

You might want to check Chapter 17, "Using a Shell," for more information on pipes.

Sun Lotion _____

If you've obtained the GNU version of *tar*, it can uncompress or gunzip files for you without your having to explicitly decompress the archive, if you use the *z* switch on the command line:

```
$ tar zxf myfile.tar.gz
$ tar zxf myfile.tar.Z
```

The *cpio* tool works slightly differently. The tool itself is short for copy in/out, but confusingly the in/out portion is in fact in from and out to standard input/output. For example, to extract files from a *cpio* archive you need to copy files in from a file:

```
$ cpio -i <myfile.cpio
```

or, as with *tar*, you can combine the command with one for decompression:

```
$ bunzip2 -c |cpio -i
```

The result in any of the above cases is a new directory matching the name of the archive you extracted. For example, extracting emacs:

```
$ gunzip -c emacs-20.7.tar.gz |tar xf -
```

provides you with a directory *emacs-20.7*.

Configuring and Building

Let's look at how to build a popular piece of free software, emacs. Emacs is not a bizarre reference to electronic rain protection devices, but is an editor and development environment originally developed by Richard Stallman (the founder and main proponent of free software). Emacs is short for *editing macros* but it does a lot more than just edit text files. You can also use it as a development environment (it has convenient wrappers for building and debugging applications), an email client, web client, and through the use of its own built-in language, you can put it to a myriad of other uses. Although the editor itself was first developed in 1975, the package is by far the most complete and ultimately useful editor you will ever find.

It does, however, take some time to learn, but I guarantee that if you persevere with it and get used to its many tiny foibles, you will learn to love it and, like the rest of us, wonder how you ever survived without it. After *bash* it's the second thing I install on any new Unix machine. Oh, and I install versions on my Mac and Unix machines too.

Your first point of call once you've unpacked the source package should be to read the documentation. Convention puts the basic information you should need into a file called *README* (yes, capitals) or various case combinations thereof. Installation instructions are usually in *INSTALL*. If you can't find anything there, complain to the distributor of the package, and then start looking at the rest of the directory contents. For reference, take a look at the contents of the *emacs* source directory:

```
$ ll
total 1098
-rw-r--r--    1 mc      root        937 Jun 17  1994 BUGS
-rw-r--r--    1 root    other    137302 Dec  1  2000 ChangeLog
-r--r--r--    1 mc      root       4737 Apr  8  1998 GETTING.GNU.SOFTWARE
-r--r--r--    1 mc      root      30235 May 31  1999 INSTALL
-r--r--r--    1 mc      root      22464 Apr  9  1999 Makefile.in
-rw-r--r--    1 root    other      3416 Dec  1  2000 README
-r--r--r--    1 mc      root       8467 Aug  4  1999 config.bat
...
```

We're in luck, a README and INSTALL document. Read them before you go any further. Although the process should be fairly automatic, it's always a good idea to read these documents before you go on.

Emacs uses the fairly ubiquitous GNU *autoconf*. Remember I talked about the difficulties of working with source code because of all the differences? Well, *autoconf* tries to make the entire process as easy as possible. The system uses a script supplied with the package that knows how to look for and determine all the different elements needed by the software, and from that it can work out how the software can be configured for building.

Most software now uses some form of automatic script. The GNU system is the most often used as it's backed up by one of the largest repositories of information on what is and isn't available on different platforms and how to get around some of the problems. To use it, change to the directory containing the source you just extracted and then type *configure*. Here's the output generated by the configure script for *emacs* under Solaris—it'll take some time:

```
$ ./configure
creating cache ./config.cache
checking host system type... i386-pc-solaris2.9
checking for gcc... gcc
checking whether the C compiler (gcc  ) works... yes
checking whether the C compiler (gcc  ) is a cross-compiler... no
...
creating src/config.h
creating src/epaths.h
creating lib-src/Makefile
creating src/Makefile
```

Okay, I've cropped the output again (trust me, it really isn't that interesting). But you get the idea.

The result, as you should spot from the bottom of the output, is a file called *Makefile*. If you are a programmer you'll know that this is a configuration file for a program called *make*. The information in the file tells *make* how to compile, link, and install the application.

In fact, *make* is quite powerful. Not only can you configure it to build the application and a whole host of other tasks, it's also intelligent enough to know that it doesn't need to compile things that it's already compiled. That shouldn't affect you, as you only need to compile once, but for programmers it saves hours.

There's nothing more you need to do now except type *make* to build the application:

```
$ make
cd lib-src; make all  \
  CC='gcc' CFLAGS='-g -O' CPPFLAGS='' \
  LDFLAGS='-L/usr/openwin/lib' MAKE='make'
make[1]: Entering directory `/usr/local/contrib/emacs-20.7/lib-src'
gcc -DHAVE_CONFIG_H -I. -I../src -I/usr/local/contrib/emacs-20.7/lib-src
-I/usr/local/contrib/emacs-20.7/lib-src/../src -L/usr/openwin/lib  -g -O
-o test-distrib /usr/local/contrib/emacs-20.7/lib-src/test-distrib.c
./test-distrib /usr/local/contrib/emacs-20.7/lib-src/testfile
gcc -DHAVE_CONFIG_H -I. -I../src -I/usr/local/contrib/emacs-20.7/lib-src
-I/usr/local/contrib/emacs-20.7/lib-src/../src -L/usr/openwin/lib  -g -O
/usr/local/contrib/emacs-20.7/lib-src/make-docfile.c -lsocket -lnsl
-lkstat -lkvm -lelf -o make-docfile
gcc -DHAVE_CONFIG_H -I. -I../src -I/usr/local/contrib/emacs-20.7/lib-src
-I/usr/local/contrib/emacs-20.7/lib-src/../src -L/usr/openwin/lib  -g -O
/usr/local/contrib/emacs-20.7/lib-src/profile.c -lsocket -lnsl -lkstat
-lkvm -lelf -o profile
gcc -DHAVE_CONFIG_H -I. -I../src -I/usr/local/contrib/emacs-20.7/lib-src
-I/usr/local/contrib/emacs-20.7/lib-src/../src -L/usr/openwin/lib  -g -O
/usr/local/contrib/emacs-20.7/lib-src/digest-doc.c -lsocket -lnsl
-lkstat -lkvm -lelf -o digest-doc
```

Okay, lots more relatively useless information—it's just telling you about the build process. For each source file, it calls *gcc* to compile the file into object code and then eventually gets around to building the final application. Watch for errors here—it could mean a problem somewhere in your configuration that wasn't identified during the configuration process. There's not enough space to go through the issues here, but try reading the documentation again and check to make sure you have the very latest version of the source code.

Assuming everything went okay, you can install the software by typing:

```
$ make install
```

This copies the files into a sensible place (probably */usr/local* and the directories therein, creating them if they don't already exist), including the documentation, *man* pages, and the other files needed to run the application.

Success!!

Not all processes are as easy as this, of course, but reading the documentation should help to guide you through the process. With a few exceptions the general process is the same for all source packages. For example, Perl doesn't use GNUs *autoconf* script. Instead it has its own configure script, but that, too, generates a *Makefile*. Some use a script that not only determines and configures the elements needed for a build, but also performs the build itself.

How autoconf Works

The principle of *autoconf* is actually incredibly simple, and as with all things, that's the very thing that also makes it very powerful. Basically, *autoconf* starts by knowing the different commands, libraries, functions, and header files required to build the application. This information is generated by the developer as part of the process of packaging up the source for distribution.

Then, using that list, *autoconf* tries to use the command or employ the library in a small application. For example, let's say the package requires the *ranlib* command (which sets up a library archive for use). All the script has to do is try using *ranlib*. If the command works, then you're okay; if the command doesn't, you've got a problem and the configure script fails.

For libraries, functions, and header files the script tries to compile an application that uses the library, a specific function, or imports a required header file. If the compilation fails, then there is something missing and the script terminates, reporting the problem. If it finds the necessary tools, it logs the information and goes on.

Behind the scenes, each of these processes may take place multiple times. In order to ensure that it gets the right version of an application or library, the configuration script will actually look in specific locations for the file until it finds the one it wants.

Once all the information has been deduced, the script writes that information into a configuration file and creates a suitable *Makefile* based on a template designed by the developer. The result is a *Makefile* and header file combination capable of compiling the package for your platform. Because the process is repeated on each platform before the build, *autoconf* works on any platform—including those it's never come across before—to determine the setup.

Simple, right?

The Least You Need to Know

- ◆ Use *pkgadd* to install a package on a machine.
- ◆ Use *pkgrm* to remove a package from a machine.

◆ Use *pkginfo* to find out what packages are already installed.

◆ Use *patch_install* to install a patch onto a machine.

◆ To install from a source package, first decompress and extract the package information, then for most packages type *configure*, followed by *make* and *make install* to configure, build, and install the software on your machine.

Part  Networking

No computer is an island, and whether you want to connect your Solaris machine to others in your own network or to the Internet, you need to know how to set up your machine to talk correctly to others. As well as the basic mechanics, there are also network services that you can configure to allow information to be shared—through disks, FTP, or over the web.

Connecting to a Network

In This Chapter

- ◆ Introducing the network system
- ◆ Setting up TCP/IP networking
- ◆ Connecting to computers outside your network

Sun coined the phrase "The network *is* the computer," so it's no surprise that Solaris is ready and waiting to be configured for network access. It's actually easiest to do this during the installation, but if your machine wasn't connected to a network, or you didn't have the information at hand to set it up, then you need to know what goes on behind the scenes.

I start with an overview of how the networking system employed by Solaris works. Then I'll move on to the three main components—setting up your network, communicating with the outside world, and setting up your name resolving service.

The Network System

Despite what you may think, setting up networking on a Solaris system—or indeed any system—is nowhere near as complicated as it might sound. Although I could go into all sorts of detail about the *ISO/OSI* seven layer network model, the truth is that you really don't need it (and in fact it doesn't apply to the primary networking system under Solaris anyway).

Sun Lotion

The **International Standards Organization (ISO)** produced a standard model that defines the seven basic layers of network, otherwise known as the Open Standards Interconnect model. The seven layers are (from the bottom up), physical, data link, network, transport, session, presentation, and application.

Unfortunately, it really only makes a good theoretical model—most of the modern networking protocols in use today do not conform to the seven layer model.

Ignoring the seven layer model, we can instead identify the three core components to any network system used to connect machines together: hardware, networking, and application.

The hardware is the physical equipment that you use to connect networks together. Most computers use Ethernet and Ethernet cards, and interfaces are included in many machines— including all the Sun SPARC machines ever produced—by default, as nearly everybody networks their computer to another somewhere along the chain.

The application element is the final part of the process—it's the protocol and application used to provide a particular service. For example, the File Transfer Protocol (FTP) is an application layer that allows us to transfer files between systems over a TCP/IP network. The Hypertext Transfer Protocol (HTTP) is a different application which uses TCP/IP, but instead of transferring files it transfers the information required for a website, including files (text, graphics, and others) and session and state information.

The networking element is the bit that really does the work of transferring information over the network. For Solaris, the primary networking technology is called TCP/IP. The IP element stands for Internet Protocol, and it refers to the way in which machines are addressed and how packets are routed over a network in order to reach their destination. We'll return to this in a minute.

The TCP stands for Transmission Control Protocol and is a method of communicating between two machines in an orderly fashion. TCP is actually best thought of as an equivalent of the phone system—you dial a number (called the IP address) and the other end answers and accepts your call. After that, how you communicate and in what language is entirely up to you.

There is an alternative to TCP/IP called UDP/IP. UDP/IP uses the same IP-based addressing and routing protocols, but uses a "connection-less" transport mechanism. In English, this means that when you send information using UDP/IP you have no guarantee or acknowledgement that the other end actually picked up your message. UDP/IP is roughly equivalent to the postal service—you send a letter, but have no way (without explicitly asking) of knowing if the recipient received it or not.

Going back to the IP element, all hosts on a TCP/IP network have their own unique IP address. An IP address is in the form x.x.x.x, where *x* is a number between 0 and 255. For example, my main desktop machine has the IP address 192.168.1.131. These IP addresses are logically grouped together into Class A, B, and C addresses. If your company has been given a Class C network address, then you will have been given the first three numbers—for example, 192.168.1—and the remainder of the numbers are used to identify each of the machines within your network.

Class B networks start with numbers between 128 and 191. It's possible to have 16,384 of these networks and each class B network can handle up to 65,534 IP addresses or computers. Typically Class B networks are given out only to companies with a very large number of computers, or to ISPs who need large blocks of numbers.

Class A networks start with a number between 1 and 126. Only 126 of these networks are available, however each class A network can handle 16,777,214 IP addresses or computers. Only a few companies have ever been given a Class A address (including Hewlett-Packard, who have one of the largest active IP allocations on the Internet).

To help your machines know which other machines are physically on the same single network, the IP address is combined with a network mask (or netmask), which is used as a filter to show the range of numbers that apply to your network. For example, an entire Class C network has the netmask 255.255.255.0.

Now, if a machine with the IP address 192.168.1.131 and netmask 255.255.255.0 wants to talk to a machine outside of the range 192.168.1.0 to 192.168.1.255 (that is, outside the Class C network) then it must talk to a *router*.

Solingo

A **router** is a device that routes (forwards) the packets of one or more protocols from one network to another to allow the two networks to communicate with each other. A bridge is a device that connects two networks at the hardware level, effectively allowing any protocol from either physical network to be shared across the two.

Because the Internet uses a specific protocol—TCP/IP (and UDP/IP)—you use a router to connect to the Internet, not a bridge.

The last part of the puzzle is the name resolver—this is a computer or other device on the network which is used to convert numbers—something us humans are terrible at dealing with—into the IP address required to communicate with a given machine. It's the name resolver that allows you to refer to a machine by name, and yet still communicate with it—all because behind the scenes the computer is translating that name into the information it really needs.

You can therefore summarize the main components you need to set up networking on a machine:

- ◆ An IP address.
- ◆ A netmask.
- ◆ The IP address of a router.
- ◆ The information required to contact our name resolving service.

Configuring Your Network Cards

If you didn't set up your network when you installed your machine then you will need to perform the process manually. You need to edit four files to enable TCP/IP networking on your machine:

- ◆ */etc/nodename*: The name of the machine.
- ◆ */etc/netmasks*: This should contain the netmask for your network.
- ◆ */etc/hosts* (which is actually an alias to */etc/inet/hosts*, the */etc/inet* directory holds a number of network specific configuration files): This holds a list of the hostnames and their IP addresses.
- ◆ */etc/hostname.interface*: Where *interface* is the name and number of the physical device that is being configured.

The first item is really just a nicety—it gives your machine a name so that it can identify itself. It's also the name the machine will use for itself if you configure multiple interfaces— each interface will have to have its own IP address, and therefore its own name.

The second item, the netmask, is required for your machine to know how to talk to other machines on the local network. To set this, enter the network number—that is the class C, B, or A address, and the netmask. For example, for our sample network the network number is 192.168.1.0 and the netmask is 255.255.255.0:

```
192.168.1.0 255.255.255.0
```

The third and fourth files are loosely intertwined. The */etc/hostname.interface* will contain the name or IP address for each interface in your machine. The */etc/hosts* file contains a map of the hostnames and their corresponding IP address. The system will use this information to configure each interface with its IP address. For example, if */etc/hostname. interface* contains only the name, the system will get the IP address from */etc/hosts*, and if */etc/hostname.interface* contains the IP address, the system will get the name from */etc/hosts*.

To set these two files up, you need to determine what your IP address will be. If you are a system administrator, you'll probably have the information available to you. If you are not, ask your system administrator for the information.

Now edit */etc/hosts*, adding your system's IP address and hostname. For example, to add the host *twinsol* with the address 192.168.1.135, we would add the following line to the file:

```
192.168.1.135 twinsol
```

Now you need to determine what interfaces you have attached to your machine. The interfaces are named using a combination of the driver name and a logical unit number, which increments by one for each device type. For example, if you have a machine with two Sun Ethernet interfaces, they will probably be named *le0* and *le1*. As a general rule, Ethernet interfaces in a SPARC machine are *le* or *hme* devices. Under Intel, it will depend on the Ethernet card you are using—check */var/adm/messages* to determine the name.

Solingo

The **localhost** is a special name (and a special IP address of 127.0.0.1) that allows a machine to talk to itself without having to know its own IP address or host/node name. Don't remove this entry because you don't know what it is—it's important!

To actually set the hostname or IP address, you create the corresponding file. For example, to configure our *twinsol* machine which is using an SMC Ethernet card we create the file */etc/hostname.spwr0* adding the single line:

```
twinsol
```

That's all there is to it! The easiest way to set up and enable the network is probably just to reboot your server. To set things up without rebooting, try running:

```
# /etc/init.d/network start
```

which is the same script used during boot up to configure the main network components—it may not work, depending on your existing configuration.

To test if everything worked okay, use *ping* to communicate with another machine on the network, using the IP address, rather than name, to ensure it's not a name server problem:

```
$ ping 192.168.1.127
```

Sun Lotion

If you ever have to change network configurations, that is, changing IP addresses, always do it from the console, and always reboot, rather than using */etc/init.d/network*.

It should come back and say:

```
192.168.1.127 is alive
```

which means that your computer could contact the other one. If it doesn't come back with this information, then you've done something wrong. The most common mistake is to put different hostnames in */etc/hosts* and */etc/hostname.interface*; they must match, otherwise the system will be unable to determine what the IP address of your network card should be.

If everything appears to be okay but you still can't get through, use *ifconfig -a* to get a full report on the status of your network interface:

```
# ifconfig -a
ifconfig -a
lo0: flags=1000849<UP,LOOPBACK,RUNNING,MULTICAST,IPv4> mtu 8232 index 1
        inet 127.0.0.1 netmask ff000000
pcn0: flags=1000843<UP,BROADCAST,RUNNING,MULTICAST,IPv4> mtu 1500 index 2
        inet 192.168.1.204 netmask ffffff00 broadcast 192.168.1.255
```

If the interface you just configured is not showing *UP* and *RUNNING* then there is either something wrong with the setup or with the cables.

Communicating with the Outside World

If you need to communicate with the outside world, that is, with a machine immediately outside your network, then you need to do two things:

1. Determine a way of identifying the machine or machines you want to talk to.

2. Tell your machine how to contact the router.

The first point is generally covered by one of the various naming systems. See the following section, "Resolving Names and Numbers," for more information.

Sun Lotion

If you want to use your machine either as a router or as a way of communicating with the Internet over a modem or ISDN connection, then Solaris does come with the tools to communicate using the PPP (Point to Point Protocol) used over dial-up connections.

I don't, unfortunately, have space to go through the details here (the "quick" step-by-step notes are about 15 pages long!). If you want a step-by-step guide, check the online documentation or the System Administration Guide in the AnswerBook. Alternatively, check out the web for some guides—I've used the one at http://www.kempston.net/solaris/connect.html.

The second point is a case of configuring your machine to talk to a router and to send its network packets on to another network or over the Internet. To do this, all you need to do is create a new file on your system, called */etc/defaultrouter* which contains the IP address of the router (or routers, one per line) that the machine should contact. You'll need to reboot or run */etc/init.d/network* to set the route up.

Resolving Names and Numbers

Whether you are only communicating with other computers on a single network, or whether you are using your machine to view and communicate with the Internet, you will need some way to identify the different machines on the network.

As we already know, the TCP/IP networking system employed by Solaris (and most other platforms) uses a simple set of four numbers to identify a particular machine on the network. For example, I use the IP address 192.168.1.135 for my Solaris 8 server. However, remembering that number each time is a little bit complex and it doesn't exactly trip off the tongue when you say it. When you realize that the Mac server is 192.168.1.134 or the Windows 2000 server is 192.168.1.127 you begin to realize that remembering all these numbers can be a bit cumbersome.

When you set up your machine, it will have asked you for a hostname. This is the name really used by the machine to identify itself, but there's no reason why you can't use that same name to refer to the machine when connecting to it from another on your network. You may want to name your other machines using some sort of naming scheme so that you can easily identify and remember which machine is which.

A Postcard From ...

Lots of people use a naming scheme to make the names given to their machines slightly more interesting than *sales1* or other mnemonic equivalents. For my office network I use a combination of different schemes—most of the Unix machines are named according to the operating system they are running, for example the Linux box is called *penguin*, and the main server, *twinsol*, is so called because it's a dual processor machine running Solaris.

The Windows machines are named according to words containing the letters NT, the OS I was running at the time. The main Win2K box is *Insentient*. The Mac machines are named according to their purpose—the portable is called *Nautilus* (because it's a shell design), my wife's iMac is called *Kernel* because she worked on a project called 'Nutshell' and the Mac server is called *Sulaco* after the ship in *Aliens* because it's a large box with lots of storage.

I have in the past used Disney characters (printers at one company were called Sneezy, Sleepy, Doc, Happy, and so on) and isometric shapes (Dodecahedron, Icosahedron, Pentagon, and so on). Whatever floats your boat!

There are three main ways of resolving names into their IP addresses, and vice versa: using static tables, using the Domain Name System (DNS), or using the Network Information System (NIS).

Using Static Information

Static host information is stored in the */etc/hosts* file that we've already seen. You can add as many different hosts to that file as you like, using the same format as we used to set the IP address and name for the machine itself.

```
127.0.0.1       localhost
10.1.1.2        twinfire
192.168.1.135   twinsol loghost twinsol.mcslp.pri
192.168.1.200   kernel
192.168.1.201   nautilus
192.168.1.202   atuin
192.168.1.127   insentient
192.168.1.204   penguin
```

Sun Lotion

I don't know about you, but I hate those ads that appear in web pages. If you do too, then here's a little tip. For each host responsible for serving up an ad, add an entry in the */etc/hosts* file with the IP address *127.0.0.1*. Any requests for an ad will now be directed towards your machine, not the real server. If you are supporting a web server on your machine, you might want to configure a "missing" page that is just plain blank—then the space where an ad exists will just be filled with a blank space!

Using DNS

The Domain Name System, or DNS, is the naming system used to identify hosts on the Internet. When you enter an Internet address (as a name, rather than an IP address), your machine will communicate with a DNS server (which could be your machine) and ask it to "resolve" the address. It does this by asking a number of "root" servers to tell it which machines are responsible for the domain, and then it requests direct from those servers what the real address is. The process takes milliseconds, even when connected over a modem.

The DNS system is actually quite flexible. Not only will it resolve a name to an IP address, it will also resolve an IP address back to a name. Some systems actually require this in order to validate them as valid clients or users of a system. For example, when sending an email, if the receiving server can't resolve your domain name or hostname back into an IP address, it will normally refuse to handle the mail, as it's usually a good indicator that a user is trying to send spam emails.

To set up DNS, if you didn't elect to configure it during system installation, you need to edit two files. The first is */etc/resolv.conf*, the second is */etc/nsswitch.conf*. I'll cover the use of the */etc/nsswitch.conf* file in a moment, in the section "Switching Between Systems." The file consists of a number of basic text lines which define the domain name and the IP addresses of one or more servers (typically there are at least two) that should be communicated with to resolve an IP address.

For example, on the client Solaris machine on my network I use the following in my */etc/resolv.conf* file:

> **CAUTION**
>
> **Sun Screen**
>
> In case you haven't got the idea yet, using IP addresses over names in some places is absolutely vital. In the case of configuring DNS, using a name just wouldn't work—how would the system resolve the name of the DNS server if it didn't know what its IP address was and therefore how to talk to it?

```
domain mcslp.pri
nameserver 192.168.1.135
nameserver 192.168.1.134
nameserver 192.168.1.138
nameserver 192.168.1.127
```

The *domain* line tells the DNS resolver what domain to append by default to addresses that are not qualified—that is, if I'm trying to access *twinsol*, what it actually looks up is *twinsol.mcslp.pri*.

The *nameserver* entries are the list of hosts communicated to resolve the address. In this case, I've set up my own domain name server (so I can resolve all the addresses I use on my own network)—I'll explain how to do this in Chapter 13, "Setting Up Network Services."

Using NIS/NIS+

TheNetwork Information Service (NIS) is a way of sharing host information and other databases such as user names and passwords across your network. I discuss it separately in Chapter 14, "Configuring NIS." You might also want to check back to Chapter 6, "Managing Users and Groups," where I discuss some of the benefits.

Switching Between Systems

When you request an address, how does your machine know which of the above systems to consult?

The answer is the */etc/nsswitch.conf* file. The Name Service Switch file, to give it its full name, contains a list of the major system databases on the system, and then provides a list of systems to use when looking up the information for each database. For example, here's the file used for a system using */etc/hosts* and DNS to obtain network information (I've trimmed the comments, for brevity):

```
passwd:       files
group:        files
hosts:        files dns
ipnodes:      files
networks:     files
protocols:    files
rpc:          files
ethers:       files
netmasks:     files
bootparams:   files
publickey:    files
netgroup:     files
automount:    files
aliases:      files
services:     files
sendmailvars:    files
printers:        user files
```

The important line, as far as we are concerned, is the *hosts* entry, which shows two entries, *files*, which indicates that the system should check the */etc/hosts* file, and *dns* which means the system should consult the DNS resolver. I could have also added *nis* here to have the machine search the NIS database.

The order here is important—the database types listed will be checked in the order given, so when you search for *twinsol* the machine first looks in */etc/hosts*, and then when it can't find anything, it asks the DNS system. If the DNS system comes back and says the entry is not found, then I'll get a "no such host" or similar message to indicate the problem.

Sun Lotion

Using *nsswitch.conf* to switch between systems is great, but be warned that setting the order incorrectly can cause problems, especially if just one of those elements is down. If you are using all three systems, I prefer to put them in the order *hosts nis dns*, which makes the system search the */etc/host* files first, the local network system (NIS) next, and then start searching the Internet. Hopefully any local address will have been found within the hosts or NIS system before we start talking to the rest of the world.

Putting hosts first also means that I can talk and communicate with a few key machines by name even if NIS and/or DNS are down, and I don't have to wait for the system to determine if the two are down before it goes ahead and searches the local file.

It also means that I can reassign or redirect particular names to a different IP address if I need to—useful for my little web ad trick shown earlier in this chapter!

To change the order and sources checked, just open the file in the editor of your choice and make the changes—it's that easy. You don't need to restart or kill anything—the next time the system is looking for information from one of those databases, it'll consult the file and determine which databases to examine and in which order.

The Least You Need to Know

- To configure your machine for connecting to a network, you must know its IP address, netmask, and name.

- To get your machine to talk to machines on other networks, you must set up a default route—that is, the address of a router on your network that knows where to send the packets to.

- To resolve names, you must use the local files, the DNS system, or the NIS system.

- To use a combination of local, DNS, and NIS systems, you must configure the */etc/nsswitch.conf* file.

## Chapter 12

Setting Up Email

In This Chapter

♦ Understanding how email is distributed

♦ Configuring the *sendmail* application

♦ Using the *mail* program and the *mailx* command

Today we take email for granted. Five years ago, maybe even only two years ago, the phrase "I'll email you" was something said only by a very few individuals at large corporations or the geeks with their machines at home.

Now, we send millions of emails each day. I conduct 99% of my work through sending and receiving manuscripts and contracts by email. I even suggest, make, and confirm decisions about projects all by email, even though it's only become legally binding to do so in recent history.

In this chapter I discuss the mechanisms that make email work on Solaris and most other Unix flavors, which just happen to be the same techniques employed on the Internet.

How Email Is Distributed

The email revolution was largely driven by Unix. The ability to quickly exchange information between two machines in the form of an email is something that today we take for granted; despite its apparent complexities the process is actually very simple.

First, let's consider an email address. My main email address, *mc@mcslp.com*, consists of two elements, the name (mc) and the domain (mcslp.com). When someone sends me an email, the Domain Name Service (DNS) is consulted and it looks for an MX (Mail Exchanger) record for the domain mcslp.com. Then MX record matches the domain name with one or more email hosts—that is, those machines that are configured to accept email for the domain mcslp.com.

The sender then opens a connection with one of those machines, supplies the recipient machine with the name of the sender, the recipient (mc@mcslp.com), and the message data. That's it—the email has been sent!

In reality, things are slightly more complicated. The exchange of information between the sender and recipient is handled by a standard protocol called Simple Mail Transfer Protocol, or SMTP. The SMTP protocol is purely a method for *sending* mail—you cannot *receive* email at the client end using SMTP.

What usually happens is that the email will be sent through one or more mail servers before it reaches its destination. For example, a more usual route for an email from sharon@mcwords.com to mc@mcslp.com might be:

1. Sharon sends email from her machine to a server on her network, or the server at her ISP using SMTP.

2. Sharon's server or ISP sends the email to the server for mcslp.com.

3. The server for mcslp.com sends the message to the server handling mail for mc@mcslp.com.

4. MC picks up his email from the email server using the local file method, IMAP (Internet Mail Access Protocol) or POP3 (Post Office Protocol, v3).

Steps 2 and 3 may actually be repeated a number of times, depending on how the email service is set up.

A Postcard From ...

The differences between IMAP and POP stem from how you expect to use the information. The POP protocol stores email on the server until the client accesses and downloads the email to his or her client machine. POP is therefore fairly light in requirements, as it's merely acting as the last stage in the delivery process from client to client. Most ISPs use POP for this reason—they don't need servers and lots of disk space, as the messages will only be stored until the next time the user connects.

IMAP stores all the mail on the server all of the time. When you read an email, the mail message is downloaded to the client, but only so you can read the content—the actual message stays on the server until you explicitly delete it. IMAP also allows the user to create folders on the server so they can keep and file mail there. The benefit is that users can then access the machine from potentially any client and gain access to both their active email and their filed mail.

The client protocols used to actually deliver the email to the user's email account depend entirely on the system being used. Within Unix systems, most people use the local file method, which is really just a file residing in the */var/mail* directory on their server. Users communicating to a mail server will use the POP3 or IMAP protocols to pick up the email from a server and read it on a client machine. The same basic process is used with proprietary systems such as Microsoft's Exchange server.

Configuring sendmail

In the example earlier in this chapter, the jobs of accepting email from a client by SMTP, forwarding the email by SMTP, accepting the mail by SMTP, and finally delivering it to its destination could all have been handled by an application called *sendmail*. Its job, as the name suggests, is to send mail to its destination.

Sendmail works as a daemon, sitting in the background and accepting emails both locally and over the network through SMTP. All mail messages, however they are received, are placed into a queue, which the *sendmail* daemon will process periodically to send emails. Local email is sent instantaneously, emails to other machines on the Internet are sent immediately, or queued until the next scheduled queue process run, depending on the configuration.

Your system is automatically set up to send email from the moment you first install the machine—the reason for this is that email is one of the primary ways for the system to communicate errors and problems and general information with you. For example, the *cron* system, which I'll discuss in Chapter 21, "Automating Systems," uses email to tell you when a scheduled job has completed.

The sendmail Configuration File

I don't remotely expect to describe all the facilities and complexities of the *sendmail* configuration file. You can, and indeed people have, written books on the topic of *sendmail* configuration. The software, and the configuration file on which it relies, is so complex purely because of the complexity of the email system. *Sendmail* must be able to identify the different components of an address in all their different forms, recognize the difference between a local user and a remote one, a local machine and a remote one, and to know where to send an email once it's worked out who it's for.

The *sendmail* configuration consists of just one file, */etc/mail/sendmail.cf*. The standard file supplied with Solaris is designed for a server, or the primary *sendmail* server in a network. Another version, */etc/mail/subsidiary.cf* is designed for other systems on the network that talk to this main server. If you want to use the subsidiary version you will need to copy it over */etc/mail/sendmail.cf* and then stop and restart the *sendmail* daemon.

Sun Screen _____

One of the other configuration elements of *sendmail* is the ability to determine whether the email being transferred through the system is a genuine email, or one that could potentially be spam—more officially known as Unsolicited Bulk Email (UBE).

Unfortunately, the flexibility of the email system makes it easy to send such email. *Sendmail* gets around this—as other SMTP server software does—by making decisions about whether the computer sending the email is allowed to send the email in the first place, and whether the sender or recipient matches one of the domains *sendmail* thinks it's in charge of. Setting these pieces of information correctly will allow people to send you email through your system, setting it incorrectly, or failing to set it all, will likely block and refuse email that should have been accepted.

If you look at the file, it's actually split into a number of distinct sections—only some of which you actually need to modify to get the email working:

- **Local Info:** This defines the configuration information specific to this machine, and consists of the official domain name, masquerading name, administrator's email address, and other information.

- **Options:** A number of options that define how *sendmail* accepts and validates email, message sizes and formats, and how the alias database is handled.

- **Message Precedence:** The priority used for delivering different classes of email.

- **Trusted Users:** The list of users who can administer and control the email system.

- **Format of Headers:** This defines the format of the mail headers and where the sender/recipient, subject, and routing information is located.

- **Rewriting Rules:** The rules used to extract, validate, and reassemble email addresses so that mail can actually be delivered.

Of all the above sections, you only need to make modifications to the first two to configure *sendmail* for your own needs. The file is just a standard text file—you don't need any special tools beyond a text editor to make modifications. Each configuration line is prefixed by a specific letter and a specific option letter and then contains the actual configuration data. For example, the line:

```
Fw/etc/mail/local-host-names
```

defines the location of a file for configuring local servers/clients for whom we accept email. Table 12.1 contains a list of the main configuration parameters that you will probably want or need to change to set up email for your system.

Sun Lotion _____

The *sendmail* file follows the normal convention of using the # character to denote comments—the comments in the *sendmail* configuration files are quite extensive, so you should be able to follow the instructions given to set up your system.

Table 12.1   Configurable Parameters in *sendmail*

Parameter	Description
Fw/etc/mail/local-host-names	The location of the file that contains the names of any local hosts on your network for which this *sendmail* should accept and process email. For example, if you have two machines, *twinsol* and *sol9penguin*, and *twinsol* is responsible for handling email to both machines, then */etc/mail/local-host-names* (on *twinsol*) should contain two lines, *twinsol* and *sol9penguin*.
DSmailhost$?m.$m$.	The name of the server responsible for handling all the email for this domain. On each client machine, you should set this to the name of the main *sendmail* server in your local network. Alternatively, create an entry in */etc/hosts* or with your NIS or DNS system where the *mailhost* is an alias for that server.
FR-o /etc/mail/relay-domains	The location of the file that contains the list of domains for which you accept and relay email. That is, if your machine receives email for mcslp.com, this file should contain that domain name—one per line. It's this configurable parameter that decides whether an email is genuine or possible UBE.
DR	The name of the machine responsible for handling email when the address is just a username (that is no domain, more explicitly classed as unqualified). Leave this blank for the machine handling email on your network. For all other machines, set this to the name of the machine handling the email.
DM	The name your machine will masquerade as. Effectively the domain name appended to every email message that is sent beyond the local machine. You need to set this if you want email to appear as coming from mcslp.com instead of twinsol.mcslp.com.

The Alias Database

The alias database is a simple and easy way to redirect email to other users, to set up small groups, and of course to create aliases for different people. Once a *sendmail* server has identified the email as being its responsibility, it then checks the alias database to see if there are any expansions that translate the specified recipient into a list of other users or redirect it to a different location altogether.

The format of the file is very straightforward. Each line of the file defines a single alias; the text before the colon is the string that will be expanded, and the items after the colon are the addresses, users, or other options that actually sent the email.

For example, with the alias:

```
martin: mc
```

Any email sent to *martin* will actually be put into the mail file for *mc*. Meanwhile, the alias:

```
request: mc, slp
```

would send any messages sent to *request* to both the *mc* and *slp* accounts. The item after the colon doesn't have to be a list of other users. It could be a file, as in:

```
nobody: /dev/null
```

Now email sent to *nobody* will be immediately deleted.

To actually update the database, edit the file */etc/mail/aliases* with a text editor.

When you have finished editing the file, use the *newaliases* command to convert the alias file into the DBM database used by *sendmail* when it is delivering mail.

Monitoring sendmail

You can monitor the status of the sendmail queue—which contains a list of all the messages waiting to be sent, or those that have been received but not yet delivered, by using the *mailq* command. Chances are it will probably report an empty queue if your system is working correctly—mail is normally delivered pretty much instantaneously. If it doesn't, then either your machine is busy, your Internet connection is down, or there is some problem communicating with the next machine in the chain. For example, in the output below you can see that it's reporting a problem trying to communicate with *sulaco.mcslp.pri*:

```
$ mailq
/var/spool/mqueue (1 request)
----Q-ID---- --Size-- -----Q-Time----- -----------Sender/Recipient-----------
g12ArWI00749        8 Sat Feb  2 10:53 mc
                    (Deferred: Connection refused by sulaco.mcslp.pri.)
                                      mc@sulaco.mcslp.pri
```

You can force *sendmail* to process the queue by using the *-q* option. The effect is to trigger *sendmail* to work through every item in the queue and attempt to resend it—there's no guarantee of course that it will work.

The *sendmail* system is configured to send a warning email to the sender if an email could not be forwarded on to the next machine in the chain for four hours, and to return the message to the sender with information about the error if the message could still not be sent after three days. If you want to change these figures, look for the timeout section of */etc/sendmail.cf*.

For a more in-depth view of the mail that has been sent and received by *sendmail*, check the contents of the syslog file in */var/log/syslog*. All lines containing "sendmail" relate to the *sendmail* service, and you can monitor the sender, recipient, and other data from the logs in this way.

```
Feb  1 20:59:55 twinsol sendmail[27158]: [ID 801593 mail.info] g11Kxte27158:
from=<perl6-internals-return-8235-perl-te=mcwords.com@perl.org>, size=3166,
class=-60, nrcpts=1, msgid=<Pine.OSF.4.44.0202012016040.20909-100000@ermine.
ox.ac.uk>, proto=SMTP, daemon=MTA,relay=punt-11.mail.demon.net [194.217.242.34]
Feb  1 20:59:56 twinsol sendmail[27160]: [ID 801593 mail.info] g11Kxte27158:
to=<perl-te@prluk.demon.co.uk>, delay=00:00:01, xdelay=00:00:01, mailer=cyrus,
pri=231166, dsn=2.0.0, stat=Sent
Feb  1 20:59:57 twinsol sendmail[27163]: [ID 801593 mail.info] g11Kxue27163:
from=<modperl-return-22435-perl-te=mcwords.com@apache.org>, size=2472, class=-60,
nrcpts=1, msgid=<20020201200840.70504.qmail@web20107.mail.yahoo.com>,
proto=SMTP, daemon=MTA, relay=punt-11.mail.demon.net [194.217.242.34]
Feb  1 20:59:57 twinsol sendmail[27165]: [ID 801593 mail.info] g11Kxue27163:
to=<perl-te@prluk.demon.co.uk>, delay=00:00:01, xdelay=00:00:00, mailer=cyrus,
pri=230472, dsn=2.0.0, stat=Sent
Feb  1 20:59:58 twinsol sendmail[27168]: [ID 801593 mail.info] g11Kxve27168:
from=<modperl-return-22438-perl-te=mcwords.com@apache.org>, size=2094, class=-60,
nrcpts=1, msgid=<B880590E.AADA%ian@SKYLIST.net>, proto=SMTP, daemon=MTA,
relay=punt-11.mail.demon.net [194.217.242.34]
Feb  1 20:59:58 twinsol sendmail[27170]: [ID 801593 mail.info] g11Kxve27168:
to=<perl-te@prluk.demon.co.uk>, delay=00:00:01, xdelay=00:00:00, mailer=cyrus,
pri=230094, dsn=2.0.0, stat=Sent
Feb  1 20:59:59 twinsol sendmail[27173]: [ID 801593 mail.info] g11Kxwe27173:
from=<modperl-return-22437-perl-te=mcwords.com@apache.org>, size=2776, class=-60,
nrcpts=1, msgid=<Pine.GSO.4.21.0202011227580.5676-100000@shell01.corp.tellme.com>,
proto=SMTP, daemon=MTA, relay=punt-11.mail.demon.net [194.217.242.34]
Feb  1 20:59:59 twinsol sendmail[27175]: [ID 801593 mail.info] g11Kxwe27173:
to=<perl-te@prluk.demon.co.uk>, delay=00:00:01, xdelay=00:00:00, mailer=cyrus,
pri=230776, dsn=2.0.0, stat=Sent
```

Sending and Receiving Email

Hopefully, I shouldn't need to tell you too much about sending and receiving email—you probably already do it every day and no longer think of it as anything but another tool for communicating with people.

Sun Lotion

You won't normally be notified immediately when an email has been sent to you, but whenever you log in, your mailbox will be checked for new messages since the last time your email was read, and a suitable message printed if something new has arrived. Most shells will also check your mail file periodically and notify you of new mail via a message printed before a shell prompt.

Other mail software, such as Netscape Communicator or the Mail application in CDE, will also check and notify of any new mail.

Using mail

The *mail* program is probably the easiest way to send and read your email. To send an email, just supply a list of the recipients on the command line. You'll get a blank line and it's here that you type in your email message—as soon as you've finished, put a single period as the first character on a line, or press Control-D:

```
$ mail mc mc@mcslp.com
Hello, this is a test email
.
```

You should be placed back at the command prompt—you won't get any acknowledgment that the email has been queued. One of the benefits of *mail* as a command line tool is that it will read information from standard input by default, so you can use it to send emails without interactively supplying the content—useful for scripts and scheduled jobs. For example:

```
$ echo 'Hello, this is a test email' | mail mc
```

Solingo

When using the local mail format (the default for email sent/received under Unix), the email is actually written into a single file, one file for each user, located in */var/mail*. For example, the mail for root is located in */var/mail/root*. You should ensure that the permissions on the files in this directory are 622 to allow you to read and write the file and others to write the file—required if you want others to be able to send you email!

To read email with *mail*, enter the command without any arguments—if you've got any email, the oldest email in your inbox will be displayed:

```
$ mail
From mc Sat Feb  2 11:11:49 2002
```

```
Date: Sat, 2 Feb 2002 11:11:48 GMT
From: mc
Message-Id: <200202021111.g12BBmf00800@sol9penguin.mcslp.pri>
Content-Length: 9

Problem

?
```

The *?* is a prompt—entering *?* will show you a list of the full commands, but the main ones you will want to use are:

- *d* which deletes the current message.
- *r* replies (and deletes) the current message.
- *h* lists the message headers (sender, subject, date).
- *q* quits from the program.
- *x* exits, without saving any changes (i.e., any messages marked for deletion are not deleted).
- + displays next message.
- - displays previous message.
- # shows message number.

Using mailx

The *mailx* command is an extended version of *mail*. It has a slightly less-raw interface—although it's still sequential and text based—and it is slightly more intelligent when it comes to sending and formatting email.

To send an email, just as with *mail*, you supply the names and email addresses of the recipients on the command line. The difference is that in addition to the mail text, you will also be asked to supply a subject for the email you are sending:

```
$ mailx mc
Subject: Can't log in
Despite my being here, I can't seem to log on elsewhere.
.
EOT
```

You can also set the subject through the command line, very useful if you want to send an email message automatically with a subject. To set the subject, use the *-s* option and remember to include the subject text in quotes to ensure that the subject string is treated as a single argument. For example:

```
$ mailx -s "Can't log in" mc
```

The reading interface is also more friendly. When first started you will be shown a list of the message headers, rather than the first message in the file:

```
$ mailx
mailx version 5.0 Tue Jun 19 12:33:20 PDT 2001  Type ? for help.
"/var/mail/mc": 15 messages
>O  1 Mail Delivery Subs Fri Jan 25 13:05   61/1832  Returned mail:
 O  2 Mail Delivery Subs Sat Feb  2 08:36   61/1812  Returned mail:
 O  3 mc                 Sat Feb  2 08:37   12/315
 O  4 Mail Delivery Subs Sat Feb  2 08:37   59/1792  Returned mail:
 O  5 mc                 Sat Feb  2 10:24   14/348
 O  6 Mail Delivery Subs Sat Feb  2 10:52   60/1716  Returned mail:
 O  7 mc                 Sat Feb  2 10:52   14/328
 O  8 mc                 Sat Feb  2 10:52   14/328
 O  9 mc                 Sat Feb  2 11:04   14/331
 O 10 mc                 Sat Feb  2 11:24   14/396   Can't log in
 O 11 mc                 Sat Feb  2 11:28   14/360   Login problem
 O 12 mc                 Sat Feb  2 11:33   14/343   New User Please
 O 13 mc                 Sat Feb  2 11:34   14/351   Something new
 O 14 mc                 Sat Feb  2 11:34   13/344   That file you
 O 15 mc                 Sat Feb  2 11:34   12/313
?
```

To read an email, just specify the message number or use *next* and *previous*, and to reply use *reply*—simple! Use *?* or *help* to get a full list of the commands that are available.

Beyond the Standard Tools

There are of course more email clients than those I've listed here. CDE comes with its own fairly limited email tool. For a more extensive tool, use Netscape Communicator, which is actually a standard installation component with Solaris. Netscape includes the ability to support multiple email accounts and to pick up email from the local Unix mail file, POP servers, and IMAP servers. You also get filtering and other facilities.

The Least You Need to Know

- The *sendmail* daemon accepts, delivers, and resends email.
- Configure the *sendmail* daemon using the */etc/sendmail.cf* file.
- You can monitor the status of the *sendmail* queue using *mailq*.
- You can send and read email using *mail*.
- You can also send and receive email with a slightly friendlier interface using *mailx*.

Setting Up Network Services

In This Chapter

- ◆ Introducing network services
- ◆ Setting up FTP servers
- ◆ Setting up web servers
- ◆ Configuring the DNS system

Solaris comes ready to run a number of different network services, including Telnet (for remote logins) and FTP (for file transfers). However, not everybody wants to support all of these services, so in this chapter I'll show you how you can limit their access.

The web is an ever-present part of most of our lives, and your Solaris machine is also capable of working as a web server. Solaris 9 comes with the leading web server software, Apache, as standard and is so easy to enable, you'll wonder why people make such a fuss of providing web services. Of course, just enabling the service doesn't solve the biggest problem of all—you still need to build and write your pages!

The last section of this chapter looks at how you can share hostname and IP address maps with other computers in the network using the Domain Name Service (DNS). DNS is also the service used to supply IP address information around the Internet, so I'll also discuss how you can configure your machine to operate as a DNS server for your network.

How Network Services Operate

In Chapter 11, "Connecting to a Network," you had a look at how the TCP/IP network system used under Solaris (and most other platforms, and the Internet) operates. You may recall that I talked about IP addresses and how you could communicate with a machine simply by knowing its IP address.

Although this is true, it's entirely incorrect. You need one more piece of information to actually communicate with a specific service on the remote machine. If all you needed was an IP address, then you'd only be able to talk one language (protocol) with another machine, and it would have to be able to handle all of the discussions and information that you wanted to exchange.

Obviously this isn't practical; a typical machine will be sharing files, sending email, and exchanging name and host information. That's three different services already!

The extra piece of information that you need is the port or service number. The number acts a bit like the extension number at an office. By dialing the main number and the extension number, you can go straight to the right department. By using the IP address and the port number, you can go right to the service you wanted.

Different port numbers are configured for different protocols and services. For example, the SMTP protocol we saw in the last chapter works over port 25. Telnet works over port 23, and HTTP (used for websites) works on port 80. There are too many ports and services to list here, but if you want to find out more, check out the *etc/services* file, which contains a map of the port number and a short name used to identify the port.

Solingo

Telnet is a service that allows you to use a Unix machine remotely. When you "telnet" into a machine, you are given a login prompt, just as if you were using the console, and once you've logged in you have access to a normal Unix shell. Using telnet is a great way to do remote management, access your mail, or perform work remotely. The only limitation is that telnet is a text-only system—you can't run CDE or Gnome over a telnet connection.

When you communicate with a machine using a particular protocol, you are talking to the machine at a specific IP address and port number. At the end of the connection (the server end), the server must be "listening" for a connection on this port in order to accept your request to connect to it.

There are two primary methods used by services to listen for information, self-serving and using the Internet daemon. The first method, self-serving, operates by allowing the server application providing the service to run in the background (as a daemon), listening for connections. *Sendmail* does this to listen for SMTP connections, and the NFS, DNS, and NIS systems that I discuss in Chapters 11, 13, and 14 also use the same system.

The second method, using the Internet daemon, relies on a single program called *inetd* which works as a daemon, accepting requests over a number of different ports. Once a connection has been received and accepted, either *inetd* processes the request itself or hands over the connection to an application that then services the request. For example, when using FTP the connection is answered by *inetd*, but it then lets *ftpd* (the FTP daemon) handle any further communication.

Setting up systems that use the first system is relatively easy—it's entirely up to the application how it decides it wants to operate the system, all you have to do is start the application up. The Internet daemon, *inetd*, is slightly more complicated. You need to tell *inetd* what services to provide through the */etc/inetd.conf* file. By default, this file is set up to manage a number of different services, but you may want to edit the file, either to add new services or to disable services.

The Internet Daemon

The Internet daemon, *inetd*, provides a basic network service support role, handling requests from clients and either responding with information itself or handing off the connection to the daemon used to support the service in question. Configuration is handled through the *inetd.conf* file, but you don't need to look at the contents of the file, only at the primary services and facilities that it configures for support through *inetd*. Table 13.1 contains a list of the main protocols and services supported either directly by *inetd* or handled by *inetd* before the responsibility is handed off to the real daemon.

Sun Lotion _____

The clocks in computers are notoriously inaccurate. When you think that the typical digital watch is accurate to within a few seconds each month, it's amazing to think that the typical computer is accurate only to a few seconds each day. Some of them will lose ten minutes or more over the course of the day. Obviously, this isn't practical—although if it's fast, it does enable you to go home earlier!

Although *inetd* provides information about the date and time on a machine, you can't share that information. However, you can use a system that uses the Network Time Protocol (NTP). NTP allows you to synchronize the time on your machine with the time on an NTP server somewhere on the network, and many sites offer NTP services over the Internet. These servers are accurate—they get their information from the atomic clocks that record the time officially right around the world.

Table 13.1 Services Supported Through */etc/inetd.conf*

Protocol/Service	Description
daytime	Returns the date and time on the remote machine as a string of the form Sun Feb 3 14:13:14 2002.
echo	Used by programs such as *ping* to determine if a machine is up and available on the network.
exec	Used to execute programs remotely.
finger	Returns user information (derived from the current logon status and the */etc/passwd* file) about specific users on your machine.
ftp	Allows you to transfer files to/from your computer.
login	Allows you to log in remotely.
printer	Allows other machines to use your machine as a printer server.
rquotad	Shared quota (per-user disk space) information.
rstatd	Provides availability and status information to remote machines.
rusersd	Provides a list of users currently using/logged in to your machine from a remote server.
shell	Allows you to execute a remote shell from a client computer.
sprayd	Used to return a "spray" of packets to determine network performance.
talk	Enables two users to talk to each other in an interactive session.
telnet	Allows a user to log in remotely to a machine.
time	Returns the current date/time in binary format.
walld	Allows you to send messages (one way) to all users connected to or using the machine.

You will probably never have to make modifications to the file, but you may want to limit the services that your system supports and that are configured through the *inetd* system. In particular, you may want to disable the following services to reduce the potential security threat:

- echo
- finger
- exec
- login
- ftp
- talk
- walld
- daytime
- chargen

The *telnet* system is also a potential security risk as it allows users to log in remotely over the network, including over the Internet. Unfortunately, disabling it will disable it for all users, thereby restricting you as systems administrator from using the benefits of the system. If you want to support a more secure system, then use SSH, the Secure Shell. The SSH protocol provides the same features as telnet, but it uses an encrypted link.

To disable any service, put a # character at the start of the line containing the service definition to comment out that line. You'll then need to tell *inetd* of the changes. You can do this by using *pkill* to send the "hangup" signal to the daemon, like this:

```
# pkill -HUP inetd
```

The above forces *inetd* to reload the configuration file, disabling and enabling the services it configures accordingly.

Setting Up an FTP Server

You already know from the previous section that the FTP server is set up by default. You can try connecting to your machine using FTP just by typing:

```
$ ftp localhost
Connected to localhost.
220 sol9penguin FTP server (SunOS 5.9) ready.
Name (localhost:mc):
```

FTP can therefore be a useful way of transferring files between machines without having to enable NFS or anything more complex.

You don't really need to do anything to set up the FTP server. That said, the default setup allows genuine users to access the system and it's likely that you will want to limit those users who are allowed to transfer files using FTP—after all, it's an open door to anybody who obtains a valid user's password to get into your machine.

By default, any normal user can connect to your machine using FTP. If a user is told that they are not authorized to connect, then it's probably because they are using a shell other than the Bourne, Korn, or C shells. Make sure you update the file */etc/shells*, or create the file if it does not exist. The file should contain a list of the valid shells—a requirement for FTP access—that a user can use. To ensure access for anybody with one of the four standard shells that come with Solaris, create/edit the file to match the following:

```
/usr/bin/sh
/usr/bin/ksh
/usr/bin/csh
/usr/bin/bash
```

When they log in, they are placed in their home directory, just as if they had logged in as normal, but they can move around the entire system and access or download any file to which they would normally have access. You can't, unfortunately, limit their access to their home directory. However, you can exclude these people from your system altogether by adding their name to the */etc/ftpusers* file. By default, this contains a list of all the system users, including root, therefore banning everybody but the users you add to */etc/passwd*. For reference, the default contents are:

```
Root
Daemon
bin
sys
adm
lp
uucp
nuucp
listen
nobody
noaccess
nobody4
```

Sun Screen

However tempting it might be, don't remove root, or indeed any of the other users used by the system (such as *adm, bin,* etc.) from the */etc/ftpusers* file—doing so could seriously undermine the security of your system.

If you want to add a user name to the list, just put the user name or names on additional lines at the end of the file. Any user trying to connect via FTP will be unauthorized to login, and told so during the FTP login process.

Occasionally, you'll want to do the opposite—allow users to connect to the machine over FTP, but deny them access through telnet. To do this, you need to make a few changes:

1. Ensure their names are *not* in */etc/ftpusers*.

2. Add */bin/false*—a program which returns a false value—to */etc/shells*.

3. Change the user's shell to */bin/false*.

Now, when users try to use telnet, they will be immediately logged out (because */bin/false* is not a real shell), but allowed access via FTP because according to */etc/shells* it is one of the allowed shells.

I've successfully used this for years to provide FTP drop points for clients—they can connect to a server and pick up and drop off files using FTP, while not having real access to the system supporting the FTP service.

Setting Up a Web Server

There are a number of different web server solutions available, including Sun's own offering as part of its collaboration with Netscape, called iPlanet. The most popular web server on the Internet though is Apache. Apache is an open source project and is one of the oldest open source Internet products available—it's been around for almost as long as the web and HTTP.

You can download Apache for free from www.apache.org. If you are using Solaris 9, you actually get Apache installed as part of the operating system. It comes preconfigured and ready to run with the Tomcat extensions (also from Apache) to allow you to support Java Server Pages (JSP) on your website.

To get Apache running, you need to edit the *httpd.conf* file. For Solaris 9 users a default configuration file is available in */etc/apache/httpd.conf-example*. You'll need to copy this to */etc/apache/httpd.conf*. For those of you who have earlier versions of Solaris and have downloaded Apache, you need to look in the *conf* directory of your Apache installation. By default the file will probably be in */usr/local/apache/conf/httpd.conf*.

Open up the *httpd.conf* file in an editor, and be forewarned that the file is large and complicated looking. In reality, most of the text relates to the comments used to describe the different sections and options. To get the machine working you need to set just three configurable parameters—look for the lines starting with the following strings, and then use the description to help you set the correct information:

- ◆ **ServerAdmin:** The email address of the person responsible for this server. Although not required, it's a good idea to set this if you expect other people to be using your server.

- ◆ **ServerName:** The name of the server that will be reported for the web page. This should be the name (hostname and domain name) for your machine either as it appears in your local network or as it appears in the DNS. Setting the name wrong may make your web server unavailable.

- ◆ **DocumentRoot:** The location of the HTML files that you want to serve through your website. The default is */var/apache/htdocs*.

CAUTION

Sun Screen _____

You may find that you also need to disable the Tomcat extensions if all you want is to serve standard HTML pages. In this case, find the lines starting LoadModule and comment out the line (by placing a # character at the start of the line) containing "*mod_jserv.so*", then find the line slightly further through the file that reads "*AddModule mod_jserv.c*" and comment that out, too.

Once you've edited the file, it's time to test the configuration. It's easiest to use the *apachectl* tool to start and stop your server. Under Solaris 9 this tool is located in */usr/apache/bin/apachectl*. To start the server, append *start* to the command line:

```
# /usr/apache/bin/apachectl start
```

The command should come back with:

```
/usr/apache/bin/apachectl start: httpd started
```

Now open a browser, either on your own machine or on another machine on the network, and enter the name you specified in the *ServerName* parameter in the *config* file. Assuming everything has gone okay and you used the default *DocumentRoot* setting, you should get a page like the one shown in Figure 13.1.

Figure 13.1

The default Apache web page.

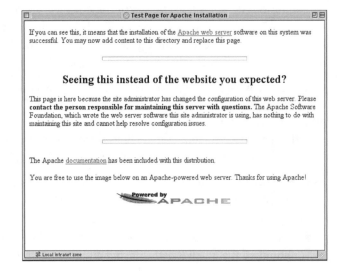

Apache will be started automatically when the machine boots up by the script linked from */etc/init.d/apache*.

Configuring DNS

I discussed the DNS system in Chapter 11 when I explained how hostnames are resolved into IP addresses. The DNS system, which is used to provide name resolving services on the Internet, is a distributed system that allows a single client to contact a known server, and for that server to ask another server which it thinks might know the answer.

If you want to host your own Internet domain name, or just want to provide a central server for the other machines to talk to when resolving both internal and external names, then you will need to set up a DNS server. If you already have a DNS server on your network, then you can probably skip this bit.

The named Service

The core to the system is the *named* daemon. The daemon does two things: first it provides resolving facilities for local domains, both to local clients and if necessary clients on the Internet. Second, it provides a forwarding ability to allow clients on the network to ask the daemon to resolve public addresses. A single *named* daemon can therefore be used to make your own name resolving and the name resolving of Internet addresses.

Configuration works initially through a single file, */etc/named.conf*. The file holds the core configuration for the named system, including the list of other hosts you talk to when trying to resolve names, plus a list of the domains for which you are responsible. You'll concentrate on setting up the file for a single, local, domain and for forwarding requests to the DNS servers of an ISP.

The first part of the file sets the global options. You can see a sample below:

```
options {
        directory           "/usr/local/adm/named";
        forwarders {
        158.152.1.58;
        158.152.1.43;
        };
};
```

The *directory* entry configures the directory which will hold information about your domain (if you have any) and caching information for the existing IP addresses and hosts that the daemon has been asked to resolve. The *forwarders* portion is a list of the other DNS servers you will query if the name can't be resolved locally. In the sample file, it lists the two IP addresses I use for my ISP. You should populate the section of the file with the corresponding information for your ISP.

The remainder of the file defines the *zone* files that will hold domain information about our local domain. There are two basic domains that you should include. The first is the cache file where already resolved names are stored. The definition for the zone looks like this:

> ### A Postcard From ...
>
> There are a number of special IP address ranges designed for use by people who do not need a genuine Internet IP address—that is, those people setting up a network that is not connected to the internet, or which is connected but through a firewall. The *192.168.1* is one such range.

```
zone "." in {
        type hint;
        file "fake/cache";
};
```

The text above sets the zone type as hint—the type for caching information—and then sets the name of the file that will be used to hold the cached data. In the example it's *fake/cache*. The name will be appended to the directory you set in the first section of the file.

The last two entries configure the real information for my local network. First, a reverse zone to map IP addresses in my network back into names, then the second defines the zone that maps names into IP addresses.

```
 zone "1.168.192.in-addr.arpa" in {
        type master;
        file "primary/1.168.192.in-addr.arpa";
};

 zone "mcslp.pri" in {
        type master;
        file "primary/mcslp.pri";
};
```

You put both files into the *primary* directory within your working directory, as these are primary zones that you are responsible for. You could have also set up *slave* zones; these are the zones that you copy from a master and then serve as if they were your own. You can use slave servers in this way to reduce the load on a single server. The basic format for a slave zone is:

```
zone "mcslp.pri" in {
        type slave;
        file "secondary/mcslp.pri";
        masters {
                192.168.1.135;
                192.168.1.127;
        };
};
```

where the IP address in the *masters* section is the list of other servers which host this domain.

To complete the process for your own domains, you need to create the two zone files, one for the reverse zone and one for the forward zone.

Basic Zone File Format

All master zone files consist of a header that defines the basic zone parameters, including the single machine and owner of the domain, the timeout values used when querying the domain, and a serial number used by slave servers to determine how up-to-date their zone file is, and whether they need to download the new version. Here's the header from our forward zone:

```
mcslp.pri. IN SOA twinsol.mcslp.pri. mc.mcslp.pri. (
      99      ; Serial number
      28800   ; Refresh after (seconds)
      7200    ; Retry after (seconds)
      604800  ; Expire after (seconds)
      86400   ; Expire after (seconds)
)
```

The first two lines should be the only two you need to change. The first line sets, in order, the domain name (mcslp.pri), the name of the machine responsible for the domain (twinsol.mcslp.pri), and the email address (using a period, rather than an **@** symbol) of the person responsible for the domain (mc.mcslp.pri). The "IN SOA" just identifies the record—in this case, it's the "Site of Authority" record. Note as well that the names are "fully qualified"—they have a period appended to the end of the name to identify them as full names that cannot be further expanded.

The serial number is just a sequential number used to identify the current version of the file. You should increment this by one each time you make a change to the file. If you want, you can include the date and time of modification here by specifying the date/time in the universal format: for example, 3 February 2002 at 3:30pm would be 200202031530.

You should also include a number of name-server entries—these list the valid name servers which hold official records for the domain. The list should include the machine that holds the main files, and any other servers which you have authorized and configured to act as secondary servers. For example, there are two official servers on my network:

```
mcslp.pri. NS twinsol.mcslp.pri.
mcslp.pri. NS penguin.mcslp.pri.
```

As you can see, the domain name is on the left, and the hostnames of the servers are on the right. Just remember to create forward records for these servers in the rest of the zone file!

For reverse zones, you must specify the reverse zone in the specification:

```
1.168.192.in-addr.arpa. IN NS twinspark.mcslp.pri.
1.168.192.in-addr.arpa. IN NS penguin.mcslp.pri.
```

Creating Forward Records

A *forward* record is a record in the forward zone file that relates a name within a domain name into an IP address. I use the full hostname and domain name in my files just to make it obvious what I'm dealing with. To identify the record as an IP address record, you must use the "IN A" (Internet Address), with the hostname/domain on the left and the IP address on the right:

```
twinsol.mcslp.pri. IN A 192.168.1.135
```

Note the hostname here—there's a period appended to the end of the name to show a fully qualified name.

You can also set up forward records that are aliases for real address records. For example, *twinsol* also acts as a web server, so an alias for the same machine would be www.mcslp.pri. Aliases are called canonical names, so they use the "CNAME" record type:

```
www.mcslp.pri. CNAME twinsol.mcslp.pri.
```

Here's a slightly longer fragment from the forward file on my machine:

```
penguin.mcslp.pri.             IN A     192.168.1.138
airport.mcslp.pri.             IN A     192.168.1.254
proxy.mcslp.pri.               CNAME    http-proxy.mcslp.pri.
linux.mcslp.pri.               CNAME    penguin.mcslp.pri.
time.mcslp.pri.                CNAME    twinsol.mcslp.pri.
```

Don't forget to create an entry for localhost:

```
localhost.mcslp.pri.           IN A     127.0.0.1
```

Creating Reverse Records

Reverse records exist within the reverse zone file and are used to relate IP addresses back to numbers. Because the zone file already contains the IP address as part of the specification, we just need to specify the end number as a *pointer* back to the real name:

```
135        IN      PTR twinsol.mcslp.pri.
```

In the above example, the "135" makes up the final part of the IP address, which points back to *twinsol*. So, when the system looks up 192.168.1.135 it should get the name *twinsol.mcslp.pri* back.

You should create a reverse mapping for each forward mapping you placed in the forward map file.

Setting Up Email Forwarding

In Chapter 12, "Setting Up Email," I explained how email is forwarded around the Internet, and I mentioned that email for mc@mcslp.com causes *sendmail* to look up the

MX (Mail Exchanger) record for the mcslp.com domain. The MX record is just another configuration line in the DNS file. From our sample file, the line looks like this:

```
mcslp.pri. MX 10     mail.mcslp.pri.
```

The *mcslp.pri* is just the domain name, and the *mail.mcslp.pri* is the name to be used when contacting the mail server. The "10" is the priority for the specified host. If you have more than one machine set up to handle email, you can set up the MX records so that different hosts are contacted according to their priority—lowest numbers first—with the other machines acting as backups.

For example, in the sample below, *mail.mcslp.pri* would be contacted first, and if no contact could be made it would then try *penguin.mcslp.pri* and then *insentient.mcslp.pri*:

```
mcslp.pri. MX 10     mail.mcslp.pri.
           MX 20     penguin.mcslp.pri.
           MX 30     insentient.mcslp.pri.
```

Starting and Reloading the Configuration

If *named* is not already started, log in as root and type *in.named* at the prompt to start the *named* service. This will load the */etc/named.conf* file and then the zones file (if there are any) and start the service. Check */var/adm/messages* for any messages logged by the system if it cannot start.

If you edit the *named* files you must tell the *named* daemon. You can do this by sending the hangup signal (HUP) to the *named* process using *pkill*:

```
# pkill -HUP named
```

See Chapter 25, "Monitoring Performance," for more information.

Checking the Name Service Records

To check that your new domain is up and running properly, make sure that the */etc/resolv. conf* file is pointing to your machine as the DNS server, and then use *nslookup* to query entries:

```
# nslookup twinsol
Server:  twinsol.mcslp.pri
Address:  192.168.1.135

Name:    twinsol.mcslp.pri
Address:  192.168.1.135

# nslookup penguin
```

```
Server:   twinsol.mcslp.pri
Address:  192.168.1.135


Name:     penguin.mcslp.pri
Address:  192.168.1.138


# nslookup 192.168.1.135
Server:   twinsol.mcslp.pri
Address:  192.168.1.135


Name:     twinsol.mcslp.pri
Address:  192.168.1.135


# nslookup -type=mx mcslp.pri
Server:   twinsol.mcslp.pri
Address:  192.168.1.135


mcslp.pri          preference = 1, mail exchanger = mail.mcslp.pri
mcslp.pri          nameserver = penguin.mcslp.pri
mcslp.pri          nameserver = twinsol.mcslp.pri
penguin.mcslp.pri          internet address = 192.168.1.138
twinsol.mcslp.pri          internet address = 192.168.1.135
```

Although the *nslookup* command queries the DNS service, it's never a guarantee that the information returned is correct. The *nslookup* command uses the information in */etc/resolv.conf* to work out which machine to contact for DNS queries. If the machine chosen from the file is not the primary server for the domain, then you may be getting the cached information from another machine, which may be from an older version of the files. If in doubt, always check on the machine, or tell *nslookup* to use the IP address of the primary server for the domain by supplying the address as the final command line argument.

The Least You Need to Know

- Many services are configured and supported through the *inetd* daemon, which is controlled by the */etc/inetd.conf* file.

- You can restrict FTP users by adding their names to the */etc/ftpusers* file.

- To enable web services, use Apache and edit the */etc/apache/httpd.conf* file to specify the hostname of your server and the location of the HTML files you want to serve.

- To set up a DNS server you must configure the */etc/named.conf* file and create suitable zone files for your local network.

Configuring NIS

In This Chapter

◆ Understanding NIS/NIS+

◆ Setting up an NIS Server

◆ Setting up an NIS Client

The Single Sign-on has been a holy grail for many client computers for a long time. There is nothing worse, from a user's point of view, than having to enter a different password each time you want to use a machine or a different service on that machine.

Although NIS does not directly resolve this problem, it makes sharing information such as user names, passwords, and host information across multiple machines significantly easier. Using NIS, you can have hundreds of machines, all of which use the same login/password database, reducing the amount of time it takes to set up individual users (you don't have to copy the info to each machine) and simplifying the user's experience. Used in combination with NFS and the *automounter* system, it can make managing a large Unix client network significantly easier. NFS and the automounter are covered in Chapter 15, "Sharing File Systems."

In this chapter I explain how to configure the NIS server, set up backup servers, and configure clients to use this information. You may find you need to refer back to Chapter 11, "Connecting to a Network," for more information on the */etc/nsswitch.conf* file.

What Is NIS/NIS+?

The Network Information Service (NIS) and its updated cousin NIS+ are both ways of sharing many of the standard information and data files used by a typical Unix system between more than one Unix machine. Using NIS/NIS+ you can reduce the difficulty of making changes to multiple machines in a network when it comes to adding users or hosts, and also reduce the frustration that users may have with using a number of different machines all of which require different passwords.

The NIS system provides a method for sharing all of the databases defined in the */etc/ nsswitch.conf* file. See Chapter 11 for more information on this file and the database it provides access and control for.

NIS systems are based on three different types of machines within the network:

♦ **Master server:** This is the machine which holds the file copies of all the information, and also where you update and manage the databases that you want to share. The master server provides information to both slave servers and clients.

♦ **Slave servers:** These act as backup servers for the master server and hold copies of the databases but have no way of updating the information they contain. These provide information to clients.

♦ **Clients:** These access the information, contacting any of the servers that have been configured for them until they find one that answers their query.

A Postcard From ...

Readers with a Windows NT or Windows 2000 background will be familiar with the idea of sharing information across different machines. In essence, the Primary Domain Controller (PDC) is no different to the NIS Master Server, and Backup Domain Controllers (BDC) are the equivalent of the Slave Servers in NIS configurations. The clients are no different from any Windows client set up to log in to a Windows domain.

Under Mac OS there is no direct equivalent, although the later versions of AppleShare IP allow you to share login information across more than one machine. Under Mac OS X the closest equivalent is the Netinfo system which was specifically designed to share information across hosts. The main difference between NIS and Netinfo is that Netinfo allows information to be more highly structured in a tree format and it's probably a closer equivalent of the tree model used by LDAP.

The NIS system works by setting up a single domain which is used as the key to identify the clients and servers which will be sharing information. These domains are not related in any way to Internet domains or the domain/hostname system employed by the Domain Name Server (DNS) system.

NIS+ is essentially the same as NIS, except that it's been extended to support a hierarchical structure, allowing you to organize domains into a rough tree structure that matches the logical layout of your organization. We won't be covering NIS+ in this manual, but check the online documentation and AnswerBook for more information.

Setting Up a Server

Setting up a server is a relatively straightforward process. First of all, you need to decide which databases—that is, which files in */etc* that contain configurable information, such as */etc/hosts* and */etc/passwd*—that you want to share with the rest of the network.

Although there is no right or wrong list of files that should be shared in this way, obvious suggestions include */etc/passwd* (and */etc/shadow*), */etc/hosts*, and */etc/mail/aliases* at the very minimum. Once you've decided, you then need to choose a master server, which will be used to create and manage the raw data that makes up the database information which will be shared, and any slave servers, which will be used to answer queries and reduce the load on the master server.

Initializing the Database

The master server uses the existing file-based databases of user names, passwords, hosts, and other information in order to build a set of database files. Although we can use the files in */etc* to directly build the databases, this is a bad idea for a number of reasons:

1. You may not want to share all of the entries in these databases. For example, the core system users such as *adm* and others do not need to be shared with machines; this information is unlikely to change and there is therefore no reason to share it.

2. The format of the source files must be perfect—you'll need to remove all the comments and extraneous information from the files before you build the databases.

3. You will probably want to trim the files in */etc*, too—they will no longer need to contain information that we'll be sharing through NIS. In particular, you should put user accounts (apart from root and your own account, in case you need to connect to the machine in an emergency) into the NIS source files, keeping the real */etc* files as light as possible. This will make administration easier in the long run.

The process is therefore:

1. Create a new directory to hold the copies of your */etc* files; you'll need separate directories for the *passwd* file and all the other files. I use */var/yp/src* and */var/yp/srcpw* for the base files and the *passwd* file, respectively.

2. Change the permissions on the directories you created above to 700.

3. Copy the files into the source directories. The exact list of files you copy depends on which databases you want to share, but includes some or all of: *bootparams*, *auto_home*, *auto_master*, *ethers*, *group*, *hosts*, *netgroup*, *networks*, *netmasks*, *protocols*, *rpc*, *service*, *shadow*.

4. Edit the files and make sure they contain only the information you want to share. While you're at it, remove any comments or special formatting, and double check that the format of all the files is okay.

5. Edit the */etc/mail/aliases* file and ensure it is up-to-date. Do not copy it into your source directory—you don't need to worry about the location of this file.

6. Change to */var/yp* and edit the *Makefile* file in that directory. Make sure that DIR is set to the source directory and that PWDIR is set to the *passwd* directory you created in step 1. Also check that the list of maps listed against the "all": entry matches the list of maps that you want to share.

7. Set the domain name for your NIS domain. You can do this by using the *domainname* command:

```
# domainname mcslp.pri
```

8. Now type:

```
# domainname >/etc/defaultdomain
```

to ensure the domain is set properly each time the machine starts up.

You are now ready to actually set up the server.

Starting Up a Master Server

Setting up the master server is a case of building those source files that you created in the previous section into a final set of databases. You do this using *ypinit*, the *-m* command line option tells the command to set us up for a master NIS server:

```
# ypinit -m
```

You'll be asked some questions—first you'll need to specify a list of the machines which will act as backup servers for this domain. Make sure that any servers that enter at this stage have corresponding entries in */etc/hosts*.

Now answer the other questions. You'll be asked if you want to terminate due to nonfatal errors, answer no (the default) and then, if a directory already exists for a domain, you will be asked to confirm the deletion of this directory. Say yes if asked, otherwise you'll need to perform the process manually.

You can see the first part of the output of a typical session below:

```
There will be no further questions. The remainder of the procedure should take
5 to 10 minutes.
Building /var/yp/mcslp.pri/ypservers...
Running /var/yp /Makefile...
updated passwd
updated group
updated hosts
updated ipnodes
updated ethers
updated networks
updated rpc
updated protocols
updated bootparams
```

Don't panic if the process raises an error like this:

```
WARNING: World writable directory /var/yp/mcslp.pri
dbm map "Alias0": unsafe map file /var/yp/mcslp.pri/mail.aliases: No such file
➥or directory
WARNING: cannot open alias database /var/yp/mcslp.pri/mail.aliases
Cannot create database for alias file /var/yp/mcslp.pri/mail.aliases
*** Error code 71
```

It's a small bug in the process which doesn't set the permissions on the directory properly. Just type:

```
# cd /var/yp
# chmod 700 mcslp.pri
```

where *mcslp.pri* is the name of your domain. The above command will set the permissions of your directory to the correct values—the default value would allow anybody to access the directory's contents!

Now type:

```
# make
```

The database-building process should start again, rebuilding all the maps and databases required. As soon as you see:

```
make[1]: Leaving directory '/var/yp'
```

You are ready to start up the NIS server. To do this, use:

```
# /usr/lib/netsvc/yp/ypstart
```

The *ypstart* command will automatically determine what sort of NIS service needs to be run and start the necessary daemons.

If you want your master server to use the NIS database—and you'll need to if you only place shared information in the NIS tables—then make sure you edit the */etc/nsswitch.conf* file to search the databases. Alternatively, copy */etc/nsswitch.nis* to */etc/nsswitch.conf*.

Starting Up a Slave Server

A slave server exists purely to hold a backup copy of the information which can then be passed on to a client if it's requested. A slave server has no control of the information in the database; it just acts as an echo station.

To set up a slave server:

1. Set the system's domain name using *domainname*, remembering to update the */etc/defaultdomain* file accordingly.

2. Update the */etc/nsswitch.conf* file to use the NIS databases you want to share. Although this isn't a required step, it's not generally a good idea to have a slave server that isn't also a client.

3. Make sure that the master server's IP address is in */etc/hosts*.

4. Run *ypinit* with the *-s* option, specifying the name of the master server:

   ```
   # ypinit -s twinsol
   ```

5. Answer the question about quitting on nonfatal errors and then wait while the slave server copies the information from the master server:

```
OK, please remember to go back and redo manually whatever fails. If you
don't, some part of the system (perhaps the yp itself) won't work.
The yp domain directory is /var/yp/mcslp.pri
There will be no further questions. The remainder of the procedure should take
a few minutes, to copy the data bases from twinsol.
Transferring mail.aliases...
...
Transferring passwd.byuid...
Transferring passwd.byname...
Transferring ypservers...

sol9penguin's nis data base has been set up

 without any errors.
```

Finally, you'll need to start up the NIS service using:

```
# /usr/lib/netsvc/yp/ypstart
```

Note that this process only copies the actual database files over from the server; the raw data files used to build the database stay on the master server.

Updating the NIS Maps

To update any of the NIS databases—for example when you add a new user or host to a database—all you need to do is edit the source files that contained the raw data used to build the maps the first time around. That makes the process as simple as:

1. Edit the file that you copied into the separate directory—that is, the file used to build the original database.

2. Change to the */var/yp* directory and run *make*.

The *make* command should check which files have been updated since the last time it was executed, and then update the maps. Any new requests should automatically obtain the new versions.

Setting Up a Client

There are really two steps to the setting up of the client. The first is configuring the */etc/nsswitch.conf* file so that it actually uses NIS maps to access information rather than using the local files. The second stage is actually to tell the client which servers to use and set up the NIS system to make queries to one or more servers. The use of multiple servers is important in large installations. Although you can still have only one master server in a network, having at least one slave server allows one of the two machines in the network to go down without it stopping everybody from connecting to the network.

Configuring the Client

Configuring a client is relatively easy. First, you should edit the */etc/nsswitch.conf* file to reflect which files you want to use the NIS maps for and which you want to use the real local files for. I tend to use the following for hosts, to ensure I pick up any local preferences first and also to ensure that if the network or NIS server is down, I still find the IP address of a host quickly:

```
hosts: files nis dns
```

For all other maps I use:

```
ethers: nis files
```

Sun Screen

Don't ever configure the /etc/nsswitch.conf file to *only* use NIS as a resolving system, especially for users and passwords. Doing so has dangerous consequences, as it can lock you out of the system entirely, even as root, because the system has no way of verifying who you are.

Sun Screen

There is one more step if you want to allow users to change their password on a client machine. You should rename the true *passwd* command (located at /usr/bin/passwd) and then copy or link /usr/bin/passwd to /usr/bin/yppasswd. Now whenever users try to change their password with *passwd* they will instead run *yppasswd* and update the copy of their password in the master server's maps.

If you want to save time, copy the /etc/nsswitch.nis file to /etc/nsswitch.conf, a standard file supplied with your system that sets up your system for accessing the information through NIS first and files as a backup.

Next, you must ensure that the real /etc/hosts file contains the hostname and IP address of the server or servers you want to use—without this information you will be unable to use a hostname when specifying an NIS server.

Then use the following steps:

1. Use *domainname* to set the domain name to match that of the server you are using as your NIS server. You may also want to place this information into /etc/defaultdomain so that the setting is configured each time the machine is switched on.

2. Run:

   ```
   # ypinit -c
   ```

   You will be prompted for the name of a server to copy the data from. Enter the name of the nearest server to you—that is, either the master server if it's on the same network, or a slave server. You can continue to enter as many servers as you like. If you are using multiple slave servers, enter those first before the master server.

3. Start the NIS service by calling /usr/lib/netsvc/yp/ypstart.

That's it! All you need to do now is try to access the information.

Viewing the Databases

The obvious way to test the databases is to try logging in with the new database using a username/password combination only broadcast by the server, or to try pinging or otherwise accessing a host specified in the host map. The easiest way is to use ping:

```
$ ping myhost
```

To view the map contents, use *ypcat*. Just supply the name of the map that you want to view on the command line. For example, to view the hosts by name map, use:

```
# ypcat hosts.byname
```

The *ypcat* command also sports a number of aliases, which you can use to access specific maps by a shorter name. You can get a list using the *-x* command line option.

```
# ypcat -x
Use "passwd"    for map "passwd.byname"
Use "group"     for map "group.byname"
Use "project"   for map "project.byname"
Use "networks"  for map "networks.byaddr"
Use "hosts"     for map "hosts.byname"
Use "ipnodes"   for map "ipnodes.byname"
Use "protocols" for map "protocols.bynumber"
Use "services"  for map "services.byname"
Use "aliases"   for map "mail.aliases"
Use "ethers"    for map "ethers.byname"
```

It's important to get to know these commands as it's the best way of checking both the content and accessibility of the NIS databases. Getting to know the aliases will just save you some time and fingertips!

The Least You Need to Know

- NIS is a system for sharing certain system databases across a number of machines over the network.

- NIS works by using a central server holding the databases. Clients communicate with the server each time they look up a piece of information. Slave servers can be used to reduce the load on the master server.

- You use the *ypinit* command to set up all three NIS machine types: master, slave, and client.

- You must configure the */etc/nsswitch.conf* file to use the NIS data once the information has been shared.

Sharing File Systems

In This Chapter

◆ Using the Network File System

◆ Sharing with Windows

◆ Sharing with Mac OS

There is nothing more annoying than moving from one machine to another and finding that you need a file from the other machine to continue working. You could use the FTP system that I introduced in Chapter 13, "Setting Up Network Services," but it would be much easier if you could access files on a remote server in the same way you access them from a local one.

Unix has had the ability to share files from one machine to another for years using the Network File System (NFS). NFS is a standard Unix feature that exists not only within Solaris but also in BSD, Linux, AIX, HP-UX, and a myriad of other Unix-like operating systems. In this chapter I'll discuss how to share and manage NFS from both the client and server sides.

Not everybody is a Unix user though; sometimes you want to be able to access the files on a Unix machine from a Windows client, and sometimes from a Mac OS client. Solaris does not support these systems directly, but you can obtain software that enables you to share your disks with other platforms using something other than NFS. I'll present two such solutions—Samba for Windows, and NetAt for Mac OS.

The Network File System

NFS is a completely transparent method of sharing files between Unix operating systems. The shares are Unix aware, so they support the owner, group, and permissions information, and unless you know it's from an NFS share, it's almost impossible to tell that the files you are accessing are on a remote machine at all.

NFS is very easy to use. You share directories by using the *share* command and unshare directories using *unshare*. You can also use a variety of commands to share and unshare all the directories from a machine, and also to monitor what is currently being shared.

Sun Screen

> You must have superuser access to share and mount file systems. None of the commands in this chapter are destructive, although you should still concentrate in case you type in the wrong directory or option! Remember, command examples with a % prefix require *root* access, examples with a $ prefix can be used by any user.

Sharing a Directory with NFS

NFS shares directories; the directories you share do not have to be the mount points for a specific file system, so if you have a file system */export/home* then you can export */export/home/mc* without exporting the rest of the file system. Conversely, if you export */export/home*, clients can mount */export/home*, */export/home/mc*, or any other directory or subdirectory within the share.

The format for the *share* command is:

```
share [-d description] [-F nfs ] [-o specific_options] pathname
```

The *-d* option gives a description to the share you are about to create. This can be useful when users want to mount a share from your server, but don't know the exact directory that they need to share—the description will be provided as part of the list.

The *-F* command is used to specify the file system format to be used when exporting the file system. At the moment, only NFS is supported in the standard system, although the potential exists for other formats.

The *specific_options* are used to set NFS-specific options to be used when sharing your directory. These help to set the operating parameters of the shared directory and control the access to it by remote clients. Table 15.1 lists the suitable options.

> ### A Postcard From ...
>
> NFS, and indeed most other shared file systems, work by using a server process which waits, listening for requests from a remote machine. The remote machine connects, associating a disk, volume, or directory with the remote server.
>
> Each time you perform an operation that requires talking to the server, a command is sent over to the server and the server responds. This process can involve fairly small amounts of information—for example, checking that the name of a directory exists when you change it—to very large amounts, such as when transferring information to or from a file on the server.
>
> Most systems, including NFS, have built-in mechanisms to cope in case there is a problem. Windows and Mac OS systems will communicate a couple of times until finally reporting an error. NFS systems using Unix can be configured to retransmit and retry operations as many times as you like—useful if the NFS server is regularly busy or at the end of WAN connection.

Table 15.1   Options for NFS Shares

Option	Description
aclok	Provides support for access control lists for NFS Version 2 clients.
anon=uid	Users who do not have a user ID that matches that of the machine sharing the disk will have their files created with this ID.
index=file	Displays the contents of *file* instead of the directory listing for WebNFS clients.
nosub	Prevents clients from mounting subdirectories of shared resources.
nosuid	Prevents clients from setting *setuid* or *setgid* access on files and directories.
ro	Provides read-only access only.
ro=list	Provides read-only access to the list of clients specified by list.
root=list	Provides root access to the list of clients specified by list.
rw	Provides read/write access.
rw=list	Provides read/write access to the list of clients specified by list.
sec=mode	Uses the security modes specified by *mode* to authenticate clients.
window=value	Sets the maximum lifetime for a client's credentials to *value* seconds.

One last option is the directory that you want to share.

For example, to share a directory without setting options you use:

```
% share /export/home
```

The command shares the directory mentioned, allowing other clients to connect to it. NFS must be running for the command to work.

Note however, that the *share* command only tells the operating system that you want to share a particular file system. The real work is handled by a separate set of daemons which service the requests of the remote clients, handling file transfers and sharing, setting permission and ownership information, and ensuring that files are not updated simultaneously. The NFS client daemons are started when the machine is executing at runlevel 2 by the script */etc/init.d/nfs.client*. Directories are not actually shared until the machine reaches runlevel 3, when the NFS server daemons are started by the */etc/init.d/nfs.server* script. The NFS server is not actually started unless there are directories that have been configured to be shared according to the contents of the */etc/dfs/dfstab* file.

It's unlikely that you will want to provide unlimited access to a shared directory from any machine. To restrict access you must specify the type and level of access to be provided to specific machines, using the *ro*, *rw*, and *root* options to the share command. For example, to share the directory read-only to all machines, use:

```
% share -o ro /export/home
```

To provide read/write access to a specific list of machines, use the *rw* option and then supply a list of machines or domain names, separated by colons, after the option:

```
% share -o rw=twinsol:penguin /export/home
```

This provides read/write access *only* to the two systems mentioned. All other machines will be denied access. You can also combine these options to provide different access to different machines by their name (including domain name, if necessary) or IP address:

```
% share -o ro,rw=.mcslp.pri,root=insentient /export/home
```

A Postcard From ...

The SunOS operating system—the precursor to Solaris—used the *exportfs* command to share disks, which is why you will often find the process of sharing a disk over NFS referred to as exporting a file system. It's also why the convention is to put the directories (and associated file systems) within the */export* directory on the host machine. Typically, all the directories in */export* are shared by some means with the outside world.

The above example provides read-only access to any machine that asks for it, read/write access to *twinsol* or *penguin*, and root access to *insentient*. Root access is special—normally when you mount an NFS disk you have access only to perform actions on files that you own or that you have been granted access to by the server. You cannot, even as root, change ownership or permissions, or delete files owned by root from a remote machine. For this, you must have root access to the NFS resource, and this is what the *root* option provides.

The *share* command is only a temporary solution—it enables you to share a particular directory; however, the information about the share is not retained over a reboot. If the machine reboots, you'll have to use *share* again to share each file system. This doesn't sound remotely friendly or Unix-like, so it won't surprise you to know that there is a solution to the problem.

In the */etc* directory there is a directory called *dfs*, and within that a file called *dfstab*. This file is used by the *nfs.server* script to export file systems for you automatically when the NFS service is started. The format of the file is actually just a list of share commands. For example, here's a file from an existing Solaris 8 machine on my network:

```
share -F nfs -o rw,root=.mcslp.pri,root=sol9linux:penguin /export/share
share -F nfs -o rw,root=.mcslp.pri,root=sol9linux:penguin /export/http
share -F nfs -o rw,root=.mcslp.pri,root=sol9linux:penguin /export/contrib
share -F nfs -o rw,root=.mcslp.pri,root=sol9linux:penguin /export/cvs
share -F nfs -o rw,root=.mcslp.pri,root=sol9linux:penguin /usr/local
share -F nfs -o ro,anon=0 /export/os/Solaris9
share -F nfs -o ro,anon=0 /export/os/Sol9Core/Solaris_9/Tools/Boot
```

The file contains standard exports (albeit with root access) to the machines on my network. For a list of the shares currently active and their options (whether they are defined in the */etc/dfs/dfstab* file or by hand) can be found in */etc/dfs/sharetab*:

```
/export/share      -     nfs     rw,root=.mcslp.pri,root=sol9linux:penguin
/export/http       -     nfs     rw,root=.mcslp.pri,root=sol9linux:penguin
/export/contrib -      nfs     rw,root=.mcslp.pri,root=sol9linux:penguin
/export/cvs        -     nfs     rw,root=.mcslp.pri,root=sol9linux:penguin
/usr/local         -     nfs     rw,root=.mcslp.pri,root=sol9linux:penguin
/export/os/Solaris9    -       nfs     ro,anon=0
/export/os/Sol9Core/Solaris_9/Tools/Boot      -      nfs      ro,anon=0
```

Solingo

DFS stands for Distributed File System. It harks back to the early days of the System V versions of Unix, which supported two different file sharing systems, NFS and the Remote File System (RFS), both referred to by the umbrella DFS title. NFS was already supported by BSD systems and a part of the Sun Unix solution. RFS fell by the wayside, leaving DFS as the term for referring to sharing file systems. If you are from a Windows background, DFS will be a familiar term for referring to file systems spread across a number of different physical machines, and in some ways NFS is not really all that different in similar situations.

Unsharing a Disk

To unshare a disk, use the *unshare* command, followed by the path to the directory you want to unshare. For example:

```
% unshare /export/home
```

Note that the directory will be unshared and unavailable to any client systems that have it mounted, but the systems won't be notified—in fact, client systems will only identify that there is a problem when they can't access a file or directory on the system they thought was available.

Mounting an NFS Disk

From your clients, all you need to do when mounting an NFS disk is to specify the host and directory that you want to mount, and the mount point. For example, to mount your */export/home* directory at the same location on a client you use:

```
% mount sol9penguin:/export/home /export/home
```

The standard *mount* command line options apply, and in addition there are a number of NFS-specific options listed in Table 18.2.

Table 18.2   NFS-Specific Options for *mount*

Option	Description
hard	Always attempts to remount if the server does not respond. Useful where the availability of the disk is vital, for example over remote links.
intr	Allows the keyboard interrupt (Control-C) to kill the process trying to mount the file system if the *hard* option is used.
nointr	Does not allow keyboard interrupts to kill the process while waiting for a *hard* mount.
public	Mounts a directory exported publicly.
retrans=n	Retransmits an NFS request up to *n* times.
retry=n	Retries the mount operation up to *n* times.
ro	Mounts the share read only.
rw	Mounts the share read/write.
soft	Tries to mount the disk, terminating with an error if the mount operation did not complete.
timeo=n	Sets the timeout for operations to *n* tenths of a second.

For example, you can attempt to mount a remote directory up to 100 times using:

```
% mount -F nfs -o soft,retry=100 twinsol:/export/home /home
```

To set a shared directory to be mounted each time a machine is switched on you need to add a suitable entry to the */etc/vfstab* file. The format of the file is:

```
devtomount devtofsck mountpoint type fsckpass atboot options
```

So to replicate the above *mount* command you use:

```
twinsol:/export/home - /home nfs - yes -o soft,retry=100
```

Note that once an NFS share has been added to */etc/vfstab*, you can mount all the shares of a particular type using the *-a* and *-F* command line options. For example, to mount all the NFS directories you can use:

```
% mount -a -F nfs
```

Sun Lotion

If you specify more than one host in the device to mount a field within */etc/vfstab*, then if one of the hosts goes down, the client will automatically switch between the other hosts that were specified. For example, if you use *twinsol,penguin: /export/home, penguin* will be used to mount */export/home* if *twinsol* cannot be contacted.

The system only works if behind the scenes *twinsol* and *penguin* are replicating the contents of */export/home* between themselves.

Unmounting an NFS Share

To unmount an NFS share, use the *umount* command:

```
% umount /export/home
```

To unmount all the NFS shares, use:

```
% umount -a -F nfs
```

Getting Information About Mounted NFS Disks

All the usual commands for interacting with a file system and its contents work as normal. You can use *ls* to list files and directories. Just as with any other file on the system, you can also refer to the file directly using its path. This is the benefit of having a single file system instead of separate volumes or disks.

To get a list of the mounted NFS disks, you can use the *mount* command as normal; the NFS mounted disks can be easily identified:

```
/ on /dev/dsk/c0d0s0 read/write/setuid/intr/largefiles/onerror=panic/
➥dev=1980000 on Tue Jan 15 15:38:37 2002
...
/export/contrib on twinsol:/export/contrib remote/read/write/setuid/dev=2f40002
➥on Tue Jan 15 15:38:52 2002
/export/share on twinsol:/export/share remote/read/write/setuid/dev=2f40001 on
➥Tue Jan 15 15:38:52 2002
/usr/local on twinsol:/usr/local remote/read/write/setuid/dev=2f40003 on Tue
➥Jan 15 15:38:52 2002
```

Also as expected, the *df* command shows you the disk statistics for the machine:

```
% df -k
Filesystem              kbytes     used   avail capacity  Mounted on
/dev/dsk/c0d0s0         246463    34433  187384     16%   /
/dev/dsk/c0d0s6        1785654   476566 1255519     28%   /usr
/proc                        0        0       0      0%   /proc
mnttab                       0        0       0      0%   /etc/mnttab
fd                           0        0       0      0%   /dev/fd
/dev/dsk/c0d0s3         246463    26794  195023     13%   /var
swap                    672872       16  672856      1%   /var/run
/dev/dsk/c0d0s5         458087       15  412264      1%   /opt
swap                    672856        0  672856      0%   /tmp
/dev/dsk/c0d0s7         192423      107  173074      1%   /export/home
/dev/dsk/c0d0s1         492422   175808  267372     40%   /usr/openwin
twinsol:/export/contrib
                       2863911  1545010 1261623     56%   /export/contrib
twinsol:/export/share
                       8813061  6071772 2653159     70%   /export/share
```

Determining What's Available

You can find out which directories are being shared on the current or a remote machine by using the *dfshares* command. Without any arguments, it reports the list of directories currently being shared by the local machine:

```
$ dfshares
RESOURCE                            SERVER ACCESS    TRANSPORT
   twinsol:/export/share            twinsol  -          -
   twinsol:/export/http             twinsol  -          -
   twinsol:/export/contrib          twinsol  -          -
   twinsol:/export/cvs              twinsol  -          -
   twinsol:/usr/local               twinsol  -          -
```

```
twinsol:/export/os/Solaris9              twinsol  -           -
twinsol:/export/os/Sol9Core/Solaris_9/Tools/Boot      twinsol  -           -
```

If you want more specific information about the shared directories on the local machine, the easiest way to do this is to examine the */etc/dfs/dfstab* file. This will contain information about the shares and options and any restrictions on the directories that have been shared.

If you supply one or more hostnames or IP addresses to the command, then it returns the list of shares on a remote machine. For example, you can get the list of shares from our Solaris 9 server using:

```
$ dfshares sol9penguin
RESOURCE                             SERVER ACCESS    TRANSPORT
sol9penguin:/export/home             sol9penguin  -           -
sol9penguin:/usr/openwin             sol9penguin  -           -
```

Sun Lotion

If you are using something other than Solaris, then the *dfshares* command may not be available. On these systems you can use the *showmount* command. Supplied with the name of a machine, the command will provide a list of all the servers currently using shares on the remote server.

If you use the -e command line option then it will display a list of the directories exported by the machine instead.

Another option is to use the *dfmounts* command. This command lists the directories shared by a machine, and which machines are currently using them:

```
$ dfmounts
RESOURCE      SERVER PATHNAME                 CLIENTS
  -           twinsol /export/contrib
198.112.10.141,nautilus.mchome.com,nautilus.mcslp.pri,nautwired.mcslp.pri,
penguin.mcslp
.pri,sol9insentient,sol9linux
  -           twinsol /export/cvs             penguin.mcslp.pri
  -           twinsol /export/home/MC         penguin.mchome.com
  -           twinsol /export/home/MCSLP      penguin.mchome.com
  -           twinsol /export/home/SLP        penguin.mchome.com
  -           twinsol /export/home/etc        198.112.10.141,nautilus.mchome.com
  -           twinsol /export/http            penguin.mcslp.pri
  -           twinsol /export/os/Sol9Core/Solaris_9/Tools/Boot sol9insentient
  -           twinsol /export/os/Solaris9     sol9insentientvpc,sol9linux
  -           twinsol /export/os/Solaris9/Solaris_9/Tools/Boot
insentient,sol9insentientvpc,sol9linux,soldhcp0,soldhcp1
```

192.168.2.13

```
    -          twinsol /export/share
nautilus.mcslp.pri,penguin.mcslp.pri,sol9insentient,sol9linux
    -          twinsol /usr/local              sol9linux
```

As with *dfshare*, you can supply the name of a machine to get the share list of a remote server without having to log in remotely.

WebNFS

The WebNFS system extends the accessibility of the NFS file sharing system to allow web browsers and Java applets to access NFS shared resources. Using WebNFS you can access a shared file system from a client using a URL of the form *nfs://server/path*.

Two options when sharing a directory directly relate to WebNFS sharing. The first is the *index* option; you use this to specify the name of a file in the shared directory which should be supplied back to the client when they access the shared directory.

The *public* option changes the way that a directory is made available to a client. If specified, it allows the user to use a shortened URL. For example, if you share */export/home* with the public option switched on, then you can access */export/home/mc* using the URL *nfs://server/mc*.

Improving Performance

NFS, as with any network file system, is relatively resource hungry. In order to keep the file system open over a network connection, information needs to be transferred over the network all the time. Obviously, the moment you start exchanging information, transferring files, and reading and writing information to the shared disk, the network traffic increases.

A Postcard From ...

An NFS client and server will regularly exchange information with each other, even if you are not actually using the shared resource at all. The information exchanged includes the "heartbeat" operation, used simply to verify that the server and client still exist and are still able to communicate with each other.

These exchanges continue even when you are transferring information between the two machines; they are used by both ends to prevent corruption and to ensure that users don't try to perform operations on a shared directory that does not exist.

On a busy network, the amount of information that will be transferred will be quite extensive, but depending on a combination of the files being transferred, the size, and the frequency, coupled with the abilities of your network and server, your machine may be more than capable of providing the information.

This does not mean that performance does not cause problems. Transferring data over a network is a time-consuming task whatever the data, and anything that you can do to reduce the network traffic is obviously an advantage.

Luckily, Solaris provides a solution in the form of a special type of file system, called CacheFS, which caches the files that you access on a remote server locally on the hard disk of the client. That way, each time you access a file it is looked for in the cache first. Using CacheFS prevents the system from regularly transferring files, speeding up the client access, and reducing the network load and the load on the server.

I won't go into too much detail on CacheFS, except to say that it is easy to use. All you do is specify CacheFS as the file system type, and supply the NFS information and a directory in which to hold the cached files. Thus to enable CacheFS on our *export/home* shared directory from a client we would change the command:

```
% mount -F nfs sol9penguin:/export/home /home
```

to:

```
% mount -F CacheFS -o backfstype=nfs,cachedir=/mnt/cache
   sol9penguin:/export/home /home
```

The example above places the cache into the local directory */mnt/cache*, although it could be located anywhere.

Sun Lotion

For the absolute maximum in NFS access speed, you might want to consider putting the cache directory on a file system mounted using the *swapfs* file system. The *swapfs* system uses the machine's own RAM and the OS swap file system as the storage facility. When combined with *CacheFS,* it means that the data is cached in RAM instead of on a relatively slow hard disk, providing the fastest possible access. By default, the */tmp* directory is mounted as a *swapfs* file system.

However, be warned that RAM is not an unlimited resource and it should be used primarily for running applications. If you specify cache sizes which use up too much memory, then you may be sacrificing application speed for NFS speed.

Using Automounter

NFS is often used to share resources from a small number of central servers with a large number of clients, particularly in development houses, universities, and research organizations. Using a system configured this way allows users to log in to any machine and access their files, even though the machine they are using is unlikely to be the same machine that holds their files.

For the system to work, though, you would have to configure every machine in the network to mount the NFS shares from a server each time they start up. Now think back to earlier in this chapter when we talked about the NFS "heartbeat." For a small (10 clients) network this is not a problem; for a medium network (up to say 100 clients) the amount of traffic generated, even when the machine is idle, is significant. Go above about 200 clients, and even on a fast network the traffic starts to become a problem.

The Auto File System (AutoFS) makes the process easier because it monitors the directories requested on a client and automatically mounts the directories from a remote share that it needs. For example, if we share */export/home* on the server, it will only be mounted by a client when the client wants to access a file or directory within the */export/home* share. Because the mounting process is automatic, it also means that anybody can gain access to the shared directories that they need without requiring the *root* privileges normally required to mount remote directories.

To help with the network overhead reduction, the shared paths are also automatically dropped when they have not been used for 10 minutes. They are of course remounted the moment the file or directory is accessed again.

AutoFS works through a daemon called *automountd* and an associated command called *automount*. The automount system uses a series of three "map" files which provide the connection between an accessed directory and the real server and shared directory.

There are three types of map file, the *auto_master* map, direct maps, and indirect maps. The *auto_master* map resides in */etc/auto_master*. It's used to associate directories with indirect maps and also references the direct and indirect maps that configure the rest of the system. The *auto_master* map consists of three fields:

♦ **Mount point:** The initial portion of the pathname to which an NFS resource will be mounted.

♦ **Map name:** The name of an indirect or direct map, or the name of an internal special map, indicated by a leading hyphen.

♦ **Mount options:** Zero or more comma-separated NFS-specific mount options.

For example, let's look at the map below:

```
+auto_master
/net           -hosts          -nosuid,nobrowse
/home          auto_home       -nobrowse
/-             auto_direct
/xfn           -xfn
```

The first line indicates that this is a master map. The second line maps the */net* directory to the special *-hosts* map. You use this when you want to access a machine by changing to the directory */net/hostname*, where *hostname* is the name of the machine you want to access. When you change to one of these directories, the automounter checks the built-in hostname map (from */etc/hosts*, NIS or DNS) and mounts the appropriate server. The last line performs the same operation but uses the Federated Name Service, rather than the hosts system, to look up the host name.

The third line sets up a connection to the indirect map for directories within */home*. When a client accesses */home/mc*, for example, the entries within the *auto_home* map will be used to determine which host and shared directory should be mounted. The fourth line uses the special /- notation to indicate that the entries in the direct map *auto_direct* should be used to determine which hosts and directories should be mounted.

Direct maps provide direct associations between a local mount point and the remote server/ shared directory. The format of the file is:

- ◆ **Key:** The full pathname of the mount point to be used when the file system is mounted.

- ◆ **Mount options:** Zero or more NFS-specific mount options.

- ◆ **NFS resource:** The server/share directory specification in the form *server:path* to be mounted.

For example, the following direct map makes a connection between the paths in the first column with the shared resources in the third column:

```
/usr/local     -ro    sol9penguin:/usr/local
/export/share         twinsol:/export/share
```

Indirect maps use a combination of the prefix specified in the *auto_master* file and the *key* given in the indirect map to mount the corresponding resource. The file format is the same as that used by direct maps, except that you do not use the full pathname for the key. For example, given the following indirect map (located in the */etc/auto_home* file):

```
mc     -rw    twinsol:/export/home/mc
slp           sol9penguin:/export/home/slp
```

when a user accesses */home/mc*, the automounter will automatically mount *twinsol:/export/ home/mc*.

Sun Screen

If you are intending to use NFS shares to share user files with a large number of clients, then you should consider using NIS/NIS+ to share the user information over the network (see Chapter 14, "Configuring NIS").

Otherwise, you will need to manually update the */etc/passwd* and other files on each client when you add a new user, and it will be impossible for a user to change their password on the network, they will only be able to change their password on the local machine.

Sharing with Samba (Windows)

Microsoft Windows uses a different system for sharing its files and directories with other machines, although it is possible to obtain an NFS client to access Unix NFS shares. Windows uses a generic networking protocol called Server Message Block, or SMB, to share resources between machines. Resources include not only standard files and directories, but also printers and potentially scanners and other input devices.

SMB is a communications protocol that sits on top of a transport protocol like TCP/IP or NetBIOS. Because Solaris uses TCP/IP, we can build a communications interface on top of TCP/IP to talk SMB with Windows clients.

The tool for doing this is called Samba, a free software package available from http://www.samba.org. Follow the instructions in Chapter 10, "Managing Software," for information on how to configure, build, and install packages like Samba.

Samba enables you to share files and directories with Windows clients and recent versions also allow you to use a Samba-enabled server to act as a domain master for Windows networks. You can therefore use a Solaris server to provide nearly all the facilities of a Windows NT or 2000 server to your clients.

Sharing with NetAtalk (Mac OS)

The NetAtalk package is a free application consisting of a combination of daemons and administration tools that allow you to share directories with Apple hosts that use the AppleTalk and AppleShare File Protocol (AFP). Shared directories appear as shared volumes to a Mac OS host and can be mounted with the Chooser or Network Browser.

As with NFS, once the directories have been shared and accessed from a client it's impossible to tell the difference between a directory shared from a Unix host and one shared from another Mac OS host or AppleShare server. You can see a sample of a shared directory, here used for archiving information, in Figure 15.1.

Mac files, which consist of two forks—the data fork used to store file information, and the resource fork, which holds resource information like icons and the layouts of windows and dialog boxes—can also be copied to the shared directory. However, while the data file portion is written to the disk as normal to allow you to edit documents and other data files under Unix, the resource fork is written into a file with the same name within a special *.AppleDouble* directory.

The two forks are automatically combined when accessed from a Mac, but remain separate when viewed on the Unix side. Since the resource forks do not make any sense to a Unix machine, this separation does not cause too many problems, but be aware that deleting the data fork for a Mac file within Unix does not truly remove the file—you must also delete the corresponding resource file, if there is one.

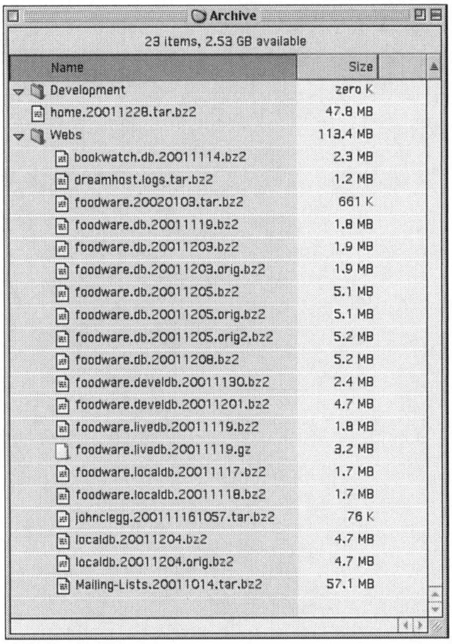

Figure 15.1

Viewing a shared directory from a Solaris host on a Mac.

You can download the NetAtalk package from Sourceforge at http://netatalk.sourceforge.net. Follow the instructions in Chapter 10 for information on how to configure, build, and install packages like NetAtalk. As well as sharing disks, the system will also share printers and act as an AppleTalk router.

A Postcard From ...

We don't actually need to use NetAtalk to share directories with Mac OS X clients. Mac OS X is the new operating system from Apple, and amongst its many features is a Unix core combined with a number of extensions. As well as supporting the traditional AppleShare volumes, as provided by NetAtalk, Mac OS X can also mount SMB and NFS shares directly without requiring additional software.

The Least You Need to Know

◆ Use *share* to share a directory and *unshare* to unshare a directory.

◆ Share directories permanently by adding share commands to the */etc/dfs/dfstab* file.

◆ Mount and unmount shared resources using *mount* and *umount*.

◆ You can improve performance by using CacheFS.

◆ You can ease the network load in complex situations by using the automount system.

Part 4

Using Solaris

If you are new to the Unix environment, then this section will help you understand the basics of the Unix and Solaris system from a user's point of view.
The Common Desktop Environment (CDE) is most people's first exposure to
the Solaris operating system. However, others will find the power of the command line far more alluring.

Using the command line, you can do everything from get file lists to basic text
processing, right up to administering and controlling the system. Because it's
command line based, you can do this all remotely, too. And because everybody
is concerned about privacy and file and data security, I'll also shine a light on
the security model used by Solaris.

## Chapter 16

Using CDE

In This Chapter

♦ Setting your display preferences

♦ Understanding the X Windows system

♦ Using CDE

WIMP—short for Windows, Icons, Menus, and Pointers—is an acronym you don't hear a lot of these days. Most people take the interface that they use to interact with their machine for granted these days. It's natural to use the mouse to point around the screen and move files and windows about.

Although Unix isn't exactly known for its graphical environment, it has for some time had a solution called the X Windows System. The system is a basic WIMP environment that was designed from the start to be easy to use and also easy to build and customize. This led to a number of different *skins* to the product, depending on which Unix vendor was supplying the Unix environment.

Over time, the different commercial companies agreed to standardize on a skin that would be easy to use and customize if necessary, while still providing the same consistent environment, and that system was the Common Desktop Environment (CDE). In this chapter I'll cover the basics of the CDE and how to use it.

Using kdmconfig

Before running X Windows for the first time, you should check the configuration and setup of your keyboard, display, and mouse using *kdmconfig*. You probably used this tool during installation to set up the system in preparation for the final configuration and installation stages.

The purpose of the tool is to tell the X Windows system about the configuration of your keyboard, so that it types the right characters; your mouse, so the buttons work properly; and the display, so you get the best resolution and color depth according to the card and monitor attached to your machine.

There's no point in my going through the steps involved here—just follow the onscreen prompts to set up the different systems. If your exact configuration doesn't exist, don't worry, use the nearest you can find. Most keyboards and mice should be supported okay—although you may have to class your mouse as a lower specification than it actually is.

Sun Screen

You must be root to use *kdmconfig*. The changes you make will apply to the entire machine—it's not possible to allow different users to use different screen resolutions.

The graphics and monitor display configuration is different—you will get the opportunity to actually test the configuration and change it if it doesn't work. Again, it's often a case of choosing the best compromise, rather than selecting the exact model if yours is not listed.

If you can't find your graphics card in the list provided, check the SunSolve patch site (sunsolve.sun.com) as a patch may exist for your card. In particular, Solaris 8 does not include drivers for the ATI Rage 128 chipset, but a patch for it does exist.

The X Windows System

The X Windows System is the core of the windowing environments under Unix. It provides a basic mechanism for allowing windows to be displayed on screen and for interaction with the mouse and keyboard. X Windows also has some other tricks up its sleeve, such as its ability to display the window for a given X application onto the display of another machine. To do this, use the *-display* argument to the command, as in:

```
$ xterm -display twinsol:0.0
```

Or change the value of your *display* environment variable. Historically this was used to allow network-based X terminals—essentially cut-down computers—to display applications executed on a central server. All the processing still takes place on the machine you run the application on, only the window displaying the applications interface is shown on the remote machine, with the keyboard and mouse passing the information back.

In a local network, this facility can also be used to allow you to execute an application such as the Solaris Management Console on one machine, while viewing it on your desktop.

Confusingly, machines that offer the ability to show the window remotely are called X Windows Servers (or simply X Servers), and the applications that you use with them are clients. You can get X Servers for many platforms, including Mac OS, Mac OS X, and Windows, so it's possible to use Unix applications right on your desktop.

X Windows in its base format is not pretty—although we can display windows and move them around, we don't have any nice window dressing, decent backgrounds, or a way to control and customize our environment to make it easier to use. Instead, X Windows allows a number of different window managers to control the environment and look and feel. There are a number of different systems to choose from, including …

- **Common Desktop Environment (CDE):** The standard environment for Solaris, CDE was an attempt to standardize the X Windows environment across the Unix community to make the machines easier to use and migrate between. CDE is the standard environment on other vendor Unix solutions, including IBM, SGI, and others.

- **OpenWindows:** The old environment favored by Sun, and still available in Solaris as an alternative to CDE. One of the biggest strengths was the use of the Display PostScript to render graphics on screen, making it attractive to publishers and design agencies, although it never really managed to usurp the already-strong position help by Mac OS.

- **Gnome:** A free software alternative made popular under Linux, since it comes with many of the Linux distributions as standard. Gnome offers an interface and suite of applications that make the typical Unix system look and feel like a typical desktop system. You can use Gnome as an alternative to the Windows desktop. Solaris 9 includes Gnome as a standard alternative to OpenWindows and CDE, and Solaris 8 comes with Gnome as a third-party installation on the Solaris Software Companion CD.

- **K Desktop Environment (KDE):** KDE is another alternative to CDE and Gnome, designed to allow a Unix machine to look and feel more like a Windows desktop, hiding the complexities of Unix within a nicer shell. KDE consists not only of the basic window manager toolkit, but also a suite of other applications including calendar, word processor, spreadsheet, and web browser.

Other systems are available, although CDE, Gnome, and KDE are the most complete alternatives. Other solutions include AfterStep, which looks like the NeXTStep OS, and WindowMaker, a relatively basic, but low-bandwidth alternative.

Solaris 8 and 9 both come with Gnome as alternatives to CDE, but they need to be installed separately before you can use them. The Solaris Companion Software CD also contains many other X Windows alternatives. If you want KDE, visit www.kde.org to download the packages—standard Solaris package formats are available.

The dtlogin System

Unless it's been disabled (see "Disabling dtlogin" later in this chapter), the first thing you will probably see when sitting in front of a Solaris machine is the login panel, an example of which you see in Figure 16.1.

Figure 16.1

The dtlogin *window, your entry point into the world of CDE and Solaris.*

Using dtlogin

At the simplest level, all you need to do is enter your login and password—if you are authorized correctly and this is the first time you have logged in, you will be asked to choose which window system you want to use. Choose Common Desktop Environment, and then it will continue to log you in and start up the CDE.

If you don't want to start up with the CDE but with a standard prompt, use the Options popup to request a command line login. You can also use this popup to select between the different available session types—CDE and OpenWindows—in case you want to try an alternative session. The system will remember which system you used last time and automatically use that session type for your next login.

One other useful feature, especially if you have multiple machines all supporting the desktop login system, is to select a remote host to log in to. If you select this and enter an alternative system name you can log in remotely to the other machine, using the current console as just the X Server.

Disabling dtlogin

If you want to disable the desktop login system, you need to delete */etc/rc3.d/S99dtlogin* or rename it to */etc/rc3.d/K99dtlogin*. The result should just be a standard text based login prompt.

Once it's been disabled, if you want to start X Windows after you have logged in (only on the console!) use:

```
$ startx
```

The Common Desktop Environment

CDE is really just a standard method and look and feel for interacting first with the X Windows System, and second with the underlying Solaris (or other Unix) operating system. CDE is a standard, so if you learn how to use CDE under Solaris you should be able to move to IBM, SGI, and other platforms and use the X Windows System in the same way.

The CDE standard is composed of two parts: the look and feel, and the CDE panel. The look and feel is just the window format, borders, and the locations and effects of the different window controls, such as minimize and maximize, and how to resize the window. The CDE panel is like the dashboard of your car—it provides the main way of starting applications, configuring the system, and working with the X Windows System to perform different tasks.

I discuss both components in this section, and how to find and start other X Windows System–compatible applications.

Getting Started with CDE

First, let's look at a basic window. You can see a simple Terminal window in Figure 16.2.

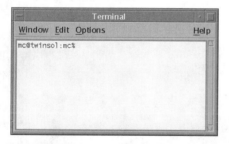

Figure 16.2

A simple Terminal window within CDE.

The usual operations are available for controlling your window. Clicking and dragging the menu bar will allow you to move the window around the screen, and you can click the bottom right-hand corner to *grow* the window. You can also grow the window by its sides—just click on any of the four sides of a window and you can resize the width and height accordingly.

The button on the top left-hand side is your window control button. Click it once, and you'll get a menu (shown in Figure 16.3) that enables you to explicitly move and resize the window. Double-click the button, and you'll close the window (and the associated application, if it was the last window for that application). The rightmost button at the top of the window *maximizes* the window to fill up the entire screen. When maximized, clicking this button again reduces it back to a normal window.

Figure 16.3

The window control menu.

The button to the left of that (which looks like a tiny dot) will *iconize* the window. This reduces the window to a tiny icon that then rests on your desktop—by default, these are placed on the left-hand side of your desktop. See Figure 16.4 for an example of both open windows and desktop icons. To restore the window, just double-click on its icon.

Figure 16.4

A CDE desktop showing iconized windows and normal windows.

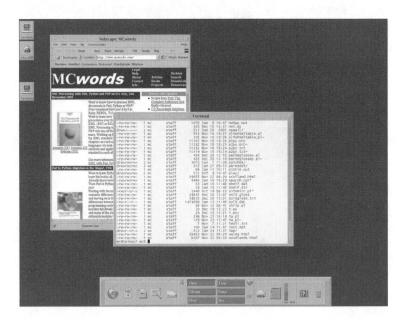

Hopefully, so far none of what I've described should be a particular shock; the system pretty much works like all other windowing systems. There are a couple of extra niceties worth mentioning. First, windows are not displayed as a collection when you switch to an application. In Mac OS and Windows when you switch to an application, all of the windows for that application are brought forward. Within CDE, windows are treated individually—that is, you switch between windows, not applications. This can cause a bit of confusion, as it's possible to switch to an application but not see all of the windows associated with it.

Windows are also all nonmodal. When an error or warning message is produced, it's displayed in a standard window. You can move that window around, even iconize the window, without it interrupting your current application. There are good and bad sides to this. The good side is that it means we can ignore a message without it stopping us from working in another application. The downside is that it's sometimes easy to lose a message window, and although it doesn't stop us from using other applications, it may well stop us from using the application that raised that warning.

Keyboard Shortcuts

The keyboard is configured with a number of standard shortcuts to control windows and to switch between the different windows. Table 16.1 provides a brief rundown of these shortcuts.

Table 16.1   Keyboard Shortcuts

Shortcut	Description
Alt-Tab	Moves to the next window or icon.
Shift-Alt-Tab	Moves to the previous window or icon.
Alt-Up Arrow	Moves the window on the bottom of the window stack to the top.
Alt-Down Arrow	Moves the window on the top of the stack to the bottom.
Tab	Within an entry window, moves the cursor to the next entry box.
Shift Tab	Within an entry window, moves the cursor to the previous entry box.
Alt-F7	Moves the current window.
Alt-F8	Resizes the current window.
Alt-F9	Minimizes the current window.
Alt-F10	Maximizes the current window.
Alt-F4	Closes the current window.

The Workspace Menu

Click with the right mouse button on any part of the desktop (that is not a window) and you should be presented with the workspace menu. The menu is really a quick way of accessing applications to save you from selecting them from the CDE panel individually. You can see a sample of the menu in Figure 16.5.

Figure 16.5

The workspace menu, a quick way of starting different applications.

The CDE Panel

At the bottom of the screen is the CDE panel, which is your main way of interacting with the machine, starting up applications, file managers, and other elements. It's split into three main sections, an application section on the left-hand side, a control and information panel on the right, and a workspace panel in the middle. You can see a close-up of the panel in Figure 16.6.

Figure 16.6

The CDE panel, your main interface to running applications and using CDE.

The workspace panel controls your main interaction with the overall CDE environment, and contains the following elements:

> **Sun Lotion**
>
> The CDE panel is just a window, like any other window within CDE. You can move it, and even minimize it, by using the same controls and methods as you would a normal window.

♦ The big buttons in the middle, which allow you to change workspaces. You can have as many workspaces as you like, and each workspace can have its own name, selection of windows, and applications within it—it's a bit like having many different desktops, but all running on the same machine. You can use this to divide up your work into usable sections—I keep separate workspaces for Internet access, office applications, file management, web development, and general use. You can switch to any panel just by clicking on its name button within the CDE panel.

◆ The padlock on the left-hand side, which
allows you to "lock" your terminal so that
you can safely leave it logged in, but not
open for anybody to use. You'll need to
enter your normal password to get access
again.

◆ The World button, which allows you to
enter a URL to visit, either on your
intranet or the Internet.

◆ The Exit button, which enables you to
quit the system.

Sun Lotion _____

An intranet is just an internal resource made avail-
able within your company
that uses Internet protocols,
so you can go and view
information and fill in forms using
your browser.

The application portion of the panel on the right-hand side provides your main way of
running applications. Above each icon is a popup menu. Clicking on the triangle will open
a menu of other options related to the icon. The menus will go away if you select an item,
but you'll need to click on the arrow again if you've clicked the wrong menu. You can see
the Files popup menu open in Figure 16.7.

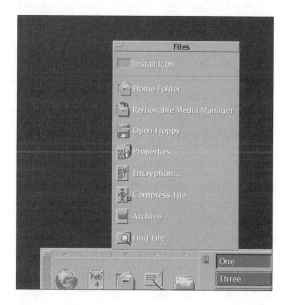

Figure 16.7

*The popup application menus
in the CDE panel.*

From left to right, the main icons, their effects when clicked, and the menus above them are:

◆ A clock, showing the current time. When clicked, it opens the Netscape Communicator Internet browser. The menu contains links for opening the browser, searching
the Internet, and viewing your personal bookmarks.

- The date pad, showing the current date. When clicked, it opens the diary/calendar application. The menu also provides you with access to the address book system, which, when used with the calendar application, allows you to book appointments.

- The file drawer icon, which opens a file manager. The menu provides quick links for instantly compressing or encrypting a file, and accessing the disk in the floppy drive.

- The notepad icon, which opens the text editor. The menu allows you to create a quick text note and a voice note (if you have a supported microphone attached to your machine). It also opens the Applications Manager.

- The mail tray icon, which shows whether you currently have new mail waiting to be read. When clicked, it opens the email application.

The right-hand panel on the main CDE panel is where all the control, monitoring, and setup icons are located. From left to right these are:

- The printer icon, which opens the print job manager. The menu above the icon allows you to open the printer.

- The options panel, which opens the control panel for setting options and configuring the look and feel of the CDE system. The menu above the icon allows you to open the configuration applications, and also to edit the workspace menu and assign hotkeys to different operations.

- The CPU/Disk bar graphs. These give you a rough idea of how busy the CPU and the disk systems are. When you click on the icon, it opens a separate performance monitor window. The menu above the icon opens different information applications and windows, including the performance monitor, a System info panel which shows the host ID and specific RAM information. The menu also allows you to open a console terminal window which will show any urgent messages broadcast to the machine's console.

- The bookshelf, which opens the help system for CDE if you click on the icon. The menu above allows you to open and search the help, and also to access the AnswerBook system if it has been installed on your machine. There are also handy links to some online resources such as SunSolve (Sun's support and patch site) and the Solaris support pages.

- The trashcan. You can drag items from within the file manager into the trash. As with trash cans on other systems you can view the contents and undelete them, as well as emptying and permanently deleting their contents.

Finding Other Applications

The Workspace menu should contain the majority of applications that you will want to run, and they are neatly organized into different groups. You can also find more applications within the Application Manager, available in the popup menu above the Text Editor icon in the CDE panel.

There's a combination of the standard desktop applications you've already seen and a series of systems administration applications, including the *admintool* and Solaris Management Console. CDE is also capable of running all the applications provided with the old OpenWindows system, including *pageview*, which allows you to view PostScript documents directly onscreen.

Most of the other applications that you may want to use will probably be third-party solutions, either supplied by Sun themselves in the Bonus Software package that came with your installation disks, or those on the Internet. A popular installation is Sun's own StarOffice application suite, which is the equivalent of Microsoft's office productivity suite. StarOffice comes with Solaris and it provides the usual word processing, spreadsheet, database, and presentation software. Not only is it equivalent to the Microsoft Office product; it's also capable of reading and writing Microsoft Office documents.

You can see an example of the word processor in StarOffice actually editing the above paragraphs in this chapter in Figure 16.8.

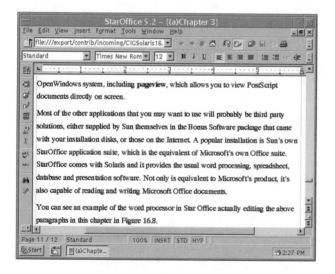

Figure 16.8

Editing a Microsoft Office document in StarOffice.

There is no reason why you cannot use StarOffice in place of Microsoft Office—the two office suites are functionally comparable and StarOffice has conversion filters that enable you to coexist in a heterogeneous environment with Microsoft Office users. With the exception of converting your current document universe to the StarOffice format, you shouldn't have too many difficulties in migrating to the StarOffice system, as most of the basic interaction and terminology is more or less identical to Microsoft Office. I've used it many times to write material for books when what I'm documenting is on a Unix system—in fact, some of the chapters in this book were produced in StarOffice!

The Least You Need to Know

- ◆ You must configure your keyboard, display, and mouse with the *kdmconfig* command.
- ◆ The main windowing system is called X Windows.
- ◆ The Common Desktop Environment (CDE) is a window manager for the X Window System.
- ◆ Other managers include KDE, Gnome, and OpenWindows.
- ◆ The main interface for starting applications and controlling CDE is the CDE Panel.

Using a Shell

In This Chapter

- ◆ Introducing different command shell types
- ◆ Using basic shell commands
- ◆ Looking at environments, redirection, and pipes

Solaris is an incredibly powerful operating system that, out of the box, includes a number of tools and utilities that could provide you with all the facilities you would ever need in a computer. Most of these facilities are available only if you are willing to use a shell. Shells, as you already know, are small applications that enable you to run other commands and applications.

This is actually a bit of a simplification. A Unix shell is capable of much more than simply executing other commands. You can also set up variables and other information; write basic programs, including the ability to iterate over a list or make decisions about different values; and it allows you to control and manipulate information.

In this chapter I'll discuss the core shell types, their main features, and some of the constructs and tricks available that you can use to make using and administering a Unix system through a shell much easier.

Shell Types

Everybody likes a bit of choice—not everybody likes the same make of car, and even if they did, they probably wouldn't all want the same color. The same is true of Unix shells; there are lots of different options available to you and which one you use depends on what you expect to do with the shell and how you intend to use your computer.

Sun Lotion

The term "shell" is actually just a reference to an item that operates as an outer shell to the operating system. A shell is therefore the primary interface between the user and computer.

Under DOS the shell was called COMMAND and you still have access to a DOS shell or Command Prompt within all versions of Windows. In essence, though, Windows is itself a kind of shell—it provides the user with the primary means of accessing and using the facilities of a computer.

In the same way, the Finder within Mac OS and OS X is a shell to the Mac OS/OS X operating systems. Under Unix you have both the command line shells that you'll be using in this chapter and the graphical shell called X Windows.

In reality, most of the facilities that people associate with a shell—listing files, manipulating the content, and so on—are actually handled by a separate series of commands and it's actually this set of external commands that generally provides the shell with most of its power and flexibility. This doesn't mean, though, that the shell is merely a dumb tool—there are some quite powerful elements to many shells to make using your machine much easier

Bourne Shell (sh)

The Bourne shell is the first shell you will ever use on Solaris, as it's the default shell for all users, including the superuser. Originally developed by Steven Bourne at AT&T Bell Laboratories, it was the first true shell provided with the Unix operating system. As well as being the default shell, the Bourne shell is also one of the easiest shells to understand and use, and many people will never find themselves limited by its abilities. Those who want to edit their commands once entered, or write programs using a shell may want to try the C, Korn, or Bourne Again shells.

Korn Shell (ksh)

The Korn shell is a beefed-up version of the Bourne shell and was written by David G. Korn at AT&T. It was based on the original Bourne shell code and in fact shares much of the same syntax and usage, but it also adds some of the features of the C shell, such as the ability to re-execute a previous command and editing facilities so that you can recall and edit a command if you typed it in wrong.

C Shell (csh)

The C shell was developed by Bill Joy at the University of California, Berkeley as part of the development of the BSD platform. Unlike the Bourne and Korn shells, the C shell uses a C-like syntax, particularly useful for programming (providing you know C!). It also includes the ability to record a list of commands that have been typed in and the ability to recall and edit commands.

Bourne-Again Shell (bash)

The Bourne-Again shell was developed by the people at GNU as a free software replacement for the Bourne, Korn, and C shells available on commercial Unix platforms. It provides some of the best elements of all three shells, as well as some new and extensive features of its own. *bash* is actually the shell I prefer to use, and I've been using it now for more than ten years.

The most useful feature to me is the ability to auto-complete a directory or filename—all I have to do is press Tab and *bash* will automatically either complete what I've partially typed, or complete as much as it can and then provide me with a list of files that will match. *bash* also includes a facility called job control, borrowed from the C shell. Using this I can be running a command interactively, and then automatically place it into the background or pause and restart jobs at will.

Sun Lotion

All shells support the ability to start a job running in the background, rather than running in the foreground. Obviously this isn't useful for an ftp session or when editing a file, as these are both interactive elements. However, for operations that you don't want to wait for, such as deleting an entire directory, or copying large files from one place to another, it can be a handy way to start multiple jobs without creating multiple windows.

To start a command in the background, add an ampersand (&) character to the end of the command line. Depending on which shell you are using, you will either get a command prompt back immediately, or you'll be given a job reference number and presented back with another command prompt.

Solaris is a multitasking, multiuser operating system, so you may as well use those features!!

bash is now installed with Solaris 9 more or less as standard, and is available separately by installing the *SUNWbash* package.

Other Shells

There are a few other shells available. Solaris 9 comes with packages for the *zsh* and *tcsh* shells (installed by default if you select Everything during the installation process). The

Sun Screen

It's vital that you don't confuse the restricted Bourne shell, *rsh*, with the remote shell, *rsh*. The former is available in /usr/lib/rsh, whilst the latter is available in /usr/bin/rsh.

zsh shell was written by Paul Falstad and closely follows the *sh* and *ksh* shells, adding built-in spelling correction (it automatically suggests an alternative if you type a name that doesn't exist) and the ability to automatically complete like *bash*, only with a programmable element so you can automatically complete straight to a C source file instead of an object file. The *tcsh* shell is the free software equivalent of the C shell providing, all the facilities from all the other shells that I've already mentioned.

Shell Comparison

To help you make a choice, Table 17.1 contains a quick list of the main features and abilities of the four main shells now installed as standard in Solaris 9.

Table 17.1 Comparing Core Functionality in the Standard Solaris Shells

Feature	sh	csh	ksh	bash	Description
Aliasing	No	Yes	Yes	Yes	This feature enables you to create an alias to another command, including adding arguments and options.
Bourne-shell compatible syntax	Yes	No	Yes	Yes	The Bourne shell syntax is easier to use for nonprogrammers.
C-shell compatible syntax	No	Yes	No	Yes	The C shell syntax is easier to use for programmers, as it's based on the C language.
Default prompt	$	%	$	$	This is a quick indication of what shell you are using. All shells allow you to change the prompt if you wish.

Feature	sh	csh	ksh	bash	Description
History capability	No	Yes	Yes	Yes	This feature enables you to access (and execute) a previous command. Unlike DOS, you can go back hundreds or thousands of commands.
History Editing	No	Yes	Yes	Yes	This feature lets you modify previous commands and resubmit them.
Initialization file during login	.profile	.login	.profile	.bash_ profile	Stores the list of commands that should be executed when you log in. The files generally set the prompt, search path for commands, and other preferences.
Initialization file during shell startup	No	.cshrc	Yes	.bashrc	If you start up a shell, either manually or when starting a command tool or xterm in X Windows, a file can also be executed to set up preferences.
Inline command editing	No	No	Yes	Yes	Both *ksh* and *bash* allow you to use *vi* or emacs style editing for lines that you are entering and lines from the history.
Logout file	No	.logout	No	Yes	When you exit a shell, you may want to run a series of commands, such as emptying a directory or logging your exit.
Overwrite protection	No	Yes	Yes	Yes	You can set the *noclobber* variable—when set, the shell will refuse to overwrite files that already exist without confirmation.
Restricted version	rsh	No	rksh	No	You can set someone up with a restricted shell if you want them to be limited to their home directory and unable to redirect input or output.
Source	AT&T	Bell	AT&T	GNU	Interestingly, the C shell came from the same people who brought us the BSD version of Unix, while Bourne and Korn were from the SVR4 side.

Basic Shell Usage

The most important thing is not to panic about using a shell—in essence all you are doing is telling the computer to perform a particular command. Although the shell is powerful, and in many cases contains facilities and features that even us professionals use, it's also true to say that the shell is one of the easiest-to-use elements of Unix, if you use it in its basic format.

In this section, I'll cover the basics and some advanced techniques available to you when using a shell.

Starting a Shell

There are a number of ways in which you can start a shell, the most obvious of which is simply to log in. If you are logging in to a machine through the console (without the GUI login) or over a network, then you will probably end up in a shell. If you do get the GUI login, try going straight to a shell by selecting Command Line Login from the Options popup at the login prompt.

If you are already in CDE then you need to start up a terminal window:

1. Right-click on the workspace.
2. Select the Programs menu.
3. Select Terminal.

The result should be a window, like the one shown here in Figure 17.1. The shell is already running within the main window—you can see the shell prompt in our example.

Figure 17.1

Using Command Tool to execute a shell.

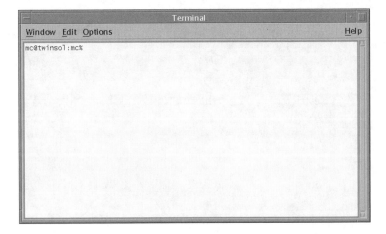

Basic Interaction

However you manage to start a shell, the result is the same. You should be shown a command prompt. The actual prompt will depend on which shell you are using. For a Bourne or Korn shell you will simply get a dollar sign, while a C shell will generally display a percent sign, usually prefixed by the hostname. In each case, the prompt tells you that the shell is waiting for you to enter a command.

> **Sun Lotion**
>
> All shells allow you to change the prompt displayed by modifying the contents of the *PS1* environment variable. The Bourne and Korn shells will also show a different prompt when you are root than when you are a standard user.
>
> The *bash* shell can be configured to display your user name and host, as well as your current directory as part of the prompt, and the Korn, C, and other shells support a similar range of options to make your prompt more useful.

If you type *ls* and then press Return, you will get a list of the files in the current directory, which might look something like this:

```
$ ls
archive.tar    news
$
```

As soon as the command has finished, you'll get another prompt, where you can enter another command. Simple, isn't it?

Changing Shells

A shell is just a command, and you can start new shells just by executing the appropriate shell command from an existing prompt. For example, below I've changed from the default Bourne shell to a Korn shell, Bourne Again shell, and C shell:

```
$ ksh
$ bash
mctest@sol9penguin:mc% csh
sol9penguin%
```

To terminate a shell either press Control+D or, if this has been disabled (or does not work), type *exit*. Be careful though, the same steps will also log you out if you use them within your login shell!

The Command Line

The command line is the information that you enter at a shell prompt to perform a particular action, whether that's setting a variable, running another command, or simply quitting from the shell.

In general, a command line is made up of one or more elements, with the exact composition depending on what you are doing. Since the majority of the operations you perform within a shell relate to executing a command, I'll use that as the basis for my examination of the command line.

In essence, all command lines that execute a program are made up of two components. The first is the name of the command you want to execute and the second is the command line arguments. The command is straightforward enough—it's just the name of the command, such as *ls*, that you want to execute. For example, the file list command is *ls*.

The command line arguments are more complex. These are a series of additional words and characters which are supplied to the command you are executing and are used to supply the command with information or set options. Command line arguments are split into two basic types, command line options, typically prefixed with a single or double hyphen, and plain words. A command line option sets a configurable option for the command. For example, the *-a* command line option to *ls* tells *ls* to list all files, including hidden files:

```
$ ls -a
./                  .bash_path~         .emacs
../                 .bash_profile       .emacs.d/
.TTauthority        .bash_vars          .netrc
.Xauthority         .bash_vars~         .profile
.bash_aliases       .bashrc             .sh_history
.bash_aliases~      .bashrc~            .solregis/
.bash_history       .dt/                archive.tar
.bash_path          .dtprofile*         news
```

Solingo

You cannot truly hide files within Solaris, but what you can do is prefix a given file with a period. By default, *ls* does not display files beginning with a period. Therefore, the startup files we've talked about in this chapter would normally be hidden from view. These hidden files, also called dotfiles, are used to store preferences and other information, and because they are essentially hidden from a typical view it's easy for a user to ignore these files until they actually need to use one.

Multiple command line options can be specified individually, as in:

```
$ ls -a -l
```

Or you can combine them:

```
$ ls -al
```

Any other arguments—that is, those that are not prefixed by a hyphen, are supplied to the command as-is. The exception to this rule is if the arguments include some form of file wildcard, in which case the supplied strings are expanded by the shell into a list of matching files.

By default, commands are split on spaces, which can cause problems if you want to supply a string that includes a space. You get around this by enclosing the string in double or single quotes—this forces the shell to supply the string to the command as a single argument, rather than as a list of individual words:

```
$ echo "Hello, this is a test"
```

File Expansion

Unlike some other shells that you may have been exposed to (most notably the DOS prompt under Windows), all the Unix shells perform their own file expansion before supplying the final list of command line arguments to a command.

The effects of this expansion are probably best demonstrated by using the *echo* command, which just prints a supplied string back to the screen. If you supply the asterisk to the command the shell automatically expands the asterisk to include the list of files in the current directory:

```
$ echo *
1.npa 2.npa 26-xmlrpc.t 3.npa AdobeFnt.lst Cookie.py Cookie.py.mac Cookie.pyc
HtmlKit MyMath.pm appa.py cixt.pl cookie.out cookie.py dutdump.text.bz2 first
kdesrc kdmout last mkdhcp netdump ns_imap nsmail p0187-01.pl ssltest.pl t.l
t.out t.pl t.py table.pl table.py tmp uriescape xml.cpio xmlrpc.daemon
xmlrpcc.pl xmlrpccgi.pl xmlrpcd.pl
```

All shells support two basic wildcards for selecting files:

◆ The asterisk (*) matches any number or any character. For example, * will expand to all the files, and *.txt will expand to all the files ending in .txt.

◆ The question mark (?) matches a single character of any kind. For example, *?* will only expand to include files with one character and ??? will only expand to files with three characters.

Beyond these basic facilities are a number of more extensive facilities. Most shells include the ability to support a range of characters. You specify a list of valid characters that you want to match against with square brackets and the system includes the ability to include all characters within a range. For example, to list all the files starting with a lowercase character:

```
$ ls [a-z]*
```

You can also be more specific, only selecting files with the characters ending in a, c, or f:

```
$ ls *[acf]
```

The *bash*, *zsh*, and *tcsh* shells include the ability to specify a list of possible values separated by commas. For example, you can list all the Perl or Python files in the current directory using:

```
$ ls *.{pl,py}
```

Environment Variables

All shells use environment variables. These are a set of user-configurable values that are used to store information, and this information in turn is used both by the shell and by other applications that the shell executes. Some of the environment variables are important to the shell and other applications. For example, the PATH variable contains a list of the directories searched when you type in a command at the command line.

You can get a list of the variables within your current session using the *set* command:

```
HOME=/export/home/mc
HZ=
IFS=

LOGNAME=mctest
MAILCHECK=600
OPTIND=1
PATH=/usr/bin:/usr/ucb:/etc:.
PS1=$
PS2=>
SHELL=/usr/bin/sh
TERM=vt220
TZ=GB
```

The above list is from a standard Bourne shell for a brand-new user. Most of the information here has been set automatically by the global startup file for the Bourne shell. This is located at */etc/profile*. To set your own values, you should create a *.profile*, *.cshrc*, *.login*, or other startup file (see Table 17.1) and then set the variable values in there.

Bourne-like Shells

To set an environment variable within a Bourne-like shell (*sh*, *ksh*, *bash*), you use the form:

```
VARIABLE=value
```

To ensure that the variable is exported to any commands executed by the shell, you should then use:

```
export VARIABLE
```

Within *bash* you can combine both statements:

```
export VARIABLE=value
```

Note that if you want to append a value to an existing variable all you have to do is include the variable in the current definition:

```
PATH=$PATH:/usr/local/bin
```

Note here that the PATH environment variable is a special case in that you have to supply a list of directories, and you separate that list using colons.

Sun Screen

All shells use different formats for setting a variable and accessing its contents. When setting the value, you use a simple name such as VARIABLE, but when accessing the variable's contents you must prefix the variable with a dollar sign, that is $VARIABLE. Using one, or the other, in a command can have odd consequences.

C-like Shells

C shells use a C-like syntax for setting variables. To set a single value to a variable, you use *set*:

```
set prompt="mc>"
```

For variables which act like lists such as *path*, you don't separate the individual directories by a colon, but instead supply a list of values in parentheses, separated by a space:

```
set path=(/usr/local /usr/hosts $path)
```

Sun Lotion

The Bourne shell and its younger brothers such as *ksh* and *bash* use uppercase variable names in the environment, although they will support variables with any case—the uppercase is just a convention. In contrast, the C shell uses lowercase variable names and there are some differences between the names used for some variables. Most of the important ones, such as PATH (or path) remain the same.

Redirection

Within Solaris all the commands that you execute communicate with the world at large through a series of three different communication channels:

- **Standard input** (stdin) is the standard input device, generally accepted to be the keyboard.
- **Standard output** (stdout) is the standard output device, generally accepted to be the monitor or terminal display.
- **Standard error** (stderr) is a secondary output device that also typically gets displayed on the monitor or terminal display. This channel is only used to report errors.

Solingo

The true name for the channels described here is a file descriptor. The operating system uses a file descriptor to allow an application to communicate with a file of some sort on the system. As you already know, Solaris uses files to refer to all devices, and this includes the devices attached to the notional standard input, output, and error file descriptors. Within an application, each file descriptor has its own unique number, the first three having numbers zero (standard input), one (standard output), and two (standard error).

Therefore, when you type in a command to the shell you are sending the command to the standard input, and when a command reports information back it sends it to standard output. If any sort of error occurs, then it reports that information to standard error.

You can redirect the input, output, and error channels to or from files for reasons that will hopefully become obvious as you view some examples.

Redirecting Output

There are occasions when you want to redirect the information normally output to the screen into a file. A typical example here would be a file listing. Using *ls* in a large directory such as */usr/bin* creates a huge listing. To save the output that was produced, you can redirect the output to a file which can then be viewed later. To redirect the output, you use the greater-than symbol (>) followed by the file name. For example, to redirect the output from *ls* to the file *filelist.txt*, you might use:

```
$ ls >filelist.txt
```

Another example is when you are running a command in the background where you want to record the output produced. For example, using *find* to look for files with a particular name you might redirect the output into a file that you can view later, once the process has completed:

```
$ find / -name "*.html" >allhtmlfiles.lst &
```

Redirecting Errors

The problem with the previous example is that if any errors are produced by *find* they will be reported immediately, quite possibly interrupting your current session and making things somewhat confusing. You can redirect just the errors to a different file by using *2>*—the leading *2* signifies that you are redirecting file descriptor number two, which as you know is the file descriptor for the standard error channel.

 **Sun Lotion**

Occasionally you are not interested in the errors. Rather than redirecting the output to a dummy file which you will later have to delete, you can instead redirect the output to the special */dev/null* device—Solaris will automatically throw away any information sent to this device.

You can therefore rewrite the above as:

```
$ find / -name "*.html" >allhtmlfiles.lst 2>allhtmlfiles.err &
```

Now when the process completes you can check *allhtmlfiles.lst* for the actual file list and *allhtmlfiles.err* to see if there were any problems.

Redirecting Input

Just occasionally you need to redirect information to the standard input of a command. Many commands will automatically take their input from the standard input if you have not specified the name of a file on which to work. Other commands only ever read their input from the standard input and the only way in which you can process the information from a file with these commands is by using redirection.

A good example is the *tr* command, which translates characters. For example, to change every letter 'a' in a file to the letter 'b' you must use:

```
$ tr 'a' 'b' <myfile.txt >newfile.txt
```

The < operator tells the shell to redirect the standard input for the command from the supplied file. In this case, you also have to redirect the standard output, rather than displaying the changes to the screen.

Pipes

Redirecting the input and output from different files is a useful way of processing information through one or more commands, but it suffers from an increased use of files and, to be honest, a severe amount of clumsiness. For example, going back to our earlier idea of outputting a list of files to another file so you could view the list, you'd actually be doing:

```
$ ls >filelist
$ more filelist
```

In essence, you've redirected the standard output of *ls* and then opened that within another command to be able to view it. Wouldn't it be more useful if you could just connect the standard output of one command with the standard input of another?

Enter pipes. A pipe provides just such a conduit. You can therefore shorten the previous command to:

```
$ ls |more
```

You've avoided creating a temporary file, and you won't have to later delete the file when you've finished with it. The pipe symbol (|), otherwise known as the vertical bar, creates the pipe—anything after the pipe symbol is treated as a brand-new command line. In this example you've just called another command, *more*.

You can use as many pipes as you like between commands in order. Actually there is a theoretical limit of between 32 and 64 pipes on most machines, limited by the number of simultaneous processes you can generally execute comfortably, and the maximum length of a command line.

For example, here's a command line that gets a list of processes, extracts the processes with a particular name, extracts the process IDs and then calls *kill* on each one to the kill each process:

```
$ ps -ef|grep httpd|awk '{ print $2 }'|xargs kill -9
```

Solingo

The *xargs* command is one of the most useful, but frequently ignored, commands available under Unix. It converts the data supplied to it on the standard input into a list of arguments to supply to a command. In the example I've given in the text, everything up to *xargs* produces a list of process IDs on the standard output. The *xargs* command takes that and supplies it as arguments to *kill*. Neat, huh?

Loops and Conditions

There are occasions when you need to make decisions about what you are doing or where you need to iterate over a list of values. The latter can be handled by a loop—I'll actually concentrate on the most useful loop available in all shells, *for*. For the former solution you need to use *if* and a number of tests.

Loops

Many shells support a number of different loop types, but I'm only going to concentrate on one, *for*. The *for* loop will iterate over a list of values supplied on the command line and then allow you to run one or more commands for each item in the loop. For example, you can print out a message on a line-by-line basis using:

```
for word in Hello, this is a test
do
    echo $word
done
```

The *word* is the name of the variable which will be used to hold the value of each item supplied after the *in*. You can supply a list of values here—they will automatically be split when a space or newline is seen. For example, you can iterate over the days of the week:

```
for word in Monday Tuesday Wednesday Thursday Friday Saturday Sunday
do
    echo "Day is $word"
done
```

Everything between *do* and *done* is the command executed for each item in the list. Here's a more extensive example that uses *tar* and *compress* to create compressed archives of each directory:

```
for file in *
do
    tar cf $file.tar ./$file
    compress $file.tar
    echo "Compressed directory $file
done
```

Conditions

You can use conditions to determine whether a particular process should take place. For example, you can test whether a file exists and then execute a command. Generally, conditions are only of real use within a script of some kind—after all, most of the tests you can do are used to automate a process, and if you are using a shell interactively you can probably find out the information quicker and easier for yourself.

To perform a test, you use the *if* command (built into the shell) and then specify the type of test and values to compare. For example, you can test for the existence of a file using the *-f* test:

```
if [ -f /usr/bin/bash ]
then
    bash
fi
```

The square brackets are used to enclose the actual test. Everything between the *then* and *if* keywords are the commands to be executed if the test resolves to true.

The full list of tests is too extensive to include here—check the *man* page for *test* for the full list of supported tests.

Scripting

Those of you familiar with Windows may be familiar with the idea of batch files. A batch file in DOS or Windows is just a list of commands that are executed when the batch file is run. For example, the AUTOEXEC.BAT is used by DOS and early versions of Windows to set up the environment and start applications.

Script files under Unix operate in the same way—they can run a series of commands placed into a standard text file. To create a script, just put the commands that you want to execute into a standard text file. Then set the permissions of the file to be executable (see Chapter 19, "Enforcing Permissions and Security," for more details). Typically, you can just get away with:

```
$ chmod 755 myscript
```

Whenever a shell sees a file that is executable which also happens to be identified as text, it attempts to run the file as if it were a script.

If your script is written in anything other than the Bourne shell, you should also tell Unix which shell to use to execute the file. You do this by specifying the *shebang* line. For example, for a *bash* script you would put:

```
#!/usr/bin/bash
```

The leading *#* character marks the line as a comment, which is normally ignored. The *!* character tells the shell to expect the location of the application to use.

Scripts are used all over Unix for doing all sorts of jobs. You've already seen and used some scripts in the rest of the book. The scripts used for starting and stopping services, for example, are all standard Bourne shell scripts.

The Least You Need to Know

◆ There are different types of shells that offer different facilities, including the default Bourne shell (*sh*), the Korn shell (*ksh*), the C shell (*csh*), and the Bourne-Again shell (*bash*).

◆ You communicate with the shell by using a command line.

◆ The command line includes the name of a command to be executed and optional additional command line arguments to the command itself.

◆ You can select multiple files by using the * (for matching any number of any characters) or *?* (for matching a single character of any type).

◆ You can redirect information in and out of a command, and redirect the errors generated to a different location.

◆ You can use a pipe to connect between the output of one command and the input of another.

Navigating and Managing Files

In This Chapter

♦ Getting file lists

♦ Managing files and directories

♦ Finding the files you want

Files and directories are the backbone of the Solaris system. Everything, one way or another, is accessed, configured, or available through some sort of file on the system. To make use of this information though you will need to know how to get hold of a list of files, how to move and rename them, and how to navigate your way around the file system.

In this chapter, I'll look at these issues, both from the command line and CDE points of view, and I'll explain how you can find files by their name, modification time, and other criteria, just in case you forget where you saved that important document!

Getting File Lists

The most basic operation on any computer should be getting a list of files on the machine. Now we already know that Solaris (and other Unix variants) use a single-file system to hold all their files.

Sun Lotion

If your shell supports aliases (csh, ksh, bash) you might want to set up an alias that treats *ll* as *ls -l* to make getting a long listing much easier.

Using ls

The *ls* command produces a list of files. By default, it lists the files and directories in the current directory, and shows only the file names in quasi-alphabetical order. By quasi-alphabetical, I mean that it lists numbers before names and uppercase characters before lowercase. You can see the effect in the directory listing shown below:

```
$ ls
/bin/ls
09fig01.tif      cookie.out        t.out
09fig02.tif      cookie.py         t.pl
1.npa            dutdump.text.bz2  t.py
2.npa            first             table.pl
26-xmlrpc.t      kdesrc            table.py
3.npa            kdmout            tmp
AdobeFnt.lst     last              uriescape
Cookie.py        mkdhcp            xml.cpio
Cookie.py.mac    netdump           xmlrpc.daemon
Cookie.pyc       ns_imap           xmlrpcc.pl
HtmlKit          nsmail            xmlrpccgi.pl
MyMath.pm        p0187-01.pl       xmlrpcd.pl
appa.py          ssltest.pl
cixt.pl          t.l
```

The command automatically lists the files in a number of columns across the screen. The command also supports a number of command line options which are used to change the way the output is produced. You can see a list of some of the more common options in Table 18.1.

Table 18.1   Command Line Options for the *ls* Command

Option	Description
-a	Lists all files, including those starting with a single period (including the special . and .. directories).
-l	Produces a long listing, including the permissions, user and group information, and the last modification date/time for the file or directory.
-F	Shows the file type after the file name (/ for a directory, @ for a link, * for an executable file and nothing for a normal file).
-r	Reverses the order of printing, either in reverse alphabetical form or reverse modification time (if *-t* is used).

Option	Description
-R	Recursively lists files, going into each directory and listing their files, and then listing the contents of directories and so on, until the entire tree has been listed.
-t	Sort the files by their last modification time, rather than by their name.

For example, we can get a long list of the files in your current directory using the *-l* option:

```
$ ls -l
total 2478
-rw-rw-rw-   1 root     other     581004 Jan 31 14:48 09fig01.tif
-rw-rw-rw-   1 root     other     274794 Jan 31 14:48 09fig02.tif
-rw-rw-rw-   1 root     other          6 Aug 21 16:10 1.npa
-rw-rw-rw-   1 root     other          6 Aug 21 16:10 2.npa
-rw-r--r--   1 root     other        628 Jul  2  2001 26-xmlrpc.t
-rw-rw-rw-   1 root     other          6 Aug 21 16:10 3.npa
-rw-rw-rw-   1 root     other      12321 May 20  2001 AdobeFnt.lst
-rw-rw-rw-   1 root     other      24904 Apr 30  2001 Cookie.py
-rw-rw-rw-   1 root     other      24813 Apr 30  2001 Cookie.py.mac
-rw-rw-rw-   1 root     other      24095 Apr 30  2001 Cookie.pyc
drwxr-xr-x   3 cyrus    staff       2048 May  1  2001 HtmlKit/
-rw-rw-rw-   1 root     other         40 May 22  2001 MyMath.pm
-rw-rw-rw-   1 root     other        341 Jul 26  2001 appa.py
-rw-rw-rw-   1 root     other        171 Aug 21 16:12 cixt.pl
-rw-rw-rw-   1 root     other      24964 Apr 30  2001 cookie.out
-rw-rw-rw-   1 root     other        256 Apr 30  2001 cookie.py
-rw-rw-rw-   1 root     other      33854 Oct 11 10:14 dutdump.text.bz2
-rw-rw-rw-   1 root     other         25 Jan 28 10:17 first
drwxrwxrwx   2 root     other        512 Aug 25 11:23 kdesrc/
-rw-rw-rw-   1 root     other          0 Jun 24  2001 kdmout
-rw-rw-rw-   1 root     other         29 Jan 28 10:17 last
-rw-rw-rw-   1 root     other       3976 Dec 30 17:56 mkdhcp
-rw-rw-rw-   1 root     other     183604 Oct 11 10:14 netdump
drwxr-xr-x   4 root     other        512 Apr  9  2001 ns_imap/
drwx------   2 root     other        512 Apr  9  2001 nsmail/
-rw-rw-rw-   1 root     other        525 Sep  9 11:57 p0187-01.pl
-rw-rw-rw-   1 root     other        394 Jul  2  2001 ssltest.pl
-rw-rw-rw-   1 root     other       1142 Dec 15 16:42 t.l
-rw-rw-rw-   1 root     other       2048 Sep  9 11:58 t.out
-rw-rw-rw-   1 root     other         64 Nov 27 17:15 t.pl
-rw-rw-rw-   1 root     other         93 Apr 19  2001 t.py
-rw-rw-rw-   1 root     other        118 May  1  2001 table.pl
-rw-rw-rw-   1 root     other        241 May  1  2001 table.py
drwxrwxrwx   2 root     other       1024 Jan 24 13:44 tmp/
-rw-rw-rw-   1 root     other        136 May  1  2001 uriescape
```

```
-rw-rw-rw-  1 root     other        8192 Jan  6 11:02 xml.cpio
-rw-r--r--  1 root     other        2398 Jul  2  2001 xmlrpc.daemon
-rw-r--r--  1 root     other         258 Jul  2  2001 xmlrpcc.pl
-rw-r--r--  1 root     other         639 Jul  2  2001 xmlrpccgi.pl
-rw-r--r--  1 root     other         628 Jul  2  2001 xmlrpcd.pl
```

The output includes the file type (in the very first character), the file permissions, owner and group owner, the file size, and the date and time the file or directory was last modified. I'll discuss permissions and their effects in Chapter 19, "Enforcing Permissions and Security."

By specifying the files (or a file specification) after any command line options, you can also supply a list of files to show the information for. So, you can list all the Perl source files (which have the extension *.pl*) using:

```
$ ls -l *.pl
-rw-rw-rw-  1 root     other         171 Aug 21 16:12 cixt.pl
-rw-rw-rw-  1 root     other         525 Sep  9 11:57 p0187-01.pl
-rw-rw-rw-  1 root     other         394 Jul  2  2001 ssltest.pl
-rw-rw-rw-  1 root     other          64 Nov 27 17:15 t.pl
-rw-rw-rw-  1 root     other         118 May  1  2001 table.pl
-rw-r--r--  1 root     other         258 Jul  2  2001 xmlrpcc.pl
-rw-r--r--  1 root     other         639 Jul  2  2001 xmlrpccgi.pl
-rw-r--r--  1 root     other         628 Jul  2  2001 xmlrpcd.pl
```

Within CDE

Within CDE, click on the Filing Cabinet icon on your CDE panel—it's on the left-hand side. This will present you with a window like the one in Figure 18.1. You can use the familiar methods to control your files. For example, double-clicking a file will attempt to open it, and double-clicking a directory will change to that directory. Similarly dragging and dropping files allows you to copy and move them within your directories, and you can also drag them to the trash—the trash icon is on the CD panel in the bottom right-hand corner.

To change the view format—that is, to show a list of files, sizes, and permissions equivalent to the *ls -l* command, choose Set View Options from the View menu—you can see a sample in Figure 18.2.

Sun Lotion

Remember the information in Chapter 17, "Using a Shell," on file expansion—any command line element which includes some form of file expansion is automatically expanded into a list of suitable files. This is why *ls* * lists all files in the current directory.

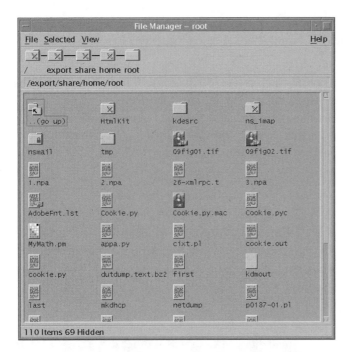

Figure 18.1

The CDE File Manager.

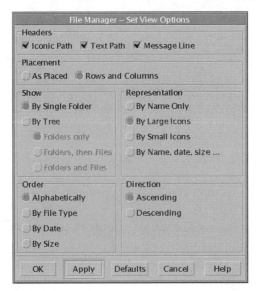

Figure 18.2

Setting viewing options within the CDE File Manager.

Managing Files

It is, in general, easier to manage files from the command line than it is to do it from within CDE. Part of this is just the speed with which you can enter a filename (and its replacement) into the command line. The other part is the way in which file names are automatically expanded, allowing you to move, copy, and delete files matching a particular specification much more quickly than you could individually drag or select the files within the File Manager.

Before looking at the specifics of moving, copying, and renaming files, you need to look at paths. All files and directories have a full pathname, which starts with a forward slash (/). The pathname is the full location of the file or directory within the file system as referenced from the root directory, /. For example, the full pathname to my home directory is */home/mc*. While I'm in my home directory—the current directory—I can refer to the file *resume.txt* in that directory using any of the following:

- *resume.txt*—this is the local or implied path to the file, based on the current directory and the filename.

- *./resume.txt*—this is the relative filename. It's relative because the name is relative to my current directory—in this case, I'm explicitly specifying the current directory using the special . directory name.

- */home/mc/resume.txt*—this is the full pathname. No matter where I am within the file system, */home/mc/resume.txt* will always provide me with access to that file.

Solingo

Unix uses two special directories to help you navigate and find your way around the system. The . directory refers to the current directory, and the .. directory refers to the parent of the current directory.

Incidentally, I can refer to other directories from my current location in the same way, that is:

- *../mc* is the relative path to my home directory from within any directory in */home*. For example, if I'm in */home/slp* I can refer to the directory for *mc* using *../mc* and */home/mc*.

- *../../tmp* is the same as */tmp*—we go up one directory (to */home*) then another (to /) and then back down into *tmp*.

Copying Files

To copy a file, use the *cp* command. To copy a single file, specify the source and the destination:

```
$ cp myfile.txt myfile.bak
```

You can also copy a number of files into a single directory by listing the files (or a file specification) after the command and putting the name of the directory as the last argument. For example, to copy all the *.c* files within the current directory into a new *source* directory you would use:

```
$ cp *.c source
```

Sun Lotion

Officially, Solaris doesn't really care about file extensions, so there is no special distinction for a file with any particular extension. However, by tradition or convention, many standard file extensions do exist, and it still remains one of the most obvious visual clues as to a file's likely contents. CDE automatically associates particular extensions with a particular application, in the same way as Windows (and Mac OS, through the File Exchange control panel) does.

The command will fail if *cp* determines that the final argument is in fact a file, not a directory.

Unfortunately, you can't use the same trick offered by DOS for changing all the file extensions for a set of files. But there is a solution available to us if you use some of the other features of the Solaris operating system. See Chapter 20, "Working with Text," and the section on the *sed* command for more information.

Renaming Files

You can rename a file by using the *mv* command—this is actually short for move, but if you think logically about what happens when you rename a file you can see that it's not that bad a command after all. You're just moving the file from one name to another. To use, supply the current name and the new name on the command line:

```
$ mv oldfile.txt newfile.txt
```

Moving Files

You've probably already guessed the answer to this—you use the *mv* command. For example, to move a file from */tmp* into */home/mc* you use:

```
$ mv /tmp/output.log /home/mc
```

If, as in the above, you only specify a directory name, then the file retains its name and just changes its directory.

You can also move it into my current directory by using the special . reference. For example, assuming I'm already in my home directory, you could rewrite the previous command as:

```
$ mv /tmp/output.log .
```

As with *cp*, specifying a list of files (or wildcard that expands to a list) and a directory will move all of the files into that directory.

Deleting Files

To delete a file on the command line, you use the *rm* command:

```
$ rm myfile
```

You can only delete a file that either you own or that is in a directory that you have write permissions to. If you are not the owner of the file, but do have permission to the directory, then you will be prompted to override the deletion. The system will refuse to delete files you don't have permissions to delete—unless you are the superuser, in which case you can delete anything!

Sun Screen

Deleting a file with *rm* is permanent. Unlike Windows and Mac OS where you have the potential of using a tool like Norton Utilities to resurrect a file, under Unix you have no such thing. If you delete a file, it's permanent. There will be no way to get it back, so make sure that you are deleting the right file or files, especially if you are using wildcards to select multiple files.

It's a good idea if you are unsure of the effect of your wildcards to use *ls* to test the file list first, then you can use *rm* or modify the specification accordingly.

The command also supports a number of different options, listed in Table 18.2.

Table 18.2   Command Line Options for the *rm* Command

Option	Description
-*i*	Interactive mode; you will be prompted to delete each file in the file list.
-*f*	Forces deletion; you will not be prompted to delete the files, even when overriding files that you do not own.
-*r*	Recursively delete a directory.

The -*i* and -*f* options should be self-explanatory, but the -*r* option demands a closer look.

When you try to delete a directory using the *rmdir* command, the directory must be empty; if not, the procedure will fail. Not only do you need to delete the files in the directory, but also any other directories, and by extension, any of the files and directories in those directories as well. You can imagine that this would be a tiresome process for a complex directory structure.

The -r option does all the work for you. If you were to use:

```
$ rm -r source
```

the command would delete the contents of *source*, including all files and other directories, and the directory itself.

CAUTION

Sun Screen _____

Probably the most dangerous command under any version of Unix is *rm -rf*, it recursively deletes all the files or directories supplied on the command line, without prompt or raising any errors. As a normal user, this shouldn't be a problem, but as the superuser, it could be fatal. They say you only do *rm -rf * * in / once. It would, after all, delete every single file on your machine, including the operating system and all of your user files.

I'm happy to say that I've never run that particular command. But I have been caught out by *rm -rf* in other situations and lived to regret it. Even now, I always double- and sometimes triple-check before pressing return after that particular sequence, whether or not I'm root.

Finding Your Way Around

It should be obvious by now (and if it isn't, you really haven't been concentrating!) that Solaris uses directories to a great effect to sort and organize files into logical groups. In order to make use of directories, though, you need to know how to find your way around.

Changing Directories

You change directories within the shell by using the *cd* command. If you don't specify any options, *cd* will take you to your home directory. If you specify the name of a directory, and you have access to it, your current directory will change to your new location. For example, to change to the */tmp* directory you would use:

```
$ cd /tmp
```

You can always find out your current directory using *pwd* (for print working directory):

```
$ pwd
/tmp
```

Sun Lotion _____

Remember that if you ever get lost you can go back to your home directory—that is, the directory you first started in when you logged in—by using the *cd* command with no options.

You can also use the special .. directory to change up to the parent directory. For example, starting from your home directory:

```
$ cd
$ pwd
/ home/mc
$ cd ..
$ pwd
/ home
$ cd mc
$ pwd
/ home/mc
```

Managing Your Directories

You can create a new directory (assuming the permissions for the current directory) using *mkdir*:

```
$ mkdir source
```

You can supply as many names as you like to the command to create all of the specified directories. You may also want to create a structure deeper than just one directory. For example, to create the directory *source/backups* you would normally have to do:

```
$ mkdir source
$ cd source
$ mkdir backups
```

Using the *-p* option you can create the entire path in one command:

```
$ mkdir -p source/backups
```

To delete any directory, use *rmdir*:

```
$ rmdir source
```

But remember that the directory must be empty (aside from the special . and .. entries). If you want to delete the directory and its contents, use the *rm -rf* command instead.

Finding the Files You Want

You don't always know the exact filename of the file that you are looking for, or you may know what you are looking for, but you need to select or identify more than a single file.

Using find

The *find* shell command provides a relatively quick and easy way of finding files by a variety of criteria, reporting the list of files found back to the standard output. The basic format of the command is:

```
find directory [options]
```

where *directory* is the path to a directory that you want to search. Without any criteria, it will list all the files and directories beneath the directory you specify:

```
$ find /usr
/usr
/usr/openwin
/usr/openwin/bin
/usr/openwin/bin/ctlconvert_txt
/usr/openwin/bin/ctlmp
/usr/openwin/bin/mp_1251
/usr/openwin/bin/mkfontdir

...
```

To find a file by its name, use the *-name* command line option. For example, to find a file called *file.txt* somewhere in the */home* directory you would use:

```
$ find /home -name file.txt
```

You can also use a file specification, providing it's quoted; for example you can look for all the HTML files in a directory structure by using:

```
$ find /var/apache/htdocs -name "*.html"
```

To search for files that have been modified or created within a specified number of days, use the *-mtime* and *-ctime* command line options respectively. For example, to find all the files changed within the current directory within the last day, use:

```
$ find . -mtime -1
```

Note the specification is *-1*, not *1*. We need to specify a negative value because we want to find those files changed in the previous day (24 hours) not the next day (24 hours). You can specify as many days here as you like. See the *man* page for *find* for more information.

You can also choose to search only for genuine files or directories, or other files of specific types. This is useful in situations where you want to get a list of files but not directories—the standard listing outputs all matching files and directories. For example, to find only files you would use:

```
$ find . -type f
```

Other types include *d* for directories and *l* for symbolic links.

You can of course combine options, so to find all of the files ending in *.html* that were modified in the last 24 hours you would use:

```
$ find /var/run/htdocs -type f -name "*.html" -mtime -1
```

Using CDE

From within the File Manager in CDE you can search for files using similar criteria to that offered by the *find* command. Just choose Find from the File menu and you should be presented with the window shown in Figure 18.3.

Figure 18.3

Finding a file with the File Manager.

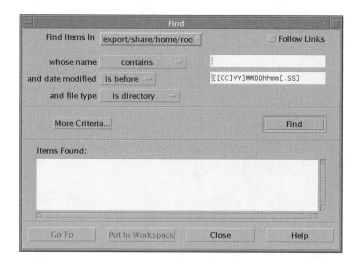

The top popup selects the directory where your search will start, and you can then specify the filename, modification time, and other criteria using the popups and selection box. When you've finished entering the criteria, click on the Find button. The list of matching files will be shown in the Items Found panel.

The Least You Need to Know

- ◆ You can get a list of files using the *ls* command.
- ◆ Alternatively, using CDE starts up a File Manager.
- ◆ You can copy, rename, move, and delete files using the *cp*, *mv*, and *rm* commands.
- ◆ You can create and delete directories using *mkdir* and *rmdir*, respectively.
- ◆ You can find a file using *find* or the Find system within the File Manager.

Enforcing Permissions and Security

In This Chapter

- Limiting access through standard file security
- Using access control lists

Everything within Solaris is generally accessible in some way through a file. When you read information off a disk, of course it's coming from a file. However, did you also realize that when copying information over USB you were accessing the device through a file? Or even that accessing the date and time potentially uses a device file to read the information from the systems clock?

Because everything is accessible through a file in some way, you can control the security and permissions of a system by controlling the permissions and security on an individual file.

Setting Standard File Security

You already know from the introduction in Chapter 6, "Managing Users and Groups," that the user and group security model employed by Unix is a powerful way of limiting access to different files on the system. The easiest way to remind yourself of this is to look at the output of *ls* in long mode (that is, with the *-l* command line option):

```
$ ls -l
total 858
-rw-rw-rw-    1 root        other             6 Aug 21 16:10 1.npa
-rw-rw-rw-    1 root        other             6 Aug 21 16:10 2.npa
-rw-r--r--    1 root        other           628 Jul  2  2001 26-xmlrpc.t
-rw-rw-rw-    1 root        other             6 Aug 21 16:10 3.npa
-rw-rw-rw-    1 root        other         12321 May 20  2001 AdobeFnt.lst
-rw-rw-rw-    1 root        other         24904 Apr 30  2001 Cookie.py
drwxr-xr-x    3 cyrus       staff          2048 May  1  2001 HtmlKit/
```

The first column contains the file permissions, the third column specifies the file's owner, and the fourth column the group owner of the file. Now I'll show you how you can modify that information.

Sun Screen

Using *chown* to change the ownership of your own files is a potentially dangerous operation. Unless you have superuser access, or are friends with the person who you've just given your files to, you will be unable to change the files back. In short, only the current owner of the file or the superuser can change the ownership to somebody else.

Owner

To change the ownership of a file, use the *chown* command. You supply the username that you want to set for the file first, followed by the list or specification of one or more files or directories that you want to change the owner of.

For example:

```
$ chown mc *.html
```

You can only change the owner of files you are the current owner of, unless of course you are the superuser, in which case you can change the owner of any file you like.

Group Owner

The group owner of a file is used to determine who can access the file when they are a member of that group. You can change the group owner of a file or directory using the *chgrp* command. The first argument should be the name of the group and the rest of the command line should list the files or directories that you want to change the owner of:

```
$ chgrp web *.html
```

Note that you can only change the group owner of a file if you are the owner, have write permissions as a group owner, or are the superuser.

File Permissions

If you recall the discussion in Chapter 6, you'll remember that the permissions column output by *ls* included a permission column that contained a sequence of "r," "w," and "x" letters. For example:

```
-rw-rw-rw-   1 root     other      12321 May 20  2001 AdobeFnt.lst
```

The permission information is the string "-rw-rw-rw-" in the previous example. The first character tells you what kind of file the listed file is. Table 19.1 shows the full list of characters used to define the file type.

Table 19.1   File Types Identified by *ls*

Letter	Description
d	The file is a directory.
D	The file is a door.
l	The file is a symbolic link.
b	The file is a block special file.
c	The file is a character special file.
p	The file is a FIFO (or "named pipe") special file.
s	The file is an AF_UNIX address family socket.
-	The file is an ordinary file.

The rwx elements show, in order, the accessibility of the file to:

1. The owner of the file or directory.

2. Members of the file's group.

3. Everybody else.

To set these permissions, you need to specify either the entire mode using *octal* or you can set specific options by specifying which class (user, group, or other). In either case, you use the *chmod* command (short for change mode).

The easiest way is to use the letter format, as humans are generally better at working with letters. To set the permissions, supply a specification that sets whether or not each class has read, write, or execute permissions, according to the following format:

```
[ugo][+-][rwx]
```

Where:

◆ u specifies the user class.

◆ g specifies the group class.

◆ o specifies the other class.

◆ a specifies all classes (equivalent to "ugo").

◆ + indicates that the permissions should be granted to the specified classes.

◆ - indicates that the permissions should be denied to the specified classes.

◆ r indicates that the specified classes should be granted or denied read permissions.

◆ w indicates that the specified classes should be granted or denied write permissions.

◆ x indicates that the specified classes should be granted or denied execute permissions.

Solingo

Octal is a format for specifying a number in a particular base. Humans typically use base 10—largely because we have 10 fingers and 10 toes in the standard model. That means that we count 0, 1, 2, 3, 4, 5, 6, 7, 8, 9; that's 10 digits. To get numbers higher than 9, we start the count again, but with two digits, that is, 10, 11, 12 and so on.

Computers use binary—applying the same rules as for decimal, we count 0, 1 and then, 10, 11, and then on to 100, 101, 110, 111, and so on. Hexadecimal counts up to 16, using letters for digits above 9. Thus we get, 0, 1, 2, 3, 4, 5, 6, 7, 8, 9, A, B, C, D, E, F. Again, once we get to 16 we combine digits, so that we get 10, 11, 12, 13, 14, 15, 16, 17, 18, 19, 1A, 1B, 1C, 1D, 1E, 1F.

Octal uses only 8 digits, so we count 0, 1, 2, 3, 4, 5, 6, 7. To get higher than 8, it follows that we would use 10, 11, 12, 13, and so on.

For example, to allow user, group, and other classes to have read access to a file you use:

```
$ chmod ugo+r myfile.txt
```

To add read/write permissions to the group ownership of a file you would use:

```
$ chmod g+rw myfile.txt
```

When using the octal permissions, you set the permissions of the file or files explicitly—that is, you define the entire set of permissions (for all classes and all modes) all at the same time. To set each permission, add the values for read, write, and execute together, and then further concatenate the numbers for each of the user, group, and other classes to produce a three-digit number. Each permission has a different value:

♦ Read permission has a value of 4.

♦ Write permission has a value of 2.

♦ Execute permission has a value of 1.

♦ No permissions has a value of 0.

Sun Lotion

The difference between using the octal mode and the letter format is that using an octal mode sets the file permissions explicitly, while using the letter form merely updates the permissions.

If you have a file with read and execute permissions for all classes (for example, 555) and you want to grant write access to the owner, you could use the mode 755 or the letter form r+x, no problems. However, if you want to add read/write permissions to a bunch of files that have a variety of read, write, and execute permissions, then using the explicit octal mode will cause problems.

For example, imagine two files, one an application with read and execute permissions (555) and the other a text file with read only permissions (444). Add write permissions to the owner with an octal mode and you'll have to set the modes individually, 755 for the application and 644 for the file. Using the letter form, you can specify u+w and *add* the write permission without upsetting any of the other values.

You can see from Table 19.2 how the different permissions add up to make the different octal values.

Table 19.2   Octal Values for Permissions

Read	Write	Execute	Mode
-	-	-	0
-	-	x	1
-	w	-	2
r	-	-	4
r	-	x	5
r	w	-	6
r	w	x	7

For example, to set read and write permissions for user, group, and other classes, use the octal value 666, where the first 6 refers to the user permissions, the second to the group, and the third to other. To set read and write permissions for the owner, but no permissions for anybody else, use 600.

To use with *chmod* just supply the value directly as you would supply the permission string:

```
$ chmod 600 myfile.txt
```

or

```
$ chmod 755 myfile.txt
```

The only difficulty with using the octal format is that you must specify the full permission information for user, group, and other, all at the same time. Using a two digit or one digit number will not only not work, if it was supported, *chown* would have no way of determining which class you were trying to set the permissions for.

Setuid/Setgid and Sticky Bits

I have, up to now, been slightly economical with the truth—the read, write, and execute settings are not the only modifications you can make to the permissions of a file. There are three other settings I have not yet discussed. These are the setuid, setgid, and sticky bits:

◆ The **setuid** bit affects the operation of an executable file—it has no effect on a file that is not executable. With the *setuid* bit set, the user automatically changes to have the effective user ID of the owner of the file when they execute an application. For example, the user *mc* when executing an application owned by *root* with the *setuid* bit set would give the application *root* privileges and abilities during its execution. As soon as the application terminates, the user is back to normal.

◆ The **setgid** bit works like *setuid*, except that it sets the user's effective group ID to the same as that of the group owner of a given application.

◆ The **sticky** bit was used to specify that a file or application should stay in physical memory. Today, the sticky bit is used to control the abilities of a user on a directory. If a directory is writable and has the sticky bit set, then you can only rename or remove the file if one or more of the following are true:

  ◆ The user owns the file.
  ◆ The user owns the directory.
  ◆ The file is writable by the user.
  ◆ The user is a privileged user.

> **A Postcard From ...**
>
> Some of the standard Unix commands are actually *setuid* or *setgid*—without them most users would be unable to use certain parts of the system. The classic example is *passwd*, which is a *setuid* program owned by root. Without such a program, or the ability for it to be run by root, other users would be unable to change their password.

The sticky bit is used on the */tmp* directory to allow anybody to read, write, or delete the files *they* place into that directory without having the ability to delete or rename anybody else's files.

To actually set the *setuid*, *setgid*, or sticky bit, you use extra options to the permissions setting we saw earlier. When using the letter form ...

- ◆ *u+s* grants *setuid*.
- ◆ *g+s* grants *setgid*.
- ◆ and *a+t* sets the sticky bit.

Using octal modes ...

- ◆ 4 grants *setuid*.
- ◆ 2 grants *setgid*.
- ◆ and 1 sets the sticky bit.

These are prefixes to the standard permission value, hence the real values are 4000, 2000, and 1000, respectively. For example, to grant *setuid* privileges on a file and also to set read and execute permission to all users, use:

```
$ chmod 4555 myapplication
```

Note that the normal permissions still apply in each case. If an application has been given *setuid* permissions then only those classes with execute permissions can actually execute the file. That is, a file with the permissions 4550 can only be executed by the owner and members of the file's group owner.

Sun Screen

> The *setuid* and *setgid* systems are very useful as they allow you to grant access to a user running an application, or provide special abilities on a directory, without granting them full access to a system.
>
> Unfortunately, they are also a potentially lethal backdoor that provides people with access to your system. Change the permissions on a shell or other application that supports the ability to run another command to include *setuid*, especially if the owner of the file is root, and anybody using that application can potentially do anything the superuser can. Unless you know what you are doing, it's best to leave the *setuid* and *setgid* programs that do exist on your system as they are, and not to create any new ones.

Default File Settings

When you create a file or directory it is created with the permissions and ownership settings according to your current effective user and group. The terms "current" and "effective" are significant because you can change your current user or group:

- Your **real user ID** is the one you used to log in to the machine.
- Your **effective user ID** is the one in force because you used *su* to change your user or because you are executing a *setuid* application.
- Your **real group ID** is the default group configured in */etc/passwd*.
- Your **effective group ID** is the one in force because you used *su* to change users (and therefore the default group), because you changed groups using *newgrp*, or because you are executing a *setgid* application.

You can determine your current real and effective user ID information by using the *id* command:

```
$ id
uid=1001(mc) gid=10(staff)
```

The permissions of a file are set according to your current *umask*. This is an *octal* value that is used as a mask against the permissions when the file is created. In essence, the value of the *umask* is removed from the permission value of the file that is created.

By default, all files are created with a mode of 666, and the default *umask* is 000, thus files are created with the final mode 666. If you set a *umask* of 022, then the files are created with a mode of 644. Note that you can't have negative values, so the recommended *umask* value of 077 never creates a file that is readable, writable, or executable by anybody but its creator.

To actually set the *umask*, use the *umask* command, supplying it the octal value you want to use:

```
$ umask 077
```

I highly recommend that you put such a line into your profile or other startup file.

Working with Access Control Lists

I have once again been mildly economical with the truth. The permissions and user/group/other class system is not the only method you can use to control access to your files. One of the limitations of the standard system is that you can only grant access to a single user, a group, or everybody else.

For the majority of systems this is fine, and I have to admit that I've never suffered any real problems using the basics on all but one occasion. However, just occasionally you may find yourself wanting to grant access to a file or directory for more than one single user or group.

Now you can argue in these cases that you can create a specific group to handle this situation, but the situations start to become unmanageable as the number of users and groups increases. For example, to grant two departments with 400 users each access to a single directory would require you to create a new group with 800 people. Furthermore, it becomes even more difficult if you find you want to provide two different groups with two different types of access.

In these situations an access control list (ACL) is the solution. Using an ACL, you can add read, write, or execute permissions for a list of users or list of groups, including the ability to set specific permissions for each user or group you specify. In addition, you can specify a *umask* for a given file that applies either to the entire file, or only to a specific user or group using the file. You can also specify a default user or group for a given file or directory, ensuring that the file is always owned by the right person.

Setting ACLs

You set or modify the permissions using the *setfacl* command. The first required argument is the type of ACL operation you want to perform:

- ◆ *-s* explicitly sets the ACL, removing all old ACL information (equivalent to setting the file permissions using an octal).
- ◆ *-a* or *-m* adds the ACL you supply to the existing ACL information.
- ◆ *-d* deletes the ACL matching the ACL you supply.

The next arguments should be the ACL specification—that is, the actual definition of the ACL that you want to set. You can supply multiple ACL specifications by separating them with a comma. Table 19.3 shows a list of the supported arguments.

Table 19.3   ACL settings

ACL Specification	Description
u[ser]::perms	File owner permissions.
g[roup]::perms	File group owner permissions.
o[ther]:perms	Permissions for users other than the file owner or members of file group owner.
m[ask]:perms	The ACL mask. The mask entry indicates the maximum permissions allowed for users (other than the owner) and for groups. The mask is a quick way to change permissions on all the users and groups.
u[ser]:uid:perms	Permissions for a specific user. For *uid*, you can specify either a user name or a numeric UID.

continues

Table 19.3 ACL settings (continued)

ACL Specification	Description
g[roup]:gid:perms	Permissions for a specific group. For *gid*, you can specify either a group name or a numeric GID.
d[efault]:u[ser]::perms	Default file owner permissions.
d[efault]:g[roup]::perms	Default file group owner permissions.
d[efault]:o[ther]:perms	Default permissions for users other than the file owner or members of the file group owner.
d[efault]:m[ask]:perms	Default ACL mask.
d[efault]:u[ser]:uid:perms	Default permissions for a specific user. For *uid*, you can specify either a user name or a numeric UID.
d[efault]:g[roup]:gid:perms	Default permissions for a specific group. For *gid*, you can specify either a group name or a numeric GID.

For example, we can add read access to an individual user of a file using:

```
$ setfacl -m user:spenfold:r-- myfile.txt
```

Solingo

The **uid** and **gid** are just the short names used for the user ID and group ID respectively.

Getting ACLs

You can get the ACL for a file using the *getfacl* command—just supply the name of the file you want to obtain the ACL for on the command line. The following example shows the output of a standard file—one that has not had any ACL information appended to it:

```
$ getfacl myfile.txt
# file: news
# owner: mc
# group: staff
user::rw-
group::rw-              #effective:rw-
mask:rw-
other:rw-
```

Here's the same report for a file that has had a user access ACL added to it:

```
$ getfacl news

# file: news
# owner: mc
# group: staff
```

```
user::rw-
user:spenfold:r--        #effective:r--
group::rw-               #effective:rw-
mask:rw-
other:rw-
```

The Least You Need to Know

◆ You can set the owner of a file using *chown*.

◆ You can set the group owner of a file using *chgrp*.

◆ You can set the permissions on a file using *chmod*.

◆ You can set the default mode used to store a file by using the *umask* command.

◆ You can set specific permissions by setting up an access control list for a file.

Working with Text

In This Chapter

◆ Viewing files

◆ Working with editors

◆ Extracting and combining file contents

◆ Using the search and replace command

◆ Working with awk

◆ Sorting information in files

You're not going to get very far with Unix if you decide that you never need to view a file. Sure, if you are using CDE or Gnome, the chances are that you may never need to use a command tool or the shell to do what you want. However, if you want to use the power of the Unix operating system, you will need to learn how to work with some basic text viewing and editing tools.

There is more to editing and viewing text under Unix than just firing up an editor and changing the contents. What happens if you want to search for a piece of text across a lot of files? Or change the content of a number of files? Are you going to fire up an editor for each file and do the search and replace yourself?

If you want to save time, the answer to that question is no, and the solution to the problem is the suite of tools available under Unix. In this chapter I'll introduce the main tools available that can be used to search and process a text file, as well as some neat tricks along the way that quite possibly aren't strictly text manipulation.

Viewing Files

You don't always want to open an editor to view a file—frequently you just want to take a quick look at the contents to make sure that it contains what you expected. There are two commands that will help here, *cat* and *more*.

Using cat

The *cat* command actually concatenates files together—in its basic form it will concatenate a single file, sending the output to the screen, thus allowing you to view the file:

```
$ cat myfile.txt
```

If you supply more than one file and then redirect the output, you can use it to create one, big, massive file, particularly useful when combining lots of log files:

```
$ cat syslog* >syslog.full
```

The only problem with *cat* (when used without redirection) is that if the file is larger than the size of your window then the contents will skim past so quickly you won't be able to read what's really in the file. In this case, you need something that displays information screen by screen—you know, something that shows a bit of the file, then shows you a little bit more, then a little bit more ...

Using more

The *more* command determines the size of your window—whether you are using the console, connecting through telnet, or using xterm—and then displays one window full of information before providing you with a prompt, which you can then use to move around the file. A space will move the file on one full page, and return will move things forward just a single line.

Solingo

There is a freely available version of the *more* command, distributed by GNU, called *less*. The basic abilities of the two commands are identical—they both display files in a paged format so that can view the information without it flying too fast past your eyes. The main benefit of *less* was the ability to go backwards through a file, as well as forwards, although this is now standard in the Solaris version of *more*.

To use the *more* command, just supply the names of the files that you want to view:

```
$ more myfile.txt
```

When a page has been displayed, you'll be prompted with something like:

```
--More--(4%)
```

The percentage figure shown tells you how far you are through the document. Once at this prompt, use one of the keys shown in Table 20.1 to change your position within the file.

Table 20.1   Moving Around with *more*

Key	Description
<space>	Move forward one page.
Return	Move forward one line.
[0-9]s	If you supply a number and then press S you will skip over that number of lines and display a new page. For example, typing 100s will skip one hundred lines.
Control-B	Go back one page.
/string Return	Search for the next occurrence of string.
h	Show the help screen.
q	Quit viewing the current file.

If you have specified more than one file on the command line, you will always be prompted before the next file is displayed.

Using Editors

One way or another, Unix always requires at least some editing of some file or another. In reality, you'll also probably want to create your own files, whether it's for writing an application or writing a letter. There are quite a few editors available for Unix; the primary one is vi and a popular alternative is emacs.

ed

Just stay away. Trust me, ed is one of the most difficult editors to use—although it was pretty amazing 30 years ago, most people will find it so difficult to use that it's not even worth looking at it. However, the term ed is frequently used in Unix/Solaris to refer to a group of editors which keep a common base. These include ed, ex, vi, and sed. I'll discuss the two most useful from the collection, vi and sed.

A Postcard From ...

If you think operating system evangelism is the epitome of the flame war, you've never seen anything like the battles over which editor is the best. I've seen people argue over the merits of vi, emacs, and many, many others. All involved frequently forget that choosing the editor you use is as much about which you prefer to use as it is about features.

Not everybody wants radical search and replace, a built-in programming language, or the ability to customize every single element of the system to suit their particular way of working. Some people just want an editor. For the record, I use emacs on Windows and Unix machines and BBedit on the Mac, and less occasionally Pepper under BeOS and Mac OS. And before you ask, I use Microsoft Word for writing.

---

vi

I'll admit, I'm no fan of vi—it's not the friendliest or most convenient of applications to use, but it is a standard editor on just about every Unix system ever released, including Solaris, and therefore it's worth learning just in case you ever need it. The full name for vi is "Visual Editor" because it has a more visually interactive version of the ed command. The limitation of ed is that you can only edit a single line at a time and you are limited in what you can do.

The vi editor works very simply—you open a file and vi displays it. Once within vi there are two modes, command mode and editing mode.

- In **command** mode you can move freely about the file, delete lines and characters, and save and quit from the application.

- In **editing** mode, you can add new text, overwrite text, or delete the text you have written in this session, but you cannot move around, delete pre-existing text or exit/save the file.

Table 20.2 shows the commands available to you (primarily in command mode only).

Table 20.2 Controlling vi

Command/Key	Description
l or Right Arrow	Move forward (right) one character.
h or Left Arrow	Move backwards (left) one character.
j or Down Arrow	Move down one line.
k or Up Arrow	Move up one line.

Command/Key	Description
w	Move forward (right) one word.
b	Move backward (left) one word.
i	Insert text under current cursor position (change to editing mode).
x	Delete the character under the cursor.
dd	Delete the current line.
a	Append text starting with the character immediately after the current cursor position (change to editing mode).
o	Open a new line after the current line and start inserting text (change to editing mode).
O	Open a new line before the current line and start inserting text (change to editing mode).
u	Undo previous change.
ZZ	Exit vi, saving changes.
:w	Save changes.
:q	Quit (you'll be unable to quit if the file has been modified).
:q!	Quit (ignoring any changes).
:wq	Write file and quit.
Escape	Change from editing mode back to command mode.

Whenever in editing mode you can of course type any characters or lines to introduce them into the file. If you use Backspace during this time to delete what you've entered, then you can retype it; if you quit back to command mode using Escape, then anything you deleted will be removed. However, you *must* change back to command mode to perform any other deletion, to move about within the file from your current line, and to quit vi altogether.

Most of the confusion and frustration with vi happens because of these two modes—in particular, the limitation of not being able to move within the document once you have entered editing mode is one of the chief reasons that people start to look for something else. You can make life easier, however, if you tell vi to indicate when it is in insert mode. To do this, create (or edit) the file .exrc in your home directory and add the line:

```
set showmode
```

to it. This will force vi to show INSERT MODE, APPEND MODE, or OPEN MODE in the status line (the last line on the screen) if you are in any edit mode. In command mode, it shows nothing.

emacs

The emacs tool was written by Richard M. Stallman, the man behind GNU and the Free Software Foundation. At its heart, emacs is just an editor—it allows you to edit a text file and save it back. However, what distinguishes emacs from a basic text editor, and in fact most other editors on any platform is its built-in language based on Lisp. Elisp enables emacs to:

◆ Automatically format a document as you are typing it—especially helpful with pro-gramming languages where emacs can automatically indent and "tidy" your code to make it easier to read and maintain. The same feature also works on HTML, XML, and SGML.

◆ Script and automate the editing and formatting of a number of files. You can also customize keyboard commands and have a keyboard command run a script for you.

◆ Open and use multiple files, all with their own mode, current location, and other information.

◆ Edit files in ways not normally possible, such as moving directly to the start and end of a code block, paragraph, or other recognizable element. The same feature allows you to move a "rectangle" of code around and swap and move entire functions or HTML sections without manually selecting the area.

◆ Act as a proper X Windows application as well as a standard terminal application. This makes it an ideal solution for editing as you can use it both "natively" within X Windows and also in a telnet or other session, and yet have access to the same features.

◆ Interactively run commands from within the editor. You can use both a complete interactive shell from within emacs or you can use many of the built-in extensions to control and process the information. For example, from within emacs you can send mail, read Usenet news, compile applications, and automatically move to the file and line that contains a particular error.

Really, I've only scratched the surface. Most people who have ever used emacs find they never want to use another editor ever again. I'm not entirely sure I'd go that far, but I would struggle to edit files—particularly Perl, Python, and C source code—without emacs. I've been using it now for over 12 years, and I haven't learned even a quarter of its abilities.

You can download pre-compiled versions of emacs from Sun Freeware (see Appendix A, "Resource Guide," for more information).

CAUTION

Sun Screen

Although one of the first applications that I install on any machine that I expect to use a lot is emacs (second only to bash if the OS doesn't have it already) it doesn't mean I don't know vi. In fact, I make a special point of using vi every now and then just to make sure that I still remember enough to be able to use it. Why?

Well, I can guarantee that the one time when I really need to edit a file, particularly a system file like /etc/vfstab or /etc/passwd, is when I don't have access to emacs. In particular, if your machine is sick and you start up in single user mode, it's highly unlikely that you will have access to emacs or whatever your favorite editor is. It's at those times when you suddenly find yourself scrabbling for a book like this one to find out how to use vi. Practice with vi—one day your life may depend on it!

Extracting and Combining Elements

There are times when you want to view or summarize the contents of a file and need to extract elements from the file in a more selective way than simply dumping the entire contents. Sometimes you also want to do the reverse.

Using cut

The cut command cuts "columns" from a file, whether they are well-defined columns using a proper separator of some kind, or whether you have to specify a range of specific characters from each line.

To use this command, you supply a definition for the columns that you want to extract (using -f and a list of column numbers), and if necessary a specification of the delimiter to use when extracting the column (using -d). For example, you can extract just the user name and home directory (fields 1 and 6) from the /etc/passwd file, which is delimited by colons, using:

```
$ cut -d':' -f1,6 /etc/passwd
root:/
daemon:/
bin:/usr/bin
sys:/
...
nobody:/
```

Using paste

If cut separates a single line into a number of individual columns, then it stands to reason that paste would combine a file containing a single column back into a single file of multiple columns. Occasionally this is useful, especially if you want to change the order of columns within a file or when extracting information from a number of columns, summarizing it and replacing the information back.

To combine the files, just supply the name of each file on the command line. The default separator between each line of each file is the tab, although you can change that. For example, if you want to combine the two "columns," one from a file (*first*) that contains:

```
Martin
Sharon
Suna
Bruce
```

and the other column from a file (*last*) that contains:

```
Brown
Penfold
Jones
Stidston
```

use:

```
$ paste first last
Martin  Brown
Sharon  Penfold
Suna    Jones
Bruce   Stidston
```

Using Search and Replace

You don't always want to view the whole file—you just want to extract specific lines or determine if the file does or doesn't contain a particular string. There are also times when you want to replace information in a file without opening up an editor to do it. Unix provides a few tools that can help you here.

Searching with grep

The *grep* command looks for a piece of text in a file and returns a list of all the lines that contain that string or regular expression. For example, you can extract a list of the lines containing "martin" using:

```
$ grep "martin" file.txt
```

The quotes are not needed on a single word like this, but are a good habit to get into. If you specify multiple files, then grep will show the filename and matching line. The *grep* command will actually extract lines based on a regular expression, although unfortunately I don't have time to look at regular expressions in detail.

Solingo

Many of the commands in Unix and modern languages like Perl and Python use a system called regular expressions. A regular expression is really just a definition for a string of text that allows you to specify additional characteristics and wildcard values. For example, let's say you wanted to replace all occurrences of "cat" with "dog." You could do this in a standard editor, but you run the risk of changing every instance of the three letters c-a-t with the letters d-o-g (for example, you may change "caterpillar" to "dogerpillar").

Herein lies the difference between a search and replace and a regular expression. With a simple search and replace you'd end up with words like dogatonic and condogenate, neither of which remotely make sense. With a regular expression you could have explicitly required to convert only the instance of "cat" where "cat" was a whole word.

If you think regular expressions might be useful then look at the *man* pages for awk or sed, the regexp(5) *man* page, or find a book on regular expressions.

Three other useful abilities are to ignore the case of the string you are looking for, to look for all lines *not* containing the text you supply, and the ability to simply provide a list of the files that contain the text you are looking for.

To ignore the case, use the *-i* command line option. For example:

```
$ grep -i 'cat' myfile.txt
```

will find all occurrences of "cat," "CAT," "cAt," and other combinations.

To look for all the lines in a file that don't contain a particular string, use the *-v* option. For example, to get a list of all the lines from a log file that don't contain "OK" you use:

```
$ grep -v 'OK' output.log
```

Finally, you can use grep to get a list of files that do or do not contain a particular string by using the *-l* command line option:

```
$ grep –l 'complete' processlogs.*
processlogs.1
processlogs.3
processlogs.4
```

You can, of course, use any combination of these and other options.

Replacing with sed

Occasionally you want to search and replace a piece of information in a file or other string without having to drop into an editor to do it. More to the point, sometimes you want to do a search and replace on a number of files without having to edit each one. The streams editor, sed, will do this for you.

The sed tool is really just an extended version of ed which is designed to iterate over every line within a file, performing one or more operations. You can use it to search (in place of grep), replace, print, and delete lines from a file, all without actually performing the changes interactively.

For our purposes, since I've covered other tools that perform those other options, I'll concentrate on the ability to search and replace information. The basic format of the command is:

```
$ sed -e ""
```

The -e tells sed to take the "script" that will be used to process the file from the string in the double quotes. To perform a search and replace, you use the substitute command, which uses the format s///. The forward slashes separate the components, so that "s/cat/dog/" would replace all occurrences of "cat" with "dog." You can also place additional options after the last slash, the most useful of which are g, which replaces all occurrences of the string in a line (the default is just to change the first) and i which ignores the case of the search string. The substitute command is actually a regular expression, so if you've learned the regular expression syntax you should be able to do some powerful substitutions.

The sed command can be used on files, in which case you must take the input and then redirect the output:

```
$ sed -e "s/cat/dog/" pets.in >pets.out
```

You can also use it for something much more mundane if you supply some output through a pipe. One of the most frustrating limitations of the majority of Unix shells is that you cannot use them to easily rename a bunch of files. This is because the shell does the command line expansion, and the ren command makes the changes. Within a DOS or Command Prompt within Windows you can do:

```
c:\> ren *.src *.txt
```

to change every file ending .src with .txt. To do this in Unix, you need to use for to iterate over each file, use sed to change the extension and then call ren to make the change:

```
$ for file in *.src
do
    newfile='echo $file|sed -e "s/\.src$/\.txt/"'
    mv $file $newfile
done
```

The newfile line is the important one. The line runs an embedded command (using back-ticks) and the embedded command uses echo to print the filename, and then sed performs a substitution to change the extension. The substitution adds some regular expression fragments you haven't covered. In short, these are the escape of a period (\.), required because a period is the character used in regular expressions to act as a wildcard for any single character, and $, which tells the substitution to only match at the end of a line—in this case our filename.

Converting Line Endings

One of the most annoying features of the three main operating systems (Unix, Windows, Mac OS) is that although they all use the same ASCII format for their text files, the characters that they use for their line endings are different. Unix uses a single linefeed character, Mac OS uses a single carriage-return character, and in typical belt and braces style, Windows use a carriage-return and linefeed character to terminate each line.

Because of this, transferring plain text files between the platforms is a pain. When transferring a Mac text file to a Unix one, for example, the information becomes unviewable, because Unix doesn't treat the carriage-return as a line end and you either end up with all the lines effectively overwriting each other, or just one massive line where it's impossible to identify the line ends.

With a Windows file under Unix, you get additional characters (that pesky carriage-return again) in the output. Luckily, the effects are somewhat reduced because you still have your required linefeed, but it's less than perfect.

Luckily, help is at hand. For converting text files from Unix to and from Windows you can use the *unix2dos* and *dos2unix* commands. For example, to convert from Windows to Unix you would use:

Solingo

ASCII stands for the American Standard Code for Information Interchange. Basically it's the standard that maps a number to a particular letter, primarily for the major roman characters (A-Z, a-z, 0-9) plus punctuation and other characters you would expect to find in a typical document.

```
$ dos2unix win.txt unix.txt
```

And back again:

```
$ unix2dos unix.txt win.txt
```

With Mac files things get slightly more complicated. There are no built-in commands for making the conversion, but you can use the *tr* command, which translates files from one format to another, to do the conversion. The command doesn't understand the notion of files, so you have to redirect to and from each time. For example, to convert from Mac text format to Unix you would use:

```
$ tr "\015" "\012" <mac.txt >unix.txt
```

And back again:

```
$ tr "\012" "\015" <unix.txt >mac.txt
```

The "\012" is the octal value of the linefeed character and "\015" is the octal value of the carriage-return character. The leading backslash and 0 indicate that you are specifying the value in octal.

Using awk

The awk programming language was one of the first programmable elements of the Unix system that could be used by just about anybody. Over the years, awk has become a well-known and often-used part of the operating system—you'll find that many of the scripts that make up the operating system use awk. Because it's a standard part, you can use it to report and summarize information without the need for another language such as Perl or Python.

> ## A Postcard From ...
>
> Never heard of gawk? Well its home is currently Israel, where my friend Aharon "Arnold" Robbins develops the GNU awk replacement. Gawk is a much more useful programming language, using awk as the lowest common denominator but now with a whole host of features not seen in the original. Gawk's only limitation is that it sits on the base of a language that was originally only designed to process text and easily identifiable columns from text files. It's not a general-purpose programming language, although it has many more capabilities than its history would suggest.
>
> Perl, which loosely stands for Practical Extraction and Reporting Language, or Practically Eclectic Rubbish Lister, was written by Larry Wall as a tool for summarizing the reports he had to produce at the time. Perl is now a more general-purpose language that you can use to develop everything from full-blown applications to small utilities. Perl has very strong text processing capabilities, making it ideal as a replacement for awk if you want to limit yourself to one language. But you don't want to do that, right?

The easiest way to use awk is as a more intelligent replacement for *cut* that also includes the facilities of a normal programming language. For example, awk naturally splits up a line by identifying the whitespace (spaces and tabs, including multiples) so that you can extract a particular column or columns without having to explicitly determine which columns or characters you need. For example, the *df* tool, as you already know, dumps out information about the size of a disk, its used space, and its device, when what you really want is a quick view of how much space is left. Using awk you can filter the output to include only the mount point and available space columns:

```
$ df -k|awk '{ print $6,"\t\t",$4 }'
Mounted             avail
/             15767
/usr          706255
/boot         8865
/var          84999
/export/contrib             528425
/export/os          272048
/export/proxy       57013
/usr/local          2424466
```

The $6 and $4 refer to the original columns output by *df*. awk automatically places each column it identifies into a variable, starting with column one in $1 and so on. Note that I've placed the program (*'{ print $6,"\t\t",$4 }'*) in single quotes. The braces around the script indicate the elements that should be executed for each line of input.

Because awk is programmable, you can also use it to summarize information for you. For example, to get an instant idea about the total amount of free space you need to add up the contents of the column and then report the total:

```
$ df -k|awk '{ s += $4  } END { print "Total free:",s }'
Total free: 25603667
```

The END indicates that the following braced block should be executed when the input has terminated. In this case, you sum up the value of column 4 and then report the final total.

awk or the free gawk are worth learning, even if it's just for the basic items like those above—it can speed up certain operations without the need to learn a full language like Perl or Python, and yet still remain relatively simplistic.

Putting Things in Order

Just occasionally you'll want the information that you extract or view to be in a more ordered format. Unsurprisingly, with all the other text processing and other tools available in Unix, there are tools that can help you organize and reduce the information to put it in a more usable format.

Sorting

File lists are automatically sorted alphabetically for you so you don't have to worry there, but there are other pieces of information that you want to sort and organize. For example, the *du* command will show you which directories are using up the most space, but the information is shown according to the names of the directories—for example, sorted alphabetically. You can sort numerically by using the *sort* command.

> **Solingo**
>
> The *du* command stands for disk usage. It accepts a list of files or directories and then reports on how much space they are using. Calculating the disk usage with *du* can be very useful when you are trying to trace where a particularly large file is, or when trying to identify who is using all the space on a user disk. Check back to Chapter 7, "Understanding Disk Management," for more information on how to use *du*.

What you want is to find out which directory is using up the most space. Solaris comes with the standard Unix command sort. By default this will sort the individual lines of input (from a file, or standard input) alphabetically, starting from the first character of each line. For example, the list:

```
Betty
Jack
Tom
Harry
Alfred
Emily
```

If you put these names into a file, names.txt and then supply the filename to sort, you should get:

```
$ sort names.txt
Alfred
Betty
Emily
Harry
Jack
Tom
```

Now let's go back to the *du* example. If you get a list of directory sizes within the */usr/local* directory (which is the default location for user contributed software), it's not immediately obvious which directory is using the most space:

```
$ du -sk
95        adm
983439    apps
170441    bin
537224    contrib
873       doc
```

```
170530   etc
34       html
2704     i386-pc-solaris2.8
10956    include
12023    info
477207   lib
1474     libexec
8        lost+found
51765    man
12883    samba
15088    sbin
156747   share
4968     ssl
```

If you run this through *sort*, you must use the *-n* command line option to indicate that you want the list sorted numerically:

```
$ du -sk|sort -n
sort -n size.lst
8        lost+found
34       html
95       adm
873      doc
1474     libexec
2704     i386-pc-solaris2.8
4968     ssl
10956    include
12023    info
12883    samba
15088    sbin
51765    man
156747   share
170441   bin
170530   etc
477207   lib
537224   contrib
983439   apps
```

The *sort* command is quite extensive—not only does it sort basic lines in alphabetical or numerical order, you can also …

- ◆ Sort lines in forward or reverse.
- ◆ Sort lines by comparing from a specific character.
- ◆ Sort lines on a particular column.
- ◆ Sort on multiple columns.

Check the *man* page for more information about the full capabilities.

Being Unique

One of the other situations where sorting is useful is when you want to determine a list of unique items from a file. For example, when examining a log file you may want to extract a list of the unique error messages in order to identify what errors occurred rather than having to trawl through the entire file to find out what the problems were.

Another use, and something that I use frequently, is when examining the log file from a web server. Often I'm not interested in performing a full diagnosis and examination of the information contained in the file; I just want an idea of which hosts have been accessing the file so I can get an idea of who has been viewing the site. If you have a look at the log file, you can see that the host information is in the first column:

```
203.195.198.254 - - [27/Jan/2002:01:03:45 -0800] "GET / HTTP/1.1" 200 1415 "-"
➥"Mozilla/4.0 (compatible; MSIE 5.0; Windows 95; DigExt)"
197.153.2.67 - - [27/Jan/2002:01:03:47 -0800] "GET /fwc.css HTTP/1.1" 200 2027
"http://www.foodware.net/" "Mozilla/4.0 (compatible; MSIE 5.0; Windows 95;
➥DigExt)"
```

You can use *cut* to extract the first column, but this will result in one big list of hosts, and you just want a list of all the deduped ones. The *uniq* command compares two lines and deletes one if the two are identical. On something like a list of hosts from a log file, the chances are that the same host may have accessed the site a number of times over an extended period. Combine *uniq* with *sort* and the entries will be sorted and deduped to arrive at a single unique list of hosts:

```
$ cut -d' ' -f1 access.log|sort|uniq
194.200.95.222
203.195.198.254
212.24.66.105
213.123.174.230
```

Alternatively you can use the *-u* command line option to *sort* to achieve the same result.

The Least You Need to Know

- ◆ You can view the contents of files without using an editor using the *more* and *cat* commands.
- ◆ The vi and emacs commands allow you to edit the file contents.
- ◆ Extracting the text from files can be achieved using *grep*.
- ◆ You can process files automatically using awk.
- ◆ You can sort and organize information using *sort* and *uniq*.

## Chapter 21

Automating Systems

In This Chapter

- ◆ Working with the crontab file
- ◆ Using the *at* command
- ◆ Monitoring jobs and security

Computers are supposed to make your life easier. But some operations on your computer are repetitive. For example, every morning you may want your machine to go off and get your email, and each week you might want to do a little spring cleaning. But if you had to tell the computer each time to do these operations, you would spend your life attached to the computer doing the same repetitive tasks each day, week, or month.

Unix comes with a built-in scheduling facility called cron, which can be set to automatically execute a given program or script either for a single execution at a set time (using the *at* command) or at regular intervals. I'll discuss both of these options in this chapter.

Using the crontab File

The cron system is merely a daemon that is used to execute specific jobs at a specific time. The cron daemon will execute jobs at regular intervals according to the contents of the crontab file. Each user can have their own crontab file (if you allow them to), and each line in the file defines the interval and command to be executed.

Sun Lotion

Your Solaris system will come already configured with some jobs set to automatically run at different intervals. Most of these relate to the management of logs—to ensure that the size of the log doesn't grow so large that it consumes the disk space on a machine—and to less-critical jobs such as updating the real time clock (part of the hardware of a machine), with the real clock being updated by the operating system.

For example, look at the following typical crontab file:

```
10 3 * * 0,4 /etc/cron.d/logchecker
10 3 * * 0   /usr/lib/newsyslog
15 3 * * 0 /usr/lib/fs/nfs/nfsfind
1 2 * * * [ -x /usr/sbin/rtc ] && /usr/sbin/rtc -c > /dev/null 2>&1
30 3 * * * [ -x /usr/lib/gss/gsscred_clean ] && /usr/lib/gss/gsscred_clean
6 4 * * * /export/http/webs/mchome/toons/getcomics.pl
0 22 * * 1,2,3,4,5 /usr/local/etc/backup/qbackup
1 * * * * /usr/local/etc/update-ntp.sh
0,15,30,45 * * * * /usr/local/etc/mediaweb/bin/status.pl
0,15,30,45 * * * * /usr/local/etc/mediaweb/bin/uptime.pl
5,20,35,50 * * * * /usr/local/etc/mediaweb/bin/collector.pl
```

There are six columns in each line. The last column is the command to be executed—you can only really execute one command (although you can separate the commands by semicolons); if you want to execute multiple commands, it's best to create a script and then place the location of the script into the crontab file. Note as well that all the entries use the full path to the script or command to be executed. This is because cron executes the commands within a bare shell—if you need to set environment variables (such as the PATH) in order for your script to execute, then you will need to set those values within the script as well.

The first five columns specify the interval. They are, in order (which is important!):

1. Minute of the hour (0–59)
2. Hour of the day (0–23)
3. Day of the month (1–31)
4. Month of the year (1–12)
5. Day of the week (0–6, where 0=Sunday)

In each case, you can specify a precise value, a list of values (separated by a comma), or a range (you specify the start and end values, separated by a hyphen; for example, 1-5 is equivalent to 1,2,3,4,5). If you specify an asterisk (*) then it's treated as a wildcard and therefore applicable to any of the possible values.

So, the specification:

```
1 * * * *
```

would execute a command at 1 minute past the hour every day.

```
1 * * * 1-5
```

would execute a command at 1 minute past the hour on Monday to Friday only.

```
0,15,30,45 8-20 * * 0
```

would execute a command every 15 minutes between 8 A.M. and 8:45 P.M. on a Sunday.

Sun Screen

Be very careful with crontab specifications—use a wildcard or value in the wrong place and you end up with a command being executed too many times, or not enough.

One of the most common is to use * 8-20 * * * and expect the job to be executed on the hour, every hour between 8 A.M. and 8:59 P.M. Instead the command will be run every minute between 8 A.M. and 8 P.M. You should instead use 0 8-20 * * *.

Another common trap is to use 0 1 31 * * to run a command at 1 A.M. on the last day of the month. In reality, it will only run the command on the last day of the month for months with 31 days. If you specifically want the last day of the month, you need three separate entries—one for months with 30 days, one for months with 31, and one for February (which has 28 or 29).

Updating Your crontab

Each user has the ability to have their own crontab (it doesn't exist until it's created). To edit your crontab, use the *-e* command line option to the *crontab* command:

```
$ crontab -e
```

This will open your existing crontab, or create a new one if it doesn't exist, in your favorite editor (vi, emacs, or other). You can then edit, add, or delete entries accordingly. When you save and exit the editor, the crontab will be checked to make sure it's valid and then the real crontab will be updated.

If you have superuser privileges, you can specify the name of a user on the command line to open and edit that user's crontab file:

```
% crontab -e mc
```

Viewing Your crontab

You use the *-l* command line option to list the contents of your crontab:

```
$ crontab -l
4 4 * * * /export/http/webs/mchome/tv/getbs.pl
6 4 * * * /export/http/webs/mchome/toons/getcomics.pl
```

Deleting Your crontab

To remove your crontab completely use the *-r* option:

```
$ crontab -r
```

Using at

Running jobs overnight is a common task used by many companies to allow them to create reports and perform other major jobs that can be executed overnight when the machine is less busy. Universities often use the system as well, to calculate large computations overnight while giving them the fastest possible times during the day.

Historically, the need to execute these jobs overnight or during specific down periods was because the computing power—generally provided by a big mainframe in the basement—was expensive, and different departments were actually charged internally for using the computer. For example, the sales department might ask the computer department to run a sales report. During the day, it might cost 50¢ to produce the report, but overnight only 25¢.

To complement the process, you also had operators whose sole job was to monitor the job overnight and ensure that the printer didn't jam or run out of paper, and that if the machine crashed, the job was resubmitted.

Today, nearly everybody in a company has access to a computer on their desk, and they have 20, 30, or more times the computing power of the old mainframes. Even complex reports can be executed in real time while the user waits—they can even be run in the background.

The Solaris cron system still allows you to assign jobs to different queues, which can be used to limit the number of simultaneous jobs executed, and projects so that you can track their execution and if necessary charge people for their usage.

The *at* command does exactly what it suggests; it executes a program or script *at* a specified time. Unlike using crontab, which sets up a regular job, the at command executes the program only once at the time you specify. You can use this for simple operations—like submitting a download or nonstandard backup to be performed overnight, as well as using the system to execute regular jobs at nonregular times.

Submitting a Job

To submit a job, you must specify the time and/or date that you want the job to be executed on the command line. The command accepts a number of different formats for this:

◆ A time, specified either by a one- or two-digit number—treated as a whole hour— or a four-digit number (including a pair of two-digit numbers separated by a colon) which will treat the time as an hour/minute value. You can specify the time in 12- and 24-hour formats.

◆ A date can be specified as a month name and number specification (for example, Feb 22).

For example, you can set a job to run at 10:00 P.M. using any of the following:

```
$ at 10:00pm
$ at 22:00pm
```

or queue a job on a specific date and time using:

```
$ at 11:00am Mar 26
```

Note that if you specify only a time, and that time has already passed, then the job is automatically scheduled for that time tomorrow. For example, if it's 9:30 A.M. and you specify that a job should be executed at 9:00 A.M., then it will execute at 9:00 A.M. tomorrow. If you specify a time in the future, then it will be scheduled for today. For example, a job submitted for 10:00 A.M. at 9:30 A.M. will be executed today at 10:00 A.M.

You can also use a number of shorthand terms for both date and time components:

◆ **now** indicates that the job should be executed immediately.

◆ **noon** indicates that the job should be executed at noon (12:00 P.M.).

◆ **midnight** indicates that the job should be executed at midnight (12:00 A.M.).

◆ **today** indicates that the job should be executed today (at the time you specify).

◆ **tomorrow** indicates that the job should be executed tomorrow (at the time you specify).

These can be combined together with standard date and time specifications, for example:

```
$ at 11:00am tomorrow
```

```
$ at midnight today
$ at noon Mar 26
```

Finally, you can also add an additional modifier that will modify the execution time. The modifier is a number preceded by a plus sign (+), with the additional quantifier of minutes, hours, days, weeks, months, or years. The word "next" is equivalent to "+ 1." For example, to schedule a job for this time next week you can use either of:

```
$ at now next week
$ at now + 1 week
```

Once you've specified the date and time that you want the job to occur, you will be presented with an at> prompt. It's here that you type in the commands that you want to execute. The interface is essentially just an inline shell—you can type in any command or phrase that you would use within your shell, just as if you had typed in the sequence at a standard command line.

What you type in is saved, and then executed as a shell script at the time you specified on the command line. For example, you might want to get a list of the processes running overnight because you want to monitor the progress of a particular job. You could do that using:

```
$ at midnight
at> ps -efl|mailx -s 'Process list' root
```

Or you could do something more complex. For example, the following code would package up the contents of */export/http/webs*, which keeps all the websites, and copies and archives them into another directory:

```
$ at midnight
at> cd /export/http/webs
at> datetime='date +%Y%m%d%H%M'
at> tar cf webs.$datetime.tar ./*
at> bzip2 -v -9 webs.$datetime.tar
at> mv webs.$datetime.tar.bz2 /export/backups
```

Once you've finished entering the commands you want executed, press Control-D to terminate the input. You'll be prompted with the exact date and time that your script will be executed, and a reference number.

Note that the commands you enter will be executed in the same environment in which they were created—that is, they will be executed using the same shell, and using the same environment variables, including the PATH. Unlike a job submitted to crontab, you can therefore just enter the commands you want to execute as you would at the command line itself—the *at* command will take care of the rest.

Repeating a Job

The *at* system isn't really designed to replace the functionality of cron when used with crontab. But that doesn't mean that you can't set up a repeating event using *at*. Let's take the previous web logging script as an example. Let's say you wanted this executed every 24 hours, but not at exactly the same time each night (which you could do with crontab). All you need to do is place the commands you entered into a script (called archive_webs), and then add a final line to the script which reads:

```
at now tomorrow <archive_webs
```

to have the script executed the next day, at the time this script terminated. When submitting the job, you supply the name of the script:

```
$ at midnight
at> archive_webs
```

When the script terminates, it will automatically resubmit itself for execution the next day.

Sun Lotion

I've used systems like this in the past to automatically resubmit a job at varying intervals depending on the state of the rest of the script. For example, logs were archived between 1 and 7 days, according to how much data was in the logs. Each time the script was run, it would check the log size—if it was large enough to archive, it would be archived and the script would be resubmitted for the next night. If it was very small, then nothing would be done, and the job would be resubmitted for 2 or more nights in advance.

During a typical working week, I'd get a log every day. When work was light, or during the holidays, I'd get a log once or twice a week according to how much work had been done. You could achieve the same by writing a complex crontab specification, but you need to keep changing it according to how busy you are, and when the holidays are each year.

Checking the Job Queue

The *at -l* command will show you a list of jobs waiting to be executed:

```
$ at -l
1011906000.a    Thu Jan 24 21:00:00 2002
1011913200.a    Thu Jan 24 23:00:00 2002
```

Note that it only shows the list of jobs for the user who invoked the command, not all the jobs waiting in the queue.

Sun Screen

It's not possible as a system administrator to get any more information about the queued jobs than a user can using the standard tools. This can be a major problem, and I've seen many people battling with a machine that seems to be continually running new jobs and soaking up resources that are affecting the machine's performance.

To find out what jobs are waiting to be executed, look in the /var/spool/cron/atjobs directory. You should find one file for each waiting job, and each file contains the environment and other settings in place when the job was created, followed by the commands that were entered.

Removing a Job

To remove a job, use the -r command line option and the job ID given when the job was created to remove the job from the queue. For example, from the job submission:

```
$ at 9:32
at> ...
commands will be executed using /usr/local/bin/bash
job 1011951120.a at Fri Jan 25 09:32:00 2002
```

You get a job ID of 1011951120.a (phew!). To remove it, use:

```
$ at -r 1011951120.a
```

You won't get any notification that the job has been removed, but you can always check the job queue using *at -l*.

Monitoring a Job

Unless you happen to be around at the time that a job is executing, the chances are that you won't be able to monitor its progress. Not to worry; there are a number of ways in which you can keep track of what your crontab and *at* jobs are doing.

With jobs submitted through crontab, any output generated by the commands will automatically be mailed to the user once the job has completed. You can turn this off by redirecting the standard output and error streams from the command in the crontab entry:

```
1 2 * * * archive_logs > /dev/null 2>&1
```

With *at* you will not normally be notified when the command completes, but you can specify the -m command line option to *at*. Using this option forces cron to email you when the job has completed.

As system administrator, you can monitor which jobs were executed and when by examining the contents of the */var/cron/log* file. You can see a sample from the following file:

```
>  CMD: /usr/local/etc/mediaweb/bin/status.pl
>  root 19284 c Thu Jan 24 04:15:00 2002
>  CMD: /usr/local/etc/mediaweb/bin/uptime.pl
>  root 19285 c Thu Jan 24 04:15:00 2002
<  root 19284 c Thu Jan 24 04:15:01 2002
<  root 19285 c Thu Jan 24 04:15:21 2002
>  CMD: /usr/local/etc/mediaweb/bin/collector.pl
>  root 19299 c Thu Jan 24 04:20:00 2002
<  root 19299 c Thu Jan 24 04:20:00 2002
```

Each CMD line is the command line used to execute the job. Lines preceded by > indicate when a job was started, and jobs preceded by < show when the job was completed. You can use this in combination with the ID number (which is actually the process ID) to determine how long each job took to complete. For example, you can see from this that the uptime.pl script took 21 seconds to complete, whereas the status.pl script took only 1 second.

Enforcing Security

You won't always want everybody to have access to the cron system. Access to the system is controlled by two files for each service; for example, */etc/cron.d/cron.allow* and */etc/cron.d/cron.deny* for crontab, and */usr/lib/cron/at.allow* and */usr/lib/cron/at.deny* for the *at* command.

Access to both systems is provided according to the following rules:

- ◆ If neither the allow or deny file exist then only the superuser or one of the administration accounts can use the system.

- ◆ If the deny file exists, and it contains the name of a user then that user is denied access.

- ◆ If the allow file exists, and the user's name is in it, the user can use the system.

- ◆ If the allow file does not exist, but the deny file does exist and does not contain the user's name, the user has access.

- ◆ If the allow and deny files exist, and the user is mentioned in the deny file, the user does not have access.

Complicated isn't it? Probably one of the most complicated sets of rules you'll come across. To make it easier, refer to Table 21.1, which shows the state of the files, whether a user is in each of the files, and what access they have as determined by the deny and allow files.

Table 21.1   User Access to the *at* and *crontab* Commands

Allow File	Deny File	User in Allow	User in Deny	User Access
No	No	-	-	No
Yes	No	No	-	No
Yes	No	Yes	-	Yes
No	Yes	-	No	Yes
No	Yes	-	Yes	No
Yes	Yes	Yes	No	Yes
Yes	Yes	No	Yes	No
Yes	Yes	Yes	Yes	Yes
Yes	Yes	No	No	No

The format of the files is simple—just a user name on each line.

The Least You Need to Know

- ◆ To schedule a job to be executed at regular intervals, use the *crontab* command.
- ◆ To schedule a job to run once at some future point in time, use the *at* command.
- ◆ You can monitor the progress of a job by examining the log files, or by receiving an email from the system when a job has completed.
- ◆ You can secure either system by specifying explicitly which users are allowed or denied access.

Part 5

Tuning and Diagnostics

No machine ever runs without some kind of fault, and diagnosing the problem can be difficult. Faults can be divided into two main types—those that affect the operation of the machine and those that affect its performance. In this section, I'll be looking at both types, including some tips on preventing and avoiding problems, along with methods for identifying and hopefully resolving any problems you might come across.

Backing Up and Restoring File Systems

In This Chapter

◆ Backing up to files with *tar*

◆ Compressing files to save space

◆ Using the *ufsdump* and *ufsrestore* commands

◆ Restoring files in emergency situations

If I had a dime for every time a user approached me and said "I've deleted one of my files, I don't suppose you'd have a copy?" I'd be a very rich man, and you probably wouldn't be reading what I'm writing here. But accidental deletions are not the only threat. Hardware failure is a possibility, however reliable a company will make out its products to be. Computers can also be stolen or damaged, and fires and other threats are unfortunately common enough to be the root of system failure.

Backing up your machine, especially if the information on it is important, should therefore be considered to be a vital part of your daily regime, as automatic as taking a shower and feeding the cat. You don't use a backup solution because you expect these problems to occur, but to act as an insurance policy in case they happen in the future. Avoid backups only if you have a reliable crystal ball!

In this chapter, I'll discuss some of the methods available for backing up your machine, including tips on reducing the size of the files that you create.

Using tar

You've already, briefly, seen the *tar* command when you looked at installing software from the source code in Chapter 4, "Installing Solaris." In that chapter, I concentrated only on extracting an entire set of files from a presupplied archive. Now it's time to look at it from the point of view of an archiving and backup solution.

Creating an Archive on Tape

You create a tar archive using the *c* option (for create!); you then need to specify the files that you want to back up. If you include a directory, then tar will include the entire contents of that directory—including any files and other directories and their contents. Also included in the archive are the owner, group, and file permissions for each file or directory—if you back up a directory with tar, you can completely recover the contents of the directory.

By default, the *tar* command will write to the first tape device specified in */etc/default/tar*—this is typically the device */dev/rmt/0n*—the first tape drive on the system. For example, you can create an archive on tape of the */etc* directory using:

```
$ tar c /etc
```

Unlike disk devices, which are identified according to the controller, device, disk, and partition, tape devices are identified by a number which increments each time a tape device has been identified as being attached to a controller, in ascending controller order. So the first tape device on controller 0 will be */dev/rmt/0*, the second on controller 0 will be */dev/rmt/1*, and a third on controller 2 will be */dev/rmt/2*.

The numeric identifier is then suffixed with a number of different letters which you use to select tape features. For example, an n in the suffix indicates that the tape should not be rewound when a tape operation completes. You use this when you want to append a number of different operations to the same tape while avoiding overwriting the contents. The c suffix switches on hardware compression, if the drive supports it.

For example, you could write without rewinding to the second tape drive using compression by using */dev/rmt/1cn*.

The exact list of supported options will depend on the tape drive you have and how it is recognized by the system. Some tape drives will require additional code or configuration to enable Solaris to support all their features, and instructions on this should come with your tape drive.

To specify an alternative tape device, use the *f* option—you must then supply the name of the device to use immediately following your options. For example:

```
$ tar cf /dev/rmt/1cn /etc
```

To monitor what happens during the archiving process, add the *v* (for verbose) option—this reports each file as it is written to tape:

```
$ tar cvf /dev/rmt/1cn /etc
a /etc/ 0K
a /etc/default/ 0K
a /etc/default/sys-suspend 1K
a /etc/default/cron 1K
```

The preceding "a" indicates the file has been added, and the trailing figure shows the size of the file.

For absolute compatibility and safety, avoid specifying the full path to the directories or files that you want to back up. Some systems will only recover those files back to the exact same location you specified. Although this is fine during a backup/recovery procedure when you want this to happen, it also has the effect of overwriting whatever was already there!

To get around this, change to the directory (or parent directory) which contains the files you want to archive and then explicitly prefix the files/directories you want to archive with *./*. This creates an archive containing files relative to the current directory:

```
$ cd /
$ tar c ./etc
```

Then when you extract the files they will be extracted into the current directory—useful if you want to recover an archive into a separate location and only copy across certain files to their proper places.

Creating an Archive on File

Okay, this is probably the easiest thing you'll learn here—to create an archive in a file, rather than on tape, just supply the name of the file you want to create in place of the name of the tape device:

```
$ tar cf archive.tar ./etc
```

The previous example creates a file called archive.tar in the current directory containing the contents of the file or directory *etc* from the current directory. You can also create archive files elsewhere, just by supplying the path:

```
$ tar tf /tmp/archive.tar ./etc
```

Note that I'm using an extension here to identify the file as a tar file—as with other parts of Unix this is not a requirement, but it is a visual aid to help you deal with the file later.

Archiving Specific Files

If you want to be more selective about the files you choose to include in the tar file you are creating then you can embed a more specific selection of files into the command line. For example:

```
$ tar cf archive.tar myfile.txt mylib.so mysource.c
```

You can also use the normal wildcards and constructs supported by the shell you are using—you can back up all the C source files and objects using:

```
$ tar cf archive.tar *.[co]
```

For archiving files according to their last modification time you can use the *find* command we used back in Chapter 18, "Navigating and Managing Files." Just embed the *find* command into the *tar* command using backticks. For example, to create an archive containing the files that have been modified in the last day, use:

```
$ tar cf archive.tar `find . -mtime -1`
```

Sun Lotion _____

The GNU version of tar incorporates a number of enhancements, including the ability to compress the archive using *compress* or *gzip* as it is being written to a file or to tape, and the ability to automatically back up files that have changed since a particular date, and to span an archive across multiple tapes. You can obtain GNU tar from the usual archives; see Appendix A, "Resource Guide," for more information.

Getting a List of Files from an Archive

The *t* option produces a table of contents within an archive:

```
$ tar tf archive.tar |more
/etc/
/etc/default/
/etc/default/sys-suspend
/etc/default/cron
/etc/default/devfsadm
```

To get extended information, including the ownership and permission information, add the *v* option:

```
$ tar tvf archive.tar |more
drwxr-xr-x   0/3         0 Jan 24 12:53 2002 /etc/
drwxr-xr-x   0/3         0 Dec 30 10:33 2001 /etc/default/
-rw-r--r--   0/3       803 Mar 29 23:41 2001 /etc/default/sys-suspend
-r-xr-xr-x   0/2        12 Dec 30 09:55 2001 /etc/default/cron
-r--r--r--   0/3       204 Dec 30 09:55 2001 /etc/default/devfsadm
-r--r--r--   0/3      3388 Dec 30 09:55 2001 /etc/default/dhcpagent
```

Extracting from an Archive

You use the *x* option, rather than *c*, to extract files from an archive, whether that archive is on tape or in a file. For example, we can extract your *etc* directory from your archive file into the current directory using:

```
$ tar xf archive.tar
```

To extract specific files, give the file's name and path *as it was stored in the archive* on the command line. For example, if you backed up */etc* using the explicit path, using:

```
$ tar cf archive.tar /etc
```

and you want to recover */etc/hosts*, use:

```
$ tar xf archive.tar /etc/hosts
```

If you archived it using:

```
$ tar cf archive.tar ./etc
```

use:

```
$ tar xf archive.tar ./etc/hosts
```

You can also use the standard wildcards to extract a range of files. For example, you can extract the contents of */etc/mail* using:

```
$ tar xf archive.tar ./etc/mail/*
```

Using tar to Copy Directories

One of the useful capabilities of tar is that you can use tar to copy the files and directory structure from one location to another, including ownership and permission information. This is similar in operation to the *cp* command when used with the *-pr* command line options, but it can be more reliable, especially over slow network links and NFS disks.

To use this method, change to the destination directory where you want the files to be copied to and then use:

```
$ (cd source; tar cfp - ./*)|tar xvfp -
```

where source is the name of the source directory where you want the files copied from. The pipe between the two commands pipes the standard output of the first *tar* to the standard input of the second, and the hyphen in place of the filename indicates the standard input/output should be used during the creation and extraction.

The *p* option tells *tar* to faithfully preserve permission, ownership, and Access Control List (ACL) information during the process. If you are root this is the default option, but only root can extract setuid and setgid files.

The other benefit of this method is that it annotates the process when you supply the *v* option to *tar*, as each file is reported. Specifying this option on both calls to *tar* will annotate both sides, providing useful visual check if something is not operating properly.

You can of course perform the same operation from the source directory:

```
$ tar cfp - ./* |(cd source; tar xvfp - )
```

Compressing Archives

One of the problems with backups is that they take up as much space (and in general, slightly more) than the size of the original files. For a drive with 2GB of files, you'll need another 2GB just to be able to back it up. The requirement for such huge amounts of space is one of the reasons we use tape, rather than additional hard disks to back up a machine—in megabytes/dollar a tape is much cheaper to use than another hard disk.

All the compression you'll see in the following section can be used to compress any file on your machine so that it takes up less space on your disk or when transferred to another machine over the Internet. Primarily, though, these tools are used to compress archives created using *tar* and *cpio*, whether they are archives, backups, or simply a collection of files being exchanged with other users.

Compression Techniques

The compression tools we will look at in this chapter are loss-less. That means if I compress a file, and then uncompress it I should get exactly the same file contents back.

On a document such as a letter this is obviously important—you don't want to compress something and then during decompression find out that it's removed every 5th word!

The same is true for any files that you decide to compress as part of a backup—the backup will be no good to you if it doesn't put you back into the state you were in when the backup was created.

There are, however, situations where you can afford to lose some quality of information and detail, without it affecting our impression and understanding. In particular, audio and video data can be compressed with lossy formats without us noticing the effects. For example, the Joint Picture Experts Groups (JPEG) format used for still images loses precise information about each individual pixel in the picture on the basis that certain elements only need to give an impression of their appearance, for example, a blue sky is a blue sky.

The Motion Picture Experts Group (MPEG) format used for video uses a similar method. Rather than recording a pixel-by-pixel representation of each frame, MPEG uses a combination of the JPEG methods and comparative analysis between frames. For example, if someone in a film moves across the screen, it's likely that some of the pixels in the two images will be shared—so the MPEG standard only records the pixels that change between each frame.

Finally, in audio, the MP3 format—currently popular as a compression tool for CDs—is a lossy compression system. The MP3 format removes the highest and lowest frequencies from an audio track and also reduces the overall resolution of the sound in order to reduce the raw track from the 60MB it takes up on an audio CD down to anything between 1 and 30MB.

Compress

The *compress* tool is one of the oldest compression mechanisms available, having been part of the Unix operating system since the early versions. The *compress* tool works by taking a character pair and creating a new multi-bit value—for example, converting the sequence 'aa' into a 9-bit value, you reduce the overall space required to store the character pair from 16 bits to 9 bits. This is an extreme example, but you can generally compress a file to about a tenth of its size using *compress* if it's a plain text file, with a lower ratio for binary files such as databases and applications.

To compress a file with *compress*, you just supply the name of the file on the command line:

```
$ compress myfile.txt
```

If you add the *-v* command line option, then you will also be told the compression ratio achieved:

```
$ compress -v dutdump.text
dutdump.text: Compression: 87.01% -- replaced with dutdump.text.Z
```

That's a compression ratio of about 8:1—not bad for a text file. The file you specify will be deleted and replaced with the compressed version, which will share the same name with .Z appended to the end.

To decompress, use uncompress:

```
$ uncompress dutdump.text.Z
```

Compress is actually a standard part of nearly all Unix flavors, making it the ideal tool to compress files for exchange with other Unix platforms. It's also supported by the StuffIt and WinZip tools under Mac OS and Windows.

Gzip

The *gzip* format was developed by GNU as a replacement for *compress* (as part of their attempt to provide free Unix tools) and to improve upon the compression abilities of compress, which are generally poor compared to other formats. Although gzip is a GNU tool, it's now provided free with Solaris—useful, as it's now the most popular format for compressing Unix-related files on the Internet.

The *gzip* system uses the Lempel-Ziv compression algorithm, as used in the WinZip, PKZip, and StuffIt applications available under both Mac OS and Windows. However, *gzip* is not compatible with these formats. Compressions ratios can be as high as 50:1 for some text files, although more usually the ratios are between 20:1 and 8:1 for text files, and slightly less than 4:1 for binary files.

Usage is identical to compress; to *gzip* a file just supply the filename:

```
$ gzip myfile.txt
```

Again, using the *-v* option gives you the compression information:

```
$ gzip -v dutdump.text
dutdump.text:            96.2% -- replaced with dutdump.text.gz
```

That's a compression ratio of about 26:1—you've compressed a 1.6MB file down to about 61KB. You can also control the priority used between speed and size when compressing the files. You do this by supplying a numeric option between one (*-1*), for speed, and nine (*-9*) for size. The default value is *-6*, a reasonable compromise between the two.

As with compress, the original file is removed and replaced with the compressed version, although this time .gz is appended to the filename.

To decompress a file compressed with *gzip*, use *gunzip*:

```
$ gunzip dutdump.text.gz
```

BZip2

Bzip2 uses the Burrows-Wheeler transform to compress files. The compression process is much more efficient than either *gzip* or *compress*, particularly on text files. Although not widely used, and certainly not as widely used as either *compress* or *gzip*, it is very popular under Linux.

The *bzip2* tool is not installed as standard with Solaris. If you are using Solaris 8 you'll need to download it from Sun Freeware or download and compile it from Freshmeat. If you are using Solaris 9, check the Early Access (EA) directory on the Solaris Software CD 2 of 2. See Appendix A for more details.

To compress a file you again use the same basic process as for *compress* and *gzip*:

```
$ bzip2 myfile.txt
```

The *-v* option also shows the compression ratio and precise information about the new and old sizes:

```
$ bzip2 -v dutdump.text
  dutdump.text: 48.047:1,  0.167 bits/byte, 97.92% saved, 1626572 in, 33854 out.
```

Even at standard compression rates, we've created a file half the size of that produced by *gzip*. The *bzip2* command also supports the same numerical option to select between compression ratios, although in general the *bzip2* tool will choose the most efficient mechanism for the type of file you are compressing.

As with the other compression tools, the original file will be deleted and replaced with a file of the same name with .bz2 suffix. To decompress, use *bunzip2*:

```
$ bunzip2 dutdump.text.bz2
```

Using ufsdump

Solaris comes with a standard backup and recovery toolset consisting of the *ufsdump* and *ufsrestore* commands. The *ufsdump* command dumps the contents of a file system on to tape or another file.

Dumping a File System to Tape

To use the *ufsdump* system you first need to appreciate how *ufsdump* decides to back up files. You specify which files to back up by supplying a "dump level" to the *ufsdump* command. The dump level is a number between 0 and 9, with 0 triggering a full dump of the file system (for example, backing up every file). Successive numbers after this only back up the files that have changed since the previous backup using a lower dump level.

Confused? Okay, not surprising—as you've already seen elsewhere, these seemingly plain and simple systems turn out to be quite difficult to understand. It's probably best to demonstrate what happens by looking at the effects of using the different dump levels on different days. Table 22.1 lists 4 different scenarios—check out of the table, and then you'll go through the effects in more detail.

Table 22.1   Dump Levels and Their Effects with *ufsdump*

Scenario	Monday	Tuesday	Wednesday	Thursday	Friday
1	0	5	5	5	5
2	0	1	2	3	4
3	0	1	5	1	5
4	0	5	5	5	1

Each of the scenarios provides different benefits, and different pitfalls. In each case, always do a full backup on the Monday, and assume that you're using a new backup tape each night:

◆ In scenario 1, from Tuesday you perform a backup of all the files that changed since Monday. For example, on Tuesday you back up all the files changed on Tuesday. On Thursday you back up all the files that were changed on Tuesday, Wednesday, and Thursday. Using this method you get a high level of resilience—you should be able to restore back to any specific day should you need to.

◆ In scenario 2, on Tuesday you back up the files changed since Monday. On Wednesday however, you only back up the files changed since Tuesday. On Thursday only those changed since Wednesday and so on. Using this method, you reduce the number of tapes and the time required to back up each night, because you only record the day's changes. However, to perform a full restore you must restore from the tape used for each day. For example, to recover to the state you were in on Friday you would have to recover from the tapes used for Monday, Tuesday, Wednesday, and Thursday night.

◆ Scenario 3 is a combination of the first two scenarios—you back up the changes since Monday on Tuesday night, and the changes since Tuesday on Wednesday night. Come Thursday, you back up the changes since Monday night again. You can now restore to any day by using only three tapes—Mondays plus Tuesday and Wednesday or Thursday and Friday.

◆ In scenario 4, you back up incrementally each night, and then produce a final backup with the changes since Monday on Friday. You can restore to any day, but you can also restore a system on a Monday morning using only two tapes—Monday's and Friday's.

The Ideal Backup System

Unless you have a particular need to or restriction on the number of backup tapes you use, the best method is to use one backup tape each day—even if you are doing full backups each day. Each tape (or tape collection, if you need more than one tape) should be used to hold backups for all the file systems.

To further improve your situation in the event of ever needing them, use two sets of tapes—one for each alternate week. This will require a minimum of ten tapes, but it will also ensure that you always have two full backup tapes and two sets of incremental tapes. If one tape set fails, you should be able to use the other tape set in an emergency—having to go back five days is better than not being able to go back at all!

Finally, you should always think about tape storage—it's no good keeping a reliable set of backup tapes and then having them stolen during a break-in or having them burn up in the fire along with the rest of your equipment. You will have wasted time and money buying the backup equipment and tapes and performing the backups.

Instead, at the very least keep your tapes in a fireproof (and hopefully locked and secure) safe on your property. You can get units fairly cheaply now that will survive house and small office fires from your local office supplies shop. In an ideal situation, you should keep your tapes off site—either in another building on site *not* connected to rest of the site, or better still, take them home. The chances of your home and office both suffering the sort of damage that would require the backup tapes is very small.

Running ufsdump

To use *ufsdump*, all you need to do is specify the dump level and any other options, plus the name of the file system or device that we want to backup. Table 22.2 lists the more commonly used options.

Table 22.2   Options for Backing Up Using *ufsdump*

Option	Description
0 through 9	The dump level.
a file	Writes the table of contents (list of files backed up) to file.
f file	Writes the dump to the specified file or device.
u	Records the dump level and date in */etc/dumpdates*.
v	Verifies the tape after the backup has completed.

CAUTION

Sun Screen

When doing a backup with *ufsdump* you should ensure that the disk is currently not in use by any users or applications. Otherwise, any changes made to the disk during the dumping process will not be reflected in the dump, and may in fact corrupt the information in the dump, rendering your backup useless. Either use *umount* to take the drive off line, or switch to single user mode before performing a backup.

For example, to run a full level dump of */opt* to the default tape device (*/dev/rmt/0*) with verification, use:

```
% ufsdump 0v /opt
```

To back up to a different tape device, use:

```
% ufsdump 0vf /dev/rmt/1cn /opt
```

The */etc/dumpdates* file can be a handy reference as it will tell you which file systems were backed up, and when and at what level. You should use this to determine the backup status of a system—assuming you are using *ufsdump* for your backup!

Restoring a File System from Tape

To restore a file system, just use *ufsrestore*. By default, it will attempt to recover the files on the default device, writing the files and directories into your current directory. For example, to recover a copy of the */etc* directory into the */tmp* directory from the default device use:

```
$ cd /tmp
$ ufsrestore
```

This creates a subdirectory in */tmp* (for example, */tmp/etc*) into which the files would be restored. To specify an alternate device or file, use the *f* option:

```
$ ufsrestore f /dev/rmt/1cn
```

To restore a file system in full, you'll need to use the *r* option to tell *ufsrestore* to completely recreate the entire file system. You'll need to insert the most recent level 0 backup tape, and then all subsequent tapes that contain changes since the level 0 dump was produced, each time using *ufsrestore* with the *r* option.

Restoring Selected Files

To restore specific files, use the *x* option:

```
$ ufsrestore x /etc/passwd /etc/default
```

Restoring in an Emergency

There are times when you will need to restore in an emergency situation when either the entire machine has failed, or when the drive holding one of the two critical file systems— / and */usr*—have failed.

In this situation, you will need to do the following:

1. Boot from a CD-ROM—the standard installation CDs should do fine. Select the option to get a command prompt so that you can run the necessary commands to rebuild the file system and disks.

2. Set up the disk or disk partition using *format* or *fdisk*.

3. Create the file system on the disk using *newfs*.

4. Mount the file system to be restored at some neutral point. I tend to use */mnt/root* or */mnt/usr* or similar.

5. Change to the directory of the new file system.

6. Run *ufsrestore* or *tar* to recover the files from tape.

7. Repeat for any other file systems that you need to recreate.

8. Unmount the new file system.

9. Use *fsck* to check its contents.

10. Modify */etc/vfstab* (remounting the file system, if necessary) to reflect the new location of the file system—this is vital for the root and */usr* file systems—if you do not change this option then your machine will fail to boot up properly.

11. If you've recovered the root file system, you need to run installboot to install the necessary boot code to allow the operating system to be found by the boot loader. Without this option, your machine will not be able to find the operating system when it switches on.

Reboot. If things don't work okay, go back to stage one and check that everything is in place—in particular, make sure the boot block and */etc/vfstab* stages (10 and 11) were completed properly.

Commercial Alternatives

The *ufsdump* and *ufsrestore* tools are a useful inclusion in the Solaris system but they are by no means a full solution to the problems of backing up. There are a number of deficiencies with the system—starting with limitations about what is and isn't backed up (it isn't possible, for example, to exclude a directory you don't need). Tape and device support are also relatively limited—although it will use most tapes and even autoloaders, there is no provision for using multiple devices.

If the information you are storing on your machine is vital to your work or business, then I would seriously recommend you investigate a commercial backup solution. There are many available, but the market leader is Legato Networker (www.legato.com). It allows you to back up a machine and any other clients on the network (kits are available for all Unix platforms, Mac OS, Windows, and Netware) and special extensions are available for safely backing up databases and email systems without risk of corruption.

One of the coolest features though is the tape backup management system. You can back up to a number of devices simultaneously, reducing your overall backup time. Better still, you can back up to a number of devices connected to a number of different servers simultaneously—so you could back up the entire network by utilizing all the tape drives across your network without having to have them all connected to the same machine.

Legato Networker is an impressive package, and Sun was so impressed that they repackaged Networker to make Solstice Backup. You shouldn't really need any more of an endorsement than that!

The Least You Need to Know

- Use *tar c* to create a tar archive on a tape.
- Add the *f* option, and a file or device, to back up to something other than the default tape device.
- Use *x* to recover information from a tar archive.
- Use *ufsdump*, a dump level, and file system name to back up a file system to tape.
- To restore the information, change to the directory where you want the file system restored to and use the *ufsrestore* command.

Solving Problems Accessing Resources

In This Chapter

- File and disk access
- Printers
- Network resources

I don't ever guarantee that you will be able to use a computer without having some kind of problem. The level of your problem or difficulty will depend entirely on a combination of your own expertise and knowledge and the way in which a particular machine has been set up.

It goes without saying that occasionally your own state of mind will affect your ability to use your computer or access a particular element—we've all been in the position where we've gone "tut" or "tsk" and rolled our eyes into the top of our heads as we realize that it was us, not the computer, doing it wrong.

In this chapter, I'll discuss some of the main problems associated with accessing and using resources. By resources I mean everything from the machine itself down to the files and services provided by that machine. It's not intended to be an exhaustive list, and if you have a query or difficulty with your machine that you can't obviously find a solution for, I suggest you visit my website (www.mcwords.com). Although I can't guarantee to have an answer, I will try to help if I can, and any queries which I think will help other people will be available on the site.

A Background to Problem Solving

Years ago (circa 1985) when I helped out at a local computer shop, we would frequently get calls from people who had just purchased their first computer. These were ZX Spectrums and Commodore 64s, and later the Atari ST and Commodore Amiga. They all worked by using the owner's TV as the monitor. Generally the calls would go something like this:

Customer: "Hi, I've just bought a new computer and it doesn't work!"

Shop: "Have you plugged it in and switched the power on?"

C: "Er, no. Does it need electricity?"

S: "Yes, check the manual."

Five minutes later, we'd get another call:

C: "I've plugged it in and switched it on, but nothing is appearing on my TV."

S: "Have you connected up the computer to the TV?"

C: "I thought it just broadcast it, you know like the TV channels?"

S: "No, you need to connect the cable up to the back of the TV. Check the manual."

And so it would go on. The moral here is that you should always …

- **Check the obvious**—just because a machine isn't working right doesn't mean it's the most complex element of the setup that's causing the problem. If your vacuum cleaner doesn't work, do you take it apart or check if it's plugged into the wall socket?

- **Read the manuals.** You'd be surprised about how much information is really in them.

- **Check your work.** More than half the problems people experience are because they typed something wrong, or because the administrator typed something wrong. If something suddenly stops working, think back to see if you've made any changes and whether that could be causing the problem.

> **A Postcard From …**
>
> If you like these sort of intelligent exchanges between users and system administrators, it won't take long for you to find some on the Internet. My own personal favorite site is www.rinkworks.com/stupid/. You'll even find a few of my submissions in there, if you know where to look!

I'll discuss some specific areas to check in the rest of the chapter.

Logging In Problems

There is nothing worse than not being able to get into the machine in the first place.

If you are entering your login and password but being denied access, then it's probably related to one of the following problems:

♦ Your user name is incorrect.

♦ Your password is incorrect.

♦ You have the Caps Lock on your keyboard switched on—both your login and password are case sensitive.

In the first two cases, you should contact your systems administrator to find out what the problems are, or to reset your password.

If you *are* the systems administrator for the machine and one of your users is having problems then use *passwd* to change their password to something else. Better still, edit their settings using *admintool* and set their password to be blank until they log on next time.

If you are sure they are using the correct user name and password, then check that the settings in the */etc/nsswitch.conf* file are correct. In particular, if you are using NIS/NIS+ to distribute user information across the network, make sure that *nsswitch.conf* is actually looking at the NIS tables and the system has been configured with the correct domain.

If the user logs in and gets the message:

```
No directory! Logging in with home=/
```

Then it means their home directory either does not exist, or they do not have the correct access permissions to the directory to be able to use it.

File Access Problems

Solaris is entirely file based, which means that everything from the files you store to the devices and systems that you communicate with are controlled by the same permissions system.

If you have trouble accessing a file, then check ...

♦ That you have permissions to actually read the file, or if you are updating the file, to write the contents back.

♦ That you at least have execute permissions on all the directories in the path to that file.

If you cannot get a list of files in a directory, check that you have read permissions to the directory, otherwise you will not be able to read the directory contents.

Printing Problems

If you are trying to print a file either from the command line or through an application, then check all of the following:

◆ Use *lpstat* to check the queue and the printer status.

◆ Make sure the printer is not disabled. If you are the administrator, use *enable* to enable printing.

◆ Ensure the printer queue has been set to accept new requests. If you are the administrator, use *accept* to allow requests to be submitted.

Sun Lotion

A few years ago I was looking for a junior administrator/assistant to help me out and I interviewed everybody, asking them a series of questions to determine whether they had a combination of knowledge and a logical mind that could be applied to problem solving. One of the questions was "You sent a job to the printer, but it's not being printed. What do you check first?"

I employed the person who correctly suggested checking the online/offline button on the printer. Despite the complexities of the modern computer and networked devices, you should always check the obvious first.

If you are an administrator and a user is having trouble printing to a particular printer, you should check ...

◆ That the user has been granted access to the printer, or conversely that they have not been explicitly denied access.

◆ If the printer is a remote device, check that the remote server has not restricted access to a particular machine, user, or machine/user combination.

NFS Shares Access Problems

If you are having problems accessing shared disks mounted over NFS, check the following:

◆ File/directory permissions. Okay, I know that's obvious, but file and directory permissions matter just as much on NFS shares as they do on traditional disks.

◆ Check that the disk has actually mounted properly.

◆ Check that the user and group IDs used on the NFS server and client are the same—use NIS if you don't want to manually share the information.

If you can't actually mount a volume from a client, check:

◆ That the directory, or one of its parents, is being shared.

◆ That you have been granted access to use the share in question—check the specification in */etc/dfs/sharetab*.

◆ That the client's IP address can be resolved properly—most network services will refuse access to hosts that they cannot put a name to (i.e., reverse lookup from the IP address to a hostname). In particular, check */etc/hosts* if it's a local server, or if you are using NIS, check that */etc/nsswitch.conf* is set to use NIS. If the client is on the Internet, make sure that the DNS service is configured correctly.

A Postcard From ...

Through the course of writing this book, I suddenly discovered that I couldn't log in remotely to a machine. I could connect, but I'd never get a login prompt. I eventually realized that the reason for this was that I'd adjusted the way the system looked up host names, and the machine couldn't reverse map my client with a real name, and so wouldn't let me in!

FTP Access Problems

If you are trying to FTP to a machine and cannot gain access, check ...

◆ That your user name and password are correct.

◆ That you have the correct machine address.

If you are an administrator, and a user is having problems connecting to a machine, check ...

◆ That the user is using the right user name/password combination.

◆ That their user name has not been added to */etc/ftpusers*.

◆ That the shell configured for the user is a valid shell listed in */etc/shells*.

If the user cannot even connect to the FTP service, check:

◆ That the FTP service is enabled in */etc/inetd.conf* and that *inetd* has been updated with the information.

- That the FTP service is configured correctly.
- That the client's IP address can be resolved properly—in particular, check */etc/hosts* if it's a local server, or if you are using NIS, check that */etc/nsswitch.conf* is set to use NIS. If the client is on the Internet, make sure that the DNS service is configured correctly.

Telnet Connection Problems

If one of your users is trying to connect to your machine with telnet then check …

- Telnet is running and configured in */etc/inetd.conf*.
- The user name and password are correct.
- If you are trying to connect as root over telnet, make sure that direct logins for root have not been disabled—check the value of the *CONSOLE* setting in the */etc/default/login* file.
- That the client's IP address can be resolved properly—in particular, check */etc/hosts* if it's a local server, or if you are using NIS check that */etc/nsswitch.conf* is set to use NIS. If the client is on the Internet, make sure that the DNS service is configured correctly.

The Least You Need to Know

- Check the obvious first—a user having problems logging in is more likely to be typing the wrong user name/password than it being a serious problem with the machine.
- Check the standard configuration files such as */etc/passwd* and the files pertaining to a particular services—for example, */etc/ftpusers* for FTP.
- Check the explicit/implicit permissions. Solaris allows you to restrict access to specific users and/or hosts, and to exclude access to all but a selected few users/hosts.
- Did I mention checking the obvious?

## Chapter 24

Fixing and Tuning File Systems

In This Chapter

- ◆ Looking inside file systems
- ◆ Checking your file system
- ◆ Tuning your file system

It's inevitable that at some point you will have some problem with the disks and file systems on your machine and you will want to diagnose the file systems to find out what's wrong. Unix comes with its own file system checker for this very purpose, and the process of checking the file system is a vital part of the operating system.

In fact, file system integrity is so important that every time you switch on your machine the file systems are checked and validated. This is one of the reasons why Unix is such a stable platform and used in situations where the data integrity is imperative—the combination of a stable OS, efficient file system, and constant checking is hard to beat.

In this chapter, I'll show you how to check the file system, and what to do if you get an error message during the boot process that a file system problem has occurred.

Inside File Systems

It's impossible to talk about checking, repairing, and tuning a file system without first looking at how a file system operates. However, the information is quite complex—but understanding the information will help you fix and diagnose problems. It's not required, though—if you don't want to read this section of the chapter, skip it.

I'll ignore the underlying disk layout, except to say that all disks are made up of a combination of platters (the physical disks which spin and are coated with magnetic material to hold the information), heads (the hardware that reads and writes the data to the disc—generally two per platter, one for each side), and cylinders (the individual concentric tracks on the disc). Cylinders are subdivided into sectors.

Information is read to and from the disk by accessing a specific sector from a specific cylinder using a specific head. These three pieces of information can identify any block of data on the disk.

A file system maps this physical information into a format that you are more familiar with—that is, files and folders. Within Solaris the primary file system type is *ufs*. The *ufs* file system uses the following terms to refer to the different elements of the file system information:

◆ A **block** is a collection of one or more sectors and the smallest amount of information addressable on the disk by the file system. Typically a block is 1K in size, but this can be adjusted.

Solingo

An **inode** is the basic component of any file system—there must be one inode for each file or directory on the disk. If you run out of inodes then you will be unable to create a new file or directory even if there is plenty of space on the disk to store the information.

◆ An **inode** is a file control block—it identifies a physical file on the disk by a unique inode number. The inode contains information such as the file owner ID, group ID, permissions, and modification and other times. It also contains the reference to the block map that identifies all of the blocks which make up the content of the file.

◆ A **directory** is a mapping which connects the inode number of a file with the character name that you recognize as the normal way of accessing the file. In addition to file-to-inode mapping, directories also refer to other directory maps, and this is how you get nested directories and directory trees.

◆ **Cylinder** groups are logical groups of file system blocks. They are created by grouping together the blocks of a disk in a vertical stripe—in essence each cylinder block is a collection of all the sectors across different heads, but within one single cylinder. Cylinder groups hold the directory maps, inode maps, and block usage maps.

The superblock contains info about the file system.

♦ A **superblock** contains information about the file system, such as the file system's size, the block size, the number of blocks per allocation unit, and summary information about the number of blocks used and available on the disk. There are multiple copies of the superblock stored on the disk, one for each cylinder group.

The layout is very efficient, and to help you understand it more, let's look at a single directory, */var/adm* from a typical system:

```
total 204
drwxrwxr-x   5 adm     adm       512 Dec 30 09:58 acct/
-rw-------   1 uucp    bin         0 Dec 30 09:55 aculog
drwxr-xr-x   2 adm     adm       512 Dec 30 09:54 exacct/
-r--r--r--   1 root    root    28056 Jan 13 16:48 lastlog
drwxr-xr-x   2 adm     adm       512 Dec 30 09:54 log/
-rw-r--r--   1 root    root    36252 Jan 13 15:14 messages
drwxr-xr-x   2 adm     adm       512 Dec 30 09:54 passwd/
drwxrwxr-x   2 adm     sys       512 Dec 30 09:58 sa/
drwxr-xr-x   2 root    sys       512 Dec 30 10:25 sm.bin/
-rw-rw-rw-   1 root    bin         0 Dec 30 09:55 spellhist
drwxr-xr-x   2 root    sys       512 Dec 30 09:54 streams/
-rw-------   1 root    root      372 Jan 13 16:48 sulog
-rw-r--r--   1 root    bin      3720 Jan 13 16:48 utmpx
-rw-r--r--   1 root    root      504 Jan 13 15:13 vold.log
-rw-r--r--   1 adm     adm     41664 Jan 13 16:48 wtmpx
```

Each of the files and directories listed here has a directory entry in the structure for */var/adm* which itself is part of the entries for the */var* directory. Each entry has its own inode, and in the case of a directory the inode contains the directory information for the next list of files.

The *vold.log* file is a directory entry which points to an inode—you can get the inode number by using the *-i* option to the *ls* command:

```
$ ls -il
total 204
 41540 drwxrwxr-x   5 adm     adm       512 Dec 30 09:58 acct/
 79297 -rw-------   1 uucp    bin         0 Dec 30 09:55 aculog
 83072 drwxr-xr-x   2 adm     adm       512 Dec 30 09:54 exacct/
 79386 -r--r--r--   1 root    root    28056 Jan 13 16:48 lastlog
 86848 drwxr-xr-x   2 adm     adm       512 Dec 30 09:54 log/
 79384 -rw-r--r--   1 root    root    36252 Jan 13 15:14 messages
 90624 drwxr-xr-x   2 adm     adm       512 Dec 30 09:54 passwd/
 56647 drwxrwxr-x   2 adm     sys       512 Dec 30 09:58 sa/
117123 drwxr-xr-x   2 root    sys       512 Dec 30 10:25 sm.bin/
 79298 -rw-rw-rw-   1 root    bin         0 Dec 30 09:55 spellhist
 94400 drwxr-xr-x   2 root    sys       512 Dec 30 09:54 streams/
```

```
79387 -rw-------    1 root    root       372 Jan 13 16:48 sulog
79299 -rw-r--r--    1 root    bin       3720 Jan 13 16:48 utmpx
79385 -rw-r--r--    1 root    root       504 Jan 13 15:13 vold.log
79300 -rw-r--r--    1 adm     adm      41664 Jan 13 16:48 wtmpx
```

In this case, the name *vold.log* points to inode number 79385, which in turn points to an area of disk that holds the information contained within the file.

Because of this different range of information at all these different levels, it's possible for any one of these items to become corrupt during a system crash or power failure. For example, if you are in the process of creating a file it's possible that the directory entry will be created but the inode won't, or for the directory entry and inode to be created, and blocks allocated to hold the data, but never associated with each other.

All of these problems also have domino effects. If the block map is incorrect, then the information in a block group will be incorrect, and possibly in the cylinder group, too. In all likelihood, this may also have affected the appropriate superblock.

In the short term, you may never notice the problem. However, if over time you continue to use the system, then more and more data may get corrupted as the data blocks and inode/block mappings will cause information to be written to the wrong parts of a disk, and you may even have files written to the same physical blocks on the disk.

Luckily, Solaris is a very stable operating system and has a relatively stable file system. It's unlikely that any information will be lost while the machine stays on. If the machine ever crashes, then the file system will be checked when the system starts up and fixed, or at least asked to be fixed during the boot process. You can also run the checks manually, which is what I'll look at next.

Sun Screen

Solaris will do its best to prevent you from doing something that will potentially damage your file system. You *must* have root privileges to run *fsck* and you will be warned about running *fsck* on a file system that is already mounted. Finally, you will also be asked to confirm each fixing operation before continuing.

Ideally you should be in Single User mode, too—this will help to ensure that nothing modifies the disk while it is being checked. Doing so would likely cause even more damage. If you *absolutely must* keep the system up, try unmounting the drive—quitting any applications that are using it first. I don't recommend doing anything to a mounted device.

If you are really worried about the disk, you can use *dd* to create an image of the raw partition before continuing. Check the *man* pages for more information.

Checking Your File System

Although most Unix file systems, including the *ufs* file system used by Solaris, are very stable and much less susceptible to random errors and corruption, it doesn't mean they are completely free of potential problems. Under Windows you have scandisk and Mac OS has Disk First Aid. Under Unix, the primary tool for checking your file system is *fsck* (short for file system checker).

In essence, *fsck* doesn't do anything different than the tools under any other operating system do; they just do it specifically for Unix file systems. One historical difference is that *fsck* is a standard part of the operating system, and is in fact used every time the machine is started up.

The command, in its basic state, is very easy to use. You just supply one of the following on the command line:

♦ The raw drive/partition device.

♦ The block special drive/partition device.

♦ The mount point of the device.

Sun Lotion

You may experience problems with file systems if you try to check one that is larger than 2GB when supplying the block, rather than raw device name. To get around this, use the raw device (which is just a case of using /dev/rdsk).

The *fsck* tool will determine the raw partition from this, then open the partition and start its checks. There are a range of different things checked when you run the *fsck* command. These include, but are not strictly limited to ...

♦ Blocks claimed by more than one inode or free block list.

♦ Blocks referenced by an inode or freelist that are outside the list of possible blocks (i.e., number too high or low).

♦ The number of links to an inode is incorrect.

♦ The size of a directory is different than that calculated.

♦ The inode is corrupt.

♦ Blocks that exist, but don't exist in either a valid inode reference or a free list.

♦ Directory entries point to an unallocated inode.

♦ Directories that neither contain the . or .. meta-directory entries as the first two entries.

♦ Block/inode mismatches in the superblock.

♦ Corrupt free block list.

♦ Total free block or free inode counts are incorrect.

Any files which are orphaned—that is, the space has been allocated but not referenced—are written into the *lost+found* directory in the root of the mounted file system. For example, */lost+found* contains the files orphaned within the root file system. The assigned name will be the inode number of the file chain.

A Standard fsck Session

Let's have a look at a typical execution, showing here a check on a file system that is perfectly healthy:

```
% fsck /opt
** /dev/rdsk/c0d0s5
** Currently Mounted on /opt
** Phase 1 - Check Blocks and Sizes
** Phase 2 - Check Pathnames
** Phase 3 - Check Connectivity
** Phase 4 - Check Reference Counts
** Phase 5 - Check Cyl groups
8 files, 15 used, 458072 free (40 frags, 57254 blocks, 0.0% fragmentation)
```

The different phases are displayed as they are being checked to help show the progress of the checking process.

The information shown at the end is more useful, because it shows …

- ◆ The number of files on the file system (8).
- ◆ The number of blocks used (15).
- ◆ The number of free blocks, excluding the minimum free (458072).
- ◆ The number of file fragments on the disk.
- ◆ The total number of file blocks—that is, the blocks that make up a file chain—on the disk.
- ◆ The overall percentage of fragmentation.

Assuming you are not prompted to approve any modifications, then the file system is okay and you can remount the file system and carry on using it.

File System with Problems

Now let's have a look at a file system that is already mounted and that you know has some problems. The *fsck* tool will always ask you before doing anything potentially lethal to your disk, as you can see from the process shown below. First of all, everything appears to proceed as normal:

```
% fsck /dev/rdsk/c1t2d0s0
** /dev/rdsk/c1t2d0s0
```

```
** Currently Mounted on /usr/local
** Phase 1 - Check Blocks and Sizes
** Phase 2 - Check Pathnames
** Phase 3 - Check Connectivity
```

Then, as you reach Phase 4, there seems to be a problem:

```
** Phase 4 - Check Reference Counts
LINK COUNT FILE I=416711  OWNER=mc MODE=0
SIZE=0 MTIME=Jan 10 01:20 2002  COUNT 0 SHOULD BE -1
ADJUST? y
```

A link file count problem means that a file is referenced but there doesn't seem to be any additional information to go with it. Probably an error occurred when a file was being created and the process never completed properly. If you adjust the link count then the file will cease to exist once the process has completed—since the file doesn't have any data attached, it's safe to adjust the count.

Other entries which will come up during these stages relate to the other items in the earlier list. For every problem you will be given a description and the fix. In 99 percent of cases, it's safe to say yes to the fix.

```
** Phase 5 - Check Cyl groups
SUMMARY INFORMATION BAD
SALVAGE? n
```

Another problem. This time it's the summary information that's wrong. The summary information holds information like the number of free blocks and used blocks—a bad reference count will usually have this domino effect.

```
FILE SYSTEM STATE IN SUPERBLOCK IS WRONG; FIX? n
```

Incorrect superblock information is usually nothing to worry about—although see the note below, "Fixing when the Superblock is corrupt." Here you are just fixing the file system state in the superblock. This determines whether the disk is clean (that is, safe to mount) or dirty (that is, needs to be checked).

Finally, you get the summary information again. As soon as this information is printed, it's safe to mount and use the file system again.

Sun Lotion

If you have a file system that has a lot of problems and you know whether you want to fix or ignore fixing those problems, you can supply the -n or -y options to the command line. The -n automatically answers no to all the questions, and -y answers yes.

```
126102 files, 2647217 used, 2512365 free (22837 frags, 311191 blocks,  0.4%
➡fragmentation)
```

Fixing When the Superblock Is Corrupt

If the file system's superblock is so corrupt that enough information from it cannot be salvaged, then you will need to determine the information about the file system layout from another superblock. Luckily all file systems contain more than one superblock, so that should one become corrupt you can use the information from the others. Every superblock is updated, although depending on when the crash occurred it will affect the quality of the information in a superblock anyway.

The alternate superblock locations are determined automatically when the file system is created, but not all file systems contain superblocks at the same location—the actual location is specifically calculated to appear on a combination of different locations within the physical disk, including different platters, different heads, and different parts of each platter—ultimately superblocks appear according to the different cylinder groups. The ultimate location will therefore be dependent on a combination of the disk's geometry and the file system size.

However, you don't have to worry about writing the information down when you create the file system. There is *always* a spare copy of the superblock at block 32, and if this block is corrupt then you can use the *newfs* command with the -*N* command. This performs the calculations required to create the file system without actually making any changes to the disk. For example, here's the output on our */usr/openwin* file system:

```
% newfs -Nv /dev/rdsk/c0d0s1
mkfs -F ufs -o N /dev/rdsk/c0d0s1 1049328 63 16 8192 1024 16 10 60 2048 t 0 -1
➥8 7
Warning: inode blocks/cyl group (67) >= data blocks (63) in last
    cylinder group. This implies 1008 sector(s) cannot be allocated.
/dev/rdsk/c0d0s1:       1048320 sectors in 1040 cylinders of 16 tracks, 63
➥sectors
        511.9MB in 65 cyl groups (16 c/g, 7.88MB/g, 3776 i/g)
super-block backups (for fsck -F ufs -o b=#) at:
 32, 16224, 32416, 48608, 64800, 80992, 97184, 113376, 129568, 145760, 161952,
 178144, 194336, 210528, 226720, 242912, 258080, 274272, 290464, 306656,
 322848, 339040, 355232, 371424, 387616, 403808, 420000, 436192, 452384,
 468576, 484768, 500960, 516128, 532320, 548512, 564704, 580896, 597088,
 613280, 629472, 645664, 661856, 678048, 694240, 710432, 726624, 742816,
 759008, 774176, 790368, 806560, 822752, 838944, 855136, 871328, 887520,
 903712, 919904, 936096, 952288, 968480, 984672, 1000864, 1017056, 1032224,
```

To make use of this information, use the -*o* option and specify the alternative superblock to use. For example:

```
% fsck -o b=194336
```

File System Checks During Startup

When you shut a Solaris machine down, part of the final stages of the shutdown process is to set the file system state for each of the file systems to "clean." The same information is set when a file system is unmounted. The "clean" setting indicates to any system that wants to mount the file system that the file system is considered to be safe to mount.

During the boot-up sequence, or when you try and mount the disk with the *mount* command, the file system state is checked first. Anything other than "clean" will indicate a problem. When using *mount*, you'll be warned the file system is not in a "clean" state, and you will be advised to run *fsck*.

During a the boot-up sequence, *fsck* will be executed on each file system—if the state is "clean" then the disk is not checked. Any other state will force *fsck* to perform a standard check. Any basic problems that can be fixed without causing damage to the file system will be fixed automatically.

Any problems which require user input will cause the system boot process to terminate and you'll be asked to run *fsck* manually so that you can diagnose and fix the problems. The actual process is exactly the same as we've been using it already. The system will already be in single user mode, so you won't need to change that. As soon as you've finished fixing the file systems, press Control+D to quit the single user shell and complete the boot process.

Note that if you've had to fix the root file system, then you should reboot before continuing.

Sun Lotion

It depends entirely on how you have split up the file systems for your system, but the two most critical file systems are / and /usr. Without these two file systems in a suitable state you cannot get a usable machine working.

Tuning Your File System

No, it's not possible to change the file system on a disk so that the continual hum from your hard drive becomes something more tuneful (although I've often thought it would be a good idea). It is, however, possible to change the parameters of the file system, as configured when you first created the file system.

If you recall how to create a new file systems on a partition (discussed in Chapter 7, "Understanding Disk Management"), you'll remember that the configurable parameters included a number of different options. Most of the time you will never adjust the settings you originally created the file system.

Occasionally though you want to change what you use your file system for—for example, you may change the file system from file storage to a development disk, so you need to change from space to speed optimizing. Alternatively, perhaps you want to store more information on the disk and reduce the minimum amount of space that the file system keeps free for emergencies.

All of these parameters can be adjusted without corrupting or affecting the information stored on the file system by using the *tunefs* command. Table 24.1 shows the list of parameters and operations that can be performed by the command.

Table 24.1 Parameters to *tunefs*

Parameter	Description
-a maxcontig	Changes the number of contiguous blocks that will be written to the disk before a rotational delay is added. Changing this parameter can affect performance—if the file system contains large files then the larger the value the more data that is read before a delay. For lots of smaller files (for example on a development system) a smaller value will improve performance.
-d rotdelay	Specifies the time (in milliseconds) to complete a transfer interrupt and then start on a new transfer.
-e maxbpg	Specifies the number of contiguous blocks that will be allocated for a single file within a single cylinder group before blocks are allocated from the next group. The default value is a quarter of the number of the blocks in the cylinder group to try and prevent a single file using all the blocks in a cylinder group and therefore affecting the performance of any other files stored in the same cylinder. Performance is generally better for files when spread across a number of cylinders. As with the *maxcontig* parameter, file systems with a small number of large files should have this set higher, higher numbers of smaller files should have lower values.
-m minfree	The minimum of space to keep free on the disk for emergencies. Not only does this affect the amount of storage space, it will also affect the performance of the drive, as the OS will be unable to reorganize and allocate blocks on the disk according to the other policy parameters. You can also use it to lower the available space on a disk and prevent users from adding more files to the disk until some files are deleted.
-o [space | time]	Change the optimization strategy for the file system. The *space* parameter conserves space at the expense of some performance, while *time* organizes files to maximize performance.

For example, to adjust the minimum free figure for a file system you would use:

```
% tunefs -m 5 /dev/dsk/c0t0d0s3
```

The Least You Need to Know

- ◆ You can use *fsck* to check and repair a disk in the event of a problem.
- ◆ The *fsck* tool is run automatically when a machine boots up to verify the quality of the disk.
- ◆ You can use *tunefs* to modify certain parameters of a file system after the file system has been created.

## Chapter 25

Monitoring Performance

In This Chapter

♦ Determining what's running

♦ Killing dead processes

♦ Monitoring system resources

Ever sat down in front of your machine and thought "What's it doing *now*?" Ever wondered why you can type in a command one minute and get an immediate response, and five minutes later have to wait a few seconds?

With a client OS like Windows or Mac OS you probably already know what you are running, so it's possible that you'll understand the slow down. On a Unix machine, there are so many background processes and services running that it can sometimes be difficult to see the wood for the trees and understand which of them is using up all your resources.

Fear not, however—Solaris comes with a veritable army of commands and solutions which can be used to find out what's going on, not only in respect to the other processes running on your machine, but also in terms of who is using it, for what, and how much disk space and memory are available.

Determining What's Running

Although it's not a hard-and-fast rule that all performance problems will be the fault of an existing process, it's not an unreasonable expectation that something you are running is having that effect. It could be that the program is a "runaway" using up resources (CPU, disk space, and so on), or you've suddenly found that 20 users have all decided to build large projects at the same time.

Taking a quick look at the process list can help you to determine what each process is doing, who is running the process, and how much memory and CPU time the process is using. There are, unsurprisingly, a number of different ways we can do this.

Using uptime

There are times when you are not interested in the specifics of what's running, but you do want to know how busy your machine is. The quickest way to get this information is to use the *uptime* command.

```
$ uptime
  2:11pm  up  2:21,  2 users,  load average: 0.02, 0.08, 0.09
```

The command returns some fairly straightforward information. In order, this includes the current time and the "uptime" (the number of days, hours and minutes that the machine has been active and available since the last reboot). You can also tell how many people are using your machine.

The load average shows the average number of processes waiting to be executed in the last minute, 5 minutes, and 15 minutes. Note that it shows the number of waiting processes, rather than an indication of how many processes have actually executed, thereby showing the load on the machine rather than its capability. In this case, the machine is currently not very busy at all, but has been busier in the recent past. If you have a look at a different machine:

```
$ uptime
  2:16pm  up 5 day(s), 20:46,  2 users,  load average: 2.02, 2.02, 2.03
```

In this example you have a machine up for a longer time, but with the same number of users, and which has been much busier consistently for the last 15 minutes.

CAUTION

Sun Screen

The load average is constantly updated based on the processes waiting to execute and a rolling 1-, 5-, and 15-minute counter. You can get different values every time you call uptime, even if you have it reporting the information every second, because of the way the information is constantly updated. Don't panic—it doesn't indicate something is wrong with your machine in any way!

If you look at a slightly busier machine, you can see that there has been a relatively recent flurry of activity:

```
$ uptime
  2:20pm  up 5 day(s), 20:50,  6 users,  load average: 4.68, 2.78, 2.30
```

The load has more than doubled in the last minute, and you've suddenly got more users. Just a few minutes later, the load has gone down again:

```
$ uptime
  2:28pm  up 5 day(s), 20:58,  6 users,  load average: 2.01, 2.62, 2.57
```

However, you can still see that the average load in the last 15 minutes has been high. As a rough guide, a load average in the last 15 minutes of $N+1$, where N is the number of CPUs in your machine, is probably an indication of a machine that is underpowered, or under an excessive load for very long periods of time. The machine in question here is my main server, handling all the mail, file, database, and web serving functions for the network. It's a dual processor machine, so to have a constant load of about two waiting processes is not taxing it too much.

If you want to find out what's really going on, you need to use the *ps* command.

A Postcard From ...

The process list is a fairly standard item on any operating system, but different operating systems treat and display that information in different ways.

All Unix variants have a *ps* command, but the options to the command differ according to the underlying flavor (BSD or SVR4) and the operating system vendor, some of which have added custom options to the commands to provide information for a specific ability of the OS or hardware.

Under Windows, the Task Manager, available under any version since Windows 95, is the closest approximation. You're provided with the ability to view a list of the running processes and if necessary force one of the processes or applications to quit. You also get a running update of the process status and the processor usage of each process.

Mac OS is less friendly. About this Macintosh will show a list of running applications, but not a list of running programs—some of which can be hidden. Mac OS X provides both a traditional application list and, through its command line interface, a complete list of all the processes running is available.

Using ps

The *ps* command (short for process status) can report a variety of information about the processes running on your machine. If you look at a typical list, you can see that your machine doesn't appear to be doing much:

```
$ ps
PID TTY        TIME CMD
  406 pts/2    0:00 ps
  397 pts/2    0:00 bash
```

In its default mode (that is, without any options) *ps* only reports a list of your processes, and then only those that relate to your active session. Had I logged in as root and used the same command, I would have still only gotten two processes reported, even though root runs lots of the background processes on a Unix machine providing network and other services.

To get a list of all the processes on a machine you need to use the command line option, *-e* which lists every process now running, regardless of who is running it and what terminal or device they are using to do so.

```
$ ps -e
PID TTY        TIME CMD
    0 ?        0:01 sched
    1 ?        0:00 init
    2 ?        0:00 pageout
    3 ?        0:01 fsflush
  371 ?        0:00 sac
  376 ?        0:03 Xsun
  203 ?        0:00 inetd
   65 ?        0:00 sysevent
   82 ?        0:01 picld
  157 ?        0:00 in.rdisc
  177 ?        0:00 keyserv
  174 ?        0:00 rpcbind
  211 ?        0:00 statd
  210 ?        0:00 lockd
  233 ?        0:00 syslogd
  225 ?        0:00 automoun
  263 ?        0:00 lpsched
  294 ?        0:00 smcboot
  251 ?        0:00 nscd
  241 ?        0:00 cron
  297 ?        0:00 vold
  295 ?        0:00 smcboot
  284 ?        0:00 utmpd
  346 ?        0:00 mountd
  348 ?        0:00 nfsd
  292 ?        0:00 sendmail
  372 console  0:00 ttymon
  355 ?        0:00 snmpdx
```

```
361 ?        0:00 dmispd
362 ?        0:00 snmpXdmi
328 ?        0:00 dtlogin
368 ?        0:00 sshd2
377 ?        0:01 devfsadm
378 ?        0:00 mibiisa
375 ?        0:00 ttymon
379 ?        0:00 dtlogin
380 ??       0:00 fbconsol
392 ?        0:01 dtgreet
423 pts/2    0:00 ps
397 pts/2    0:00 bash
393 ?        0:01 sshd2
409 pts/2    0:00 bash
```

Wow! What a lot of processes. Quite a few of these are simply the processes that go to make up the operating system itself. In particular, processes 1-4 consist of the kernel, *init*—the program responsible for running the processes on the machine that keep it running (see Chapter 8, "Starting and Stopping Services")—and the two programs responsible for swapping processes in between RAM and swap space on the disk.

All the commands with a question mark in the TTY column are background processes that were started by *init*, one of the rc scripts, or manually by root and which provide some service to the rest of the machine. For example, *lpsched* provides print services and *dtlogin* provides the graphical login screen on the machine's console.

Sun Lotion

If you have a busy machine with lots of users or background processes running, or you are just accessing a machine through a very small window, then the processes may go past so quickly that you miss them.

Don't forget that you can always pipe the output through *more* to get the process list in a paged form, or you could redirect the output to a file and then view the list at your leisure.

For the information to be really useful, you really need to get more detail about the processes that you are running, and for that you need to know the different command line options available. I've provided a quick list of the main options in Table 25.1. For full information, check the online documentation.

Table 25.1   Command Line Options for the *ps* Command

Option	Description
-a	Lists the most frequently requested processes—that is, all those associated with a terminal and/or user other than root, excluding the user's shell.
-A	Is identical to *-e*, shows every process.
-c	Prints additional scheduler priority information.
-d	Lists information about all processes except users' shells.
-e	Lists information about every process.
-f	Generates a full listing incorporating start time, time running, owner, parent process ID, and the full command line used to execute the process.
-g grplist	Generates a list of the processes owned by the process group IDs specified in *grplist*.
-G gidlist	Generates a list of processes owned by users with the group IDs in *gidlist*.
-j	Adds session ID and process group ID information for each process.
-l	Generates a long listing, adding parent process ID, priority, internal address, size, and execution time.
-L	Includes information about each light-weight process (lwp, essentially a thread).
-o format	Prints out the information according to a given format.
-ps proclist	Prints out only those processes with the process IDs given in *proclist*.
-P	Adds the number of the processor being used by the process or thread.
-s sidlist	Lists only the processes whose session leaders (shells) match the IDs in *sidlist*.
-t term	Lists only the processes associated with a particular terminal.
-u uidlist	Lists only the processes owned by the effective user IDs in *uidlist*.
-U uidlist	Lists only the processes owned by the real user IDs in *uidlist*.
-y	Under a long listing, omits the *F* and *ADDR* columns (see Table 25.2) and replaces it with an *RSS* column. Also changes *SZ* and *RSS* to report the size in kilobytes, not pages.

For example, you can get an extended list of all the processes on a system using *-efly*:

```
$ ps -efly
 S     UID   PID  PPID  C PRI NI    RSS     SZ   WCHAN      STIME TTY      TIME CMD
 T    root     0     0  0   0 SY      0      0             11:50:22 ?       0:01 sched
 S    root     1     0  0  41 20    284   1084 de94ee0e 11:50:22 ?       0:00 /etc/init -
 S    root     2     0  0   0 SY      0      0 fec48be8 11:50:22 ?       0:00 pageout
```

```
S    root      3      0   0    0 SY     0        0 fece1ce8 11:50:22 ?       0:06 fsflush
S    root    371      1   0   41 20   856     1576 de946ca8 11:50:53 ?       0:00
➥/usr/lib/saf/sac -t 300
S    root    376    328   0   40 20  4864     7964 deecfc02 11:50:54 ?       0:03
➥/usr/openwin/bin/Xsun :0 -nobanner
S    root    203      1   0   41 20  1516     2112 de5ed77a 11:50:38 ?       0:00
➥/usr/sbin/inetd -s
S    root     65      1   0   44 20  1068     1840 de94e2ae 11:50:29 ?       0:00
➥/usr/lib/sysevent/syseventd
S    root     82      1   0   88 20  1548     2356 dea5d2ce 11:50:30 ?       0:01
➥/usr/lib/picl/picld
S    root    157      1   0   40 20   532     1508 de9becb6 11:50:35 ?       0:00
➥/usr/sbin/in.rdisc -s
S    root    177      1   0   59 20  1068     2052 de5ed87a 11:50:36 ?       0:00
➥/usr/sbin/keyserv
S    root    174      1   0   41 20  1004     2004 de5ed83a 11:50:36 ?       0:00
➥/usr/sbin/rpcbind
S  daemon    211      1   0   48 20  1508     2248 de5ed6fa 11:50:38 ?       0:00
➥/usr/lib/nfs/statd
S    root    210      1   0   68 20  1292     2032 de5ed5ba 11:50:38 ?       0:00
➥/usr/lib/nfs/lockd
S    root    233      1   0   41 20  1464     3036 deb927ee 11:50:41 ?       0:00
➥/usr/sbin/syslogd
S    root    225      1   0   41 20  1652     2780 de5ed5fa 11:50:40 ?       0:00
➥/usr/lib/autofs/automountd
S    root    263      1   0   46 20   908     2916 de5ed3fa 11:50:44 ?       0:00
➥/usr/lib/lpsched
S    root    294      1   0   88 20   956     1536 de5ed37a 11:50:45 ?       0:00
➥/usr/sadm/lib/smc/bin/smcboot
S    root    251      1   0   77 20  1924     2628 dea5d12e 11:50:42 ?       0:00
➥/usr/sbin/nscd
S    root    241      1   0   47 20   884     1748 de946ee8 11:50:41 ?       0:00
➥/usr/sbin/cron
S    root    297      1   0   40 20  1716     2392 de5ed1fa 11:50:45 ?       0:00
➥/usr/sbin/vold
S    root    295    294   0   78 20   548     1536 de5ed23a 11:50:45 ?       0:00
➥/usr/sadm/lib/smc/bin/smcboot
S    root    284      1   0   41 20   564      920 de5ed33a 11:50:44 ?       0:00
➥/usr/lib/utmpd
S    root    346      1   0   66 20  1448     2308 de5ed03a 11:50:49 ?       0:00
➥/usr/lib/nfs/mountd
S    root    348      1   0   67 20  1284     1924 deecff82 11:50:50 ?       0:00
➥/usr/lib/nfs/nfsd -a 16
S    root    292      1   0   40 20  1360     2916 de5ed27a 11:50:45 ?       0:00
➥/usr/lib/sendmail -bd -q15m
S    root    372      1   0   45 20   900     1580 deecfd02 11:50:53 console 0:00
➥/usr/lib/saf/ttymon -g -h -p sol9pe
```

```
S    root   355    1   0  41 20  1184   1928 deecff02 11:50:50 ?         0:00
➥/usr/lib/snmp/snmpdx -y -c /etc/snm
S    root   361    1   0  68 20  1560   2704 de5ed1ba 11:50:50 ?         0:00
➥/usr/lib/dmi/dmispd
S    root   362    1   0  41 20  2056   3240 def3c4ce 11:50:51 ?         0:00
➥/usr/lib/dmi/snmpXdmid -s sol9pengu
S    root   328    1   0  69 20  1576   4436 deecfbc2 11:50:48 ?         0:00
➥/usr/dt/bin/dtlogin -daemon
S    root   368    1   0  47 20   944   2832 deecfe42 11:50:53 ?         0:00
➥/usr/local/sbin/sshd2
S    root   377    1   0  57 20  1448   2416 defc7d8e 11:50:54 ?         0:01 devfsadmd
S    root   378  355    0  67 20  1568   2044 defbf63e 11:50:55 ?         0:01 mibiisa -r -
➥p 8576
S    root   375  371    0  41 20   932   1572 dee3920e 11:50:53 ?         0:00
➥/usr/lib/saf/ttymon
S    root   379  328    0  49 20  1988   4612 df007bc8 11:50:56 ?         0:00
➥/usr/dt/bin/dtlogin -daemon
S    root   380  328    0  40 20  1160   2196 deecfb82 11:50:56 ??        0:00
➥/usr/openwin/bin/fbconsole -d :0
S    root   392  379    0  40 20  3980   6744 deecf942 11:51:01 ?         0:01 dtgreet -
➥display :0
O    root   428  409    1  61 20   696    860          13:17:25 pts/2     0:00 ps -efly
S      mc   397  393    0  51 20  1536   2288 df04ca94 11:51:08 pts/2     0:00 -bash
S    root   393  368    0  51 20  2104   3200 deecf982 11:51:04 ?         0:01
➥/usr/local/sbin/sshd2
S    root   409  397    0  51 20  1540   2284 df04bc94 12:04:45 pts/2     0:00
➥-bash
```

Sun Lotion _____

It is very easy to forget that *ps* shows you a "snapshot" of the list of running processes at a given time. Depending on how busy your machine is and how many processes and users are currently active, the time between the snapshot being taken and the list being presented on the screen could be as much as a minute. It's therefore quite possible to be in a situation where the process list you are viewing is so out of date, that making a decision on what to do can be difficult.

The simple rule is not to ever rely on the output of a single *ps* command to make a decision. Any process that you are mildly unsure of should be monitored for a couple of minutes with multiple *ps* commands to see if it really is a permanent resource hog, or just a temporary problem or process.

There's a lot of information here that I don't remotely expect you to take in in one go. The important part is the first line—the header line—which describes what each of the columns mean. Some of the columns are obvious; for example, UID gives the user name or ID running the process, and CMD is obviously the command executed that ran the process.

Table 25.2 provides a quick rundown of the main headers and columns.

Table 25.2   Columns Displayed from the *ps* Command

Column	Description
S	Status; *O* means process is running; *S*, process is sleeping or waiting for an event to complete; *R*, is on the run queue (waiting to be executed); *T*, the process is stopped; or *Z*, zombie state, the process has been terminated but the process's parent is not waiting for it.
UID	The effective user ID of the process (the actual login name is shown with the -*l* command line option).
PID	The process ID of the process.
PPID	The process ID of the parent process.
CLS	The scheduling class for the process.
CPU	The percentage of time that the CPU has been executing a given process.
PRI	The priority of the process. Higher numbers mean lower priority. If -*c* is in effect then higher numbers mean higher priority.
ADDR	The address in memory of the process.
SZ	The total size of the process in virtual memory.
WCHAN	The address of the event on which the process is waiting.
STIME	The time (or days and months, if started more than 24 hours ago) that the process was started.
TTY	The controlling terminal for the process, or ? when there is no controlling terminal.
TIME	The cumulative execution time from the process.
CMD	The command name or command line (with -*f*) of the command being executed.
PGID	The process ID of the process group leader.
SID	The process ID of the session leader.

For example, from the following process status fragment:

```
UID   PID  PPID  C    STIME TTY       TIME CMD
...
  mc   670   666  0 14:11:09 pts/1    0:00 -bash
root   666   368  0 14:11:08 ?        0:00 /usr/local/sbin/sshd2
root   585   573  0 13:23:29 console  1:46 /usr/java/bin/java
root   595     1  0 13:24:01 ?        0:57 /usr/java/bin/java
  mc   680   670  1 14:49:41 pts/1    0:00 ps -ef
```

you can see that the two *java* instances have been running for 1 minute and 46 seconds and 57 seconds respectively. You can also see that one of them was started from the console (because of its TTY column).

The most important piece of information that you will typically need is the process ID—this is an identifier given to every running process. The ID number is incremented each time a new process is created (and checks are made to ensure it doesn't duplicate process numbers) and then the counter is reset to 1 when the number reaches 32767.

You'll need this process ID if you want to control the processes at some later stage, something I'll discuss in more detail in the section on "Killing Processes" later in this chapter.

Another useful column is PPID, which shows the parent process ID for a given process, useful if you want to kill a command and its parent. Many system services use one "parent" process to start a number of children, killing one of the children doesn't stop the service, you must kill the parent too.

The S column, which shows the status of the process, can also come in handy. Processes with a status of R need to be executed, but are currently having to wait before doing so. If you remember back to our *uptime* discussion, the load average information was based on the number of processes in the wait queue—processes with a status of R are in that wait queue.

Using SMC

One of the problems with *ps* that I have already discussed is that it provides only a snapshot of the processes at a given time; and it requires work to keep getting a process list each time to monitor your machine. The solution, if you have access to a machine running X Windows, is to use the Solaris Management Console. Under This Computer and Processes you'll find a process list just like that produced by *ps*. Figure 25.1 shows a sample.

By default, the information is automatically updated every 30 seconds and you can reduce or increase the interval period according to your needs.

Figure 25.1

Getting a process list from the Solaris Management Console.

Sun Screen

Although it's tempting to reduce the time from 30 seconds to one second in the Solaris Management Console, the reality is that doing so would actually put an extra load on the machine, which is something that by monitoring the CPU you are trying to reduce. It's also very likely that the time taken to gather the information, particularly on a busy machine, would take longer than a second, and potentially more than 5 or 10 seconds. Thirty seconds is a much more realistic and useful value.

The information is presented and formatted in a series of columns, and you can click on a column to sort the process list by that item—useful for finding all the processes for a particular user, or for finding the process using the most memory or CPU cycles.

Killing Processes

Once you've found and identified a process that you think may be using more time or resources than it should, or that is potentially doing something it shouldn't, you need to know how to stop the process. You do that by sending it a signal. A signal is just that, an indication of a particular event to a process. Different signals exist for different purposes; there are some that control the operation of a process, one that asks a process to exit gracefully, and another that "kills" a process immediately. I'll briefly discuss these signals and how you can use them with different commands to control and terminate a process.

Signals

Signals are used through Unix to indicate events to a process. Apart from the more explicit signals such as SIGQUIT and SIGKILL there are also signals trapped by a process which are used to perform different operations. For example, the SIGHUP signal is used on a terminal connection to indicate that you want to hang up (for example, put the phone down). The same SIGHUP signal is used to tell some daemons to reload their configuration files.

You can find a full list of signals in Table 25.3.

Table 25.3   Common Control Signals

Signal Name	Number	Default Event	Description
SIGHUP	1	Exit	Hangup.
SIGINT	2	Exit	Interrupt.
SIGQUIT	3	Core	Quit.
SIGILL	4	Core	Illegal Instruction.
SIGTRAP	5	Core	Trace or Breakpoint Trap.
SIGABRT	6	Core	Abort.
SIGEMT	7	Core	Emulation Trap.
SIGFPE	8	Core	Arithmetic Exception.
SIGKILL	9	Exit	Killed.
SIGBUS	10	Core	Bus Error.
SIGSEGV	11	Core	Segmentation Fault.
SIGSYS	12	Core	Bad System Call.
SIGPIPE	13	Exit	Broken Pipe.
SIGALRM	14	Exit	Alarm Clock.
SIGTERM	15	Exit	Terminated.
SIGUSR1	16	Exit	User Signal 1.
SIGUSR2	17	Exit	User Signal 2.
SIGCHLD	18	Ignore	Child Status Changed.
SIGPWR	19	Ignore	Power Fail or Restart.
SIGWINCH	20	Ignore	Window Size Change.
SIGURG	21	Ignore	Urgent Socket Condition.
SIGPOLL	22	Exit	Pollable Event.
SIGSTOP	23	Stop	Stopped (signal).
SIGTSTP	24	Stop	Stopped (user).

Signal Name	Number	Default Event	Description
SIGCONT	25	Ignore	Continued.
SIGTTIN	26	Stop	Stopped (tty input).
SIGTTOU	27	Stop	Stopped (tty output).

Using kill

To send a signal to a process you use the *kill* command, this accepts a signal number or name (without the preceding "SIG") and the process IDs of the processes you want to send the signal to.

For example, to ask a process with an ID of 99 to quit gracefully, use:

```
$ kill -3 99
```

Or use a name:

```
$ kill -QUIT 99
```

To tell a process to terminate immediately, you use SIGKILL (signal number 9). This kills the process at the kernel level, automatically terminating the process whether it likes it or not!

```
$ kill -KILL 99 100 101
```

Using pkill

You don't always want to use *ps* to find out the process ID of a given process, and sometimes the number of process IDs that you would have to type in to kill a particular service is prohibitive. The *pkill* command gets round this. Rather than accepting a process ID number, it accepts the name of a process which will be extracted from the output of *ps* using *grep*.

For example, if I want to kill the web proxy server on my machine, I need to kill every instance of the *apache.proxy* process, or kill the parent process:

```
nobody  5694 21630  0 11:14:52 ?        0:00 apache.proxy
nobody  5681 21630  0 11:06:12 ?        0:00 apache.proxy
nobody  5677 21630  0 11:05:46 ?        0:00 apache.proxy
nobody  5671 21630  0 11:04:56 ?        0:00 apache.proxy
nobody  5670 21630  0 11:04:56 ?        0:00 apache.proxy
nobody  5669 21630  0 11:04:55 ?        0:00 apache.proxy
nobody  5692 21630  0 11:14:51 ?        0:00 apache.proxy
nobody  5682 21630  0 11:06:26 ?        0:00 apache.proxy
```

```
nobody  5693 21630  0 11:14:51 ?        0:00 apache.proxy
  root 21630     1  0    Jan 21 ?        0:00 apache.proxy
nobody  5691 21630  0 11:14:50 ?        0:00 apache.proxy
```

Instead of using *ps*, determining the number, and then killing the processes by their ID, I can instead use the *pkill* command:

```
$ pkill -QUIT apache.proxy
```

It can also be useful when getting a daemon to reload its configuration files. For example, to reload the files for the *named* service you would use:

```
$ kill -HUP named
```

Monitoring Other System Resources

Although processes are one of the main indicators of performance, there are other factors involved, such as the number of users connected to the machine (and who they are) and the disk space and swap space being used by the machine.

Using who/w

In a multi-user environment it can often be handy to find out who is using the machine. As you get to know users, it's sometimes even possible to determine how busy a machine is likely to be according to who is logged in to it.

The *who* command reports a simple list of who is logged in, and on what terminal:

```
$ who
mc         console      Jan 23 13:24    (:0)
mc         pts/3        Jan 23 14:17    (atuin.mcslp.pri)
slp        pts/5        Jan 23 14:16    (atuin.mcslp.pri)
mc         pts/6        Jan 23 13:24    (:0.0)
qdf        pts/7        Jan 23 14:17    (penguin.mcslp.pri)
npk        pts/8        Jan 23 14:17    (nautilus.mcslp.pri)
qru        pts/9        Jan 23 14:17    (sulaco.mcslp.pri)
```

The *w* command combines the output of *uptime* and *who*, also adding information about the command being executed by the user session:

```
$ w
  4:10pm  up 5 day(s), 22:40,  6 users,  load average: 0.01, 0.01, 0.02
User      tty          login@ idle   JCPU   PCPU  what
mc        console      1:24pm 2:46      1      1  /usr/dt/bin/dtexec -open 0 -
➥ttpr
mc        pts/3        2:17pm 1:48   1:04           -bash
slp       pts/5        2:16pm                       w
```

```
mc        pts/6        1:24pm  2:46                /usr/bin/bash
qdf       pts/7        2:17pm  1:47    1:17        -bash
npk       pts/8        2:17pm  1:47    1:20        -bash
qru       pts/9        2:17pm  1:50    1           -bash
```

Using df

The *df* command returns the amount of free disk space and/or inodes for all the file systems mounted by the machine. For example, on my main server:

```
$ df
/                       (/dev/dsk/c1t0d0s0 ):   130138 blocks    216905 files
/usr                    (/dev/dsk/c1t0d0s3 ): 1535674 blocks    284941 files
/boot                   (/dev/dsk/c1t0d0p0:boot):    17730 blocks        -1 files
/proc                   (/proc            ):        0 blocks      3677 files
/dev/fd                 (fd               ):        0 blocks         0 files
/etc/mnttab             (mnttab           ):        0 blocks         0 files
/var                    (/dev/dsk/c1t0d0s6 ):   222162 blocks    122610 files
/var/run                (swap             ): 1520736 blocks     43512 files
/tmp                    (swap             ): 1520736 blocks     43512 files
/export/contrib         (/dev/dsk/c1t0d0s5 ): 1176380 blocks    398610 files
/export/os              (/dev/dsk/c1t0d0s7 ):   667260 blocks    273985 files
/export/proxy           (/dev/dsk/c1t0d0s4 ):   164832 blocks    226821 files
/usr/local              (/dev/dsk/c1t2d0s0 ): 4958914 blocks    526414 files
/export/mail            (/dev/dsk/c1t3d0s0 ): 6307278 blocks    519105 files
/export/cvs             (/dev/dsk/c1t2d0s1 ): 7243552 blocks    458681 files
/export/http            (/dev/dsk/c1t3d0s1 ): 6741162 blocks    531995 files
/export/data            (/dev/dsk/c1t4d0s2 ):16232134 blocks   1110876 files
/export/share           (/dev/dsk/c1t5d0s2 ): 5310266 blocks   1070293 files
```

The output shows the number of free files (inodes) and free blocks on each file system. Blocks are not a useful measure (unless you like doing lots of calculations in your head), so instead use the *-k* command line option to show the information in kilobytes:

```
$ df -k
Filesystem              kbytes    used    avail capacity  Mounted on
/dev/dsk/c1t0d0s0       492977  427908    15772    97%    /
/dev/dsk/c1t0d0s3      2052764 1284927   706255    65%    /usr
/dev/dsk/c1t0d0p0:boot
                         10533    1668     8865    16%    /boot
/proc                        0       0        0     0%    /proc
fd                           0       0        0     0%    /dev/fd
mnttab                       0       0        0     0%    /etc/mnttab
/dev/dsk/c1t0d0s6       246493  135412    86432    62%    /var
swap                    760328      12   760316     1%    /var/run
swap                    760632     316   760316     1%    /tmp
/dev/dsk/c1t0d0s5      2863911 2275721   530912    82%    /export/contrib
```

```
/dev/dsk/c1t0d0s7    2052764 1719134  272048    87%   /export/os
/dev/dsk/c1t0d0s4     492977  410658   82319    84%   /export/proxy
/dev/dsk/c1t2d0s0    5159582 2680125 2427862    53%   /usr/local
/dev/dsk/c1t3d0s0    4406142 1252503 3109578    29%   /export/mail
/dev/dsk/c1t2d0s1    3651902   30126 3585257     1%   /export/cvs
/dev/dsk/c1t3d0s1    4405342 1034769 3326520    24%   /export/http
/dev/dsk/c1t4d0s2    8813061  696994 8027937     8%   /export/data
/dev/dsk/c1t5d0s2    8813061 6157928 2567003    71%   /export/share
```

This also, handily, gives us a percentage figure for the overall capacity used on the file system, and used and free kilobyte counts.

Using swap

Swap space is a permanent part of the Unix operating system. Any process which is waiting for an event, or is otherwise not currently executing, will be shuffled out into swap to allow running processes to have access to the maximum amount of much faster RAM. Even processes that are executing can have parts of their program and data swapped out to disk in "pages" if the OS has identified that they are not being used.

Reporting the amount of free RAM is therefore a meaningless task, as it will only tell you how much RAM is not being used by running processes. Instead, we need to look at the amount of memory being used overall by the swap system. You do that by using the *swap* command with the *-s* command line option:

```
$ swap -s
total: 68044k bytes allocated + 11984k reserved = 80028k used, 612132k
available
```

Sun Lotion

There are some aspects of resource monitoring that I don't have space for here. In particular, Solaris comes with a suite of different tools for looking at exactly how the different disks are being used in the system, how much information is being swapped in and out by the swap systems, and tools for monitoring processor load and overall system performance.

To get more information, look up the *sar* (system activity reporter) command and the *vmstat* (virtual memory statistics) and *iostat* (input/output statistics).

If you want a more holistic approach then you might want to check out some of the tools available on Sun Freeware. See Appendix A, "Resource Guide," for more information.

The information here gives us an overview of the total memory—RAM and swap space—available after the kernel and core processes have been taken into account. The different figures shown are ...

◆ **Allocated space:** The total amount of swap space allocated to running processes.

◆ **Reserved space:** The total amount of space not currently allocated, but reserved for running processes.

◆ **Used:** allocated space+reserved space.

◆ **Available space:** The space available to be allocated or reserved.

If the available space is quite low then it might mean you need to consider increasing the swap space on your machine, or better still the physical RAM. You can get a more explicit idea of how much space is being used on each swap device by using the -*l* option to *swap*:

```
$ swap -l
swapfile          dev  swaplo blocks   free
/dev/dsk/c1t0d0s1  29,65      8 1049576 1049576
```

This shows that you are not, currently, using any swap space on your only swap device.

The Least You Need to Know

◆ You can get a quick idea of how busy a machine is using *uptime*.

◆ You can get a list of processes using the *ps* command or the Solaris Management Console.

◆ You can kill a given process by using *kill* and the processes ID, or *pkill* and the command name.

◆ You can determine who is connected to a machine using *who* and *w*.

◆ You can determine disk space information using *df*.

◆ Information about swap space usage can be determined by using *swap*.

Resource Guide

Since Sun coined the term "The network is the computer" and was instrumental in providing many of the servers used to provide Internet resources, it's no wonder that Sun and Solaris are heavily supported on the Internet. Your primary port of call should be www.sun.com for generic Sun information and www.sun.com/solaris for specific information on the Solaris operating system.

The rest of this appendix contains information and pointers for specific Solaris resources and also generic Unix resources that will apply to Solaris and also to any other Unix variant such as HP-UX, AIX, or Linux.

Warning: Browsing these sites in a "spare moment" can waste hours, if not days, of your time if you are not careful. While the information in all these sites is invaluable, it's important to concentrate on the information you are specifically after. I once lost an entire day looking for performance tips for Solaris. I found lots of useful information and learned a lot, but also wasted a day that I could have spent solving the problem!

Solaris Specific Resources

As one of the most popular and heavily-used Unix operating systems, especially in the realm of Internet servers and services, Solaris is well supported across the Internet on a number of sites.

Sun Documentation

A site with all the Solaris documentation from the Sun Answerbook system in HTML format. You can browse the documentation directly or search the documentation for something specific.

> http://docs.sun.com

BigAdmin

BigAdmin is a portal site by Sun that provides a central repository of links, stories, and other information useful to Sun system administrators. In addition you'll find patch downloads, discussion groups, mailing lists, FAQs, and software downloads.

> http://www.sun.com/bigadmin

Sun Patches

As with any good software packages, Solaris has its own selection of bugs, possible security gaps, and previously unheard of features, all specially designed to trip you up right at the point you could do with it the least. Sun, however, regularly releases patches and updates to fix problems. Full access to all the patches is only available if you have a Sun support package, but you can download the important stability and security patches released by Sun for free from their Public Patches site:

> http://sunsolve.sun.com/sunsolve/pubpatches/

Sun Freeware

A site dedicated to providing easy to use precompiled binaries in both tar and package format that can be installed on your Solaris system. The site contains most of the core freeware available for the Unix platform, including the GNU tools (compilers, building tools, and editors), other utilities, and programming languages. If you want to make use of freely available software—particularly if you are used to a Linux operating environment, then you should start here. If it's not directly available on Sun Freeware you should be able to find the tools to be able to build and install the software yourself.

> http://www.sunfreeware.com

Sun Archive at Sunsite

Sunsite is the largest collection of files and information relating to Sun and other platforms. The core site resides at the University of North Carolina, Chapel Hill, USA, but there are other Sunsite mirrors around the world, including servers in the UK, Australia, many European countries, and a number of additional mirrors across the US. Many of the Sunsite servers are supported by Sun, even though the servers themselves hold information and files for a range of platforms. You can find your local Sunsite server on the Sun Sunsite page:

> http://www.sun.com/sunsite/

Usenet News Groups

Usenet is the network news and discussion group system of the Internet and it allows people to talk and discuss topics with each other right around the world. You can use these groups either to find out information by "lurking" and reading other people's messages, to download software and get tips, or to post questions, and hopefully receive answers. I've listed the primary Usenet groups related to Solaris and Unix below:

> alt.solaris.x86
>
> comp.unix.solaris
>
> comp.unix.admin
>
> comp.unix.advocacy
>
> comp.unix.cde
>
> comp.unix.internals
>
> comp.unix.misc
>
> comp.unix.programmer
>
> comp.unix.questions
>
> comp.unix.shell
>
> comp.unix.sys5.r4
>
> comp.unix.user-friendly

Solaris FAQs

The chances are that if you've come across a problem it's probably been identified by somebody else already, and it may well be a frequently asked question. There are significant numbers of FAQs out there for all sorts of topics, but the two primary Solaris FAQs are:

> http://www.wins.uva.nl/pub/solaris/solaris2
>
> http://sun.pmbc.com/faq

for SPARC and Intel platforms respectively.

For information on administrative topics try the Sun Manager's List:

> ftp://ftp.cs.Toronto.edu/pub/jdd/sun-managers/faq

General Unix Resources

Solaris is just another variety of Unix, and any of the generic Unix resources available on the Internet should at the very least provide pointers even if they don't provide specific help and command names for Solaris.

Unix Installation Tutorial

A good introduction to planning, configuring, and installing any variety of Unix on a machine, along with some tips on system administration once the machine is finally installed.

> http://www.uwsg.Indiana.edu/usail/index/index.html

The Unix Reference Desk at Geek Girl

Geek Girl holds a list of resources, searchable databases, how-to guides, and pointers to pages on other sites all about Unix. It's a great place to start if you are not entirely sure what you are looking for but need information.

> http://www.geek-girl.com/unix.html

Bugtraq Archives

Probably not for those people with a weak stomach, the Bugtraq site lists the bugs and security problems found on a variety of platforms, including Solaris. Reading them too closely could make you paranoid about how secure, or insecure, your system is!

> http://msgs.securepoint.com/bugtraq/

UnixInsider Magazine

UnixInsider magazine has absorbed the content of a number of longstanding online resources, including the old *SunWorld Online* magazine, one of the first Solaris-specific titles available.

> http://www.UnixInsider.com

Free Software Foundation/GNU

The Free Software Foundation is an organization that promotes the development and distribution of free software for all sorts of platforms, and, through the GNU name, specifically for the Unix platform. GNU tools include language compilers and replacements for most of the standard Unix command line utilities. The website includes information on the FSF's projects and information and downloads for the GNU software.

> http://www.fsf.org
>
> http://www.gnu.org

Freshmeat.net

Freshmeat is a website funded by the Open Source Developer Network (OSDN). OSDN is a group that supports the use of open source (but not necessarily free) software. Open source software, is an application that is available in its source form, which allows users to view the source and fix bugs and extend the software, usually under an agreement which supplies those changes back to the community in a new version. The vast majority of Unix software, particularly that used in Linux and that available from GNU, is Open Source.

Freshmeat is a resource which lists and catalogs free software. If you are looking for a piece of software you can try using Freshmeat first—software is cataloged and searchable not only by its name but also by different categories. While you're there, you might also want to check out the Slashdot and Sourceforge sites:

> http://www.freshmeat.net
>
> http://www.slashdot.org
>
> http://www.sourceforge.net
>
> http://www.osdn.com

Shareware.com

A good starting point to look for free software. As well as links and downloadable versions of all the popular stuff, you'll find some occasional examples of the more esoteric and unusual Unix software.

> http://www.shareware.com

The Unix Guru Universe

A portal and resource good for Unix usage in general, with specific areas on system administration and some extensive tutorial areas.

> http://www.ugu.com

Securing Internet Information Servers

If you are planning on providing Internet services with your Solaris machine, then you should be aware of the security issues—while the operating system is relatively secure by default, you'll need to spend some time changing the default information and setup to ensure the best security. The document below includes step-by-step instructions on securing anonymous FTP, Gopher, and WWW services on your Solaris machine.

> http://www.ciac.org/ciac/documents/ciac2308.html

Glossary

The pound or hash sign (depending on which side of the water you come from). Often used to start a comment in a text configuration file.

$ The dollar sign is used as a prefix for environment variables when you want to retrieve the environment variable's value.

$HOME   The environment variable which holds the path to the current user's home directory.

$PATH   The environment variable which holds a list of colon-separated directories to be searched when you enter a command at the command line.

/   The forward slash (or simply slash) is used to separate the directory names in a path. A single slash on its own (/) relates to the root of the directory structure. For example, */usr/bin* refers to the *bin* directory within the *usr* directory within the *root* directory.

/etc files   Most of the configuration information for a typical machine is located in the */etc* directory. Also included here are the startup scripts and vital system information required to get your machine into a running state. Some of the information in these files can be handled by another system; for example hosts can be handled by DNS and NIS/NIS+ while user, group, and email information may be handled by the NIS/NIS+ or LDAP services. But all machines have core configuration information such as the host's name, IP address, and root password in the files stored in this directory.

****   The backslash is used when you want to "escape" a character, for example \n inserts a newline character. The backslash is *not* used as it is under Windows as a directory separator.

;   The semicolon is a shell metacharacter used to separate individual commands within a single command line.

!   The bang (exclamation mark) is used within the C shell to recall previously executed commands by their number within a history.

*   The asterisk is used to match any character within a file specification within the shell. Within applications that support regular expressions (such as awk, sed, or Perl) the * character matches zero or more repeats of the previous expression.

?   The question mark matches a single character within a file specification.

@   Used in Perl to refer to an array, or used to separate the name and domain or hostname portions of an email address (for example, mc@mcwords.com).

<   The less-than symbol is used to redirect the standard input to the specified file or process.

>   The greater-than symbol is used to redirect the standard output from a process to the specified file.

>>   The double-greater-than symbol is used to redirect the standard output from a process appending the output to an existing file, or creating a new file if it doesn't already exist.

absolute path   The full path to a file. For example, when you are within the */usr/bin* directory, the local path to the file *zip* is simply *zip* or *./zip*. The absolute path is */usr/bin/zip*.

access control   Access control is any mechanism that governs a user's or application's ability to access a file or resource. Within Solaris and other Unix variants the primary method of resource access is through the file permissions system. Since most resources, including devices, are accessed through the file system you can control their availability by changing the corresponding file's permissions.

Access Control List (ACL)   Solaris 8 and 9 include the ability to set additional levels of access control on different files. In addition to the basic user/group/other model of the file permissions system you can also grant specific users and groups read/write/execute access on a file or directory using an access control list.

Address Resolution Protocol (ARP)   A protocol used to map the Ethernet address of a machine to an IP address.

alias   A nickname for a command. Supported by the Korn and Bash shells.

anonymous FTP   An FTP service available to the public that allows users to log in with the user *anonymous* and their email address. Used on the Internet to provide download sites for files.

ANSI   The American National Standards Institute, responsible for setting standards for all areas of life, including computers. Visit www.ansi.org.

architecture   The hardware (CPU and other elements) associated with a specific computer. For example a PC compatible, Sun SPARC, or Apple Macintosh are all considered to be individual architectures. Within Solaris, further division is made between the different varieties of SPARC platforms. Older, single processor solutions are sun4c, and the recent multi-processor platforms introduced with the SPARC 10 are classed as sun4m.

argument   A single word or other value that you supply to an application on the command line.

ASCII   The American Standard Code for Information Interchange. ASCII is the mapping of character numbers to the English letters you are reading now.

authorization   The right to access a specific resource or perform a specific action.

AutoClient   A network client that uses the local disk to hold cached copies of mounted file systems and swap space, but uses the disk space and operating system from a network server.

AutoFS   Both a network service and type of file system. The AutoFS system allows file systems to be automatically mounted when they are used, rather than permanently mounting the file system. Especially useful when mounting file systems over remote links.

AutoFS map   The file used to configure the AutoFS server. The files map directories and mount points and the associated NFS resources.

awk   A pattern scanning and processing language.

background   A space where programs are executed without producing any output. Solaris (and indeed most operating systems) run a number of programs in the background. You can also set applications to run in the background by adding an ampersand (&) to the end of a command line.

bit   A single value that can either be on or off. Computers use bits to store information— by stringing a number of bits together you can make a byte (8 bits), which has the ability to store 256 different values.

boot server   A server that provides the files necessary to allow a client to boot and then install the Solaris operating system during a network installation. The boot server includes the information to resolve a host's IP address, the kernel, and enough information to start the installation process. As soon as the boot process has completed, the installation process is handled by an install server. Typically the boot and install server are the same machine.

Bourne shell (sh)   A version of the Unix shell developed by Steven Bourne from AT&T Bell Labs. The Bourne shell is the default shell for the Solaris operating system.

Bourne-Again shell   The Bourne-Again shell, from the GBU project. Bash is compatible with *sh*, *csh*, and *ksh* and provides a number of useful enhancements such as command line editing and job control.

BSD Berkeley Systems Division, one of two "standards" in the Unix-compatible operating system arena. BSD was used as the basis for the SunOS and Solaris 1 Unix operating systems from Sun. System V Release 4 (SVR4) has been the base for all versions since Solaris 2. There is a BSD compatibility layer built into Solaris.

byte A byte is the basis for storing most of the information in your computer and a single byte can be thought of as a single letter.

C A computer programming language, often used to write and then later support operating systems. Unix and Windows were written in C.

C++ An object oriented programming language using the same basic syntax as C, and developed by Bjarne Stroustrup.

C shell (csh) A shell that uses C-like syntax for setting variables and for the built-in scripting language facilities.

CacheFS A file system used to store information temporarily to help improve the speed of access. CacheFS file systems can be used to cache information from NFS or CD file systems.

cc The Unix C compiler. Solaris does not come with a C compiler as standard, but the Forte for C compiler is available as part of the pack supplied with the Solaris operating system. If you need a C compiler see Appendix A, "Resource Guide," for information on how to obtain GCC, the GNU C compiler.

cd The command used to change between directories.

CD-R CD Recordable, a form of compact disk that can be written to once using a special CD-R drive. Once written, the information can be read from the CD-R using any standard CD-ROM drive.

CD-ROM Compact Disk Read Only Memory, capable of storing 650 MB of data or the equivalent of 74 minutes of music, or 700 MB of data, the equivalent of 80 minutes of music. CD-ROMs are generated with a mechanical process and cannot be modified.

CD-RW CD Rewritable, a form of compact disk that can be written to and later erased ready for reuse, using a special CD-RW drive. Once written, the information can be read in any CD-ROM drive.

client A computer or application that uses resources or information provided by a server. For example, when you browse the Internet your machine is acting as a client to the Internet server.

client/server An operational model where one or more servers provides information to multiple clients. A web server is an example of a client/server model.

client-side failover   An automatic system supported by the NFS server that allows the connection to the server to be automatically switched to an alternative server if the current server becomes unavailable.

Common Desktop Environment (CDE)   A windowed desktop environment built on top of the X Windows System. The CDE provides a common environment for interacting with applications under X Windows. CDE is now a standard part of many Unix operating systems.

concatenated striped virtual device   A striped disk device that has had additional disk slices added (concatenated) to the device.

concatenated virtual device   A device consisting of two or more slices. The slices can be on the same physical disk or on several physical disks.

core dump   The file generated by the operating system when an application terminates unexpectedly. A core dump contains a complete image of the application as it existed in memory (hence core dump). You can sometimes use a core dump to debug the program after it has terminated.

cracker   A malicious computer user who unlawfully breaches the security of a computer or application. Compare with *hacker*.

csh   *See* C shell.

Custom JumpStart   An automated installation method that uses a text file to set the rules and one or more profiles to determine the system configuration to install. Using JumpStart will make installing a number of machines simultaneously much easier, as you should be able to get by with simply switching the machines on—the JumpStart system will handle the booting, configuration, and installation required.

daemon   A background task or process that provides system or network services.

dataless client   A dataless client has its operating system and swap space configured on the local disk, but all the user data is stored on a central server.

device aliases   An OpenBoot feature that lets you assign an alias to a full physical device pathname.

device driver   A small piece of software that provides a conduit for communicating between a physical device and operating system.

direct map   A type of AutoFS configuration file that identifies the full path to mount points and associated NFS resources.

directory   An area of a disk used to hold a group of files. Think of a filing cabinet—a folder within a drawer (and any folders which it contains) can be considered as directories. In fact, the term folder is an alternative name for a directory.

disk group   A collection of Volume Manager (VM) disks that share a common configuration.

disk label   The label of a disk holds the configuration information for the partitions on the disk.

diskless client   A network client that does not have a hard disk of its own. Instead, everything—including the operating system—is loaded remotely from a server on the network.

domain   A group of systems belonging to a specific department, group, or company.

Domain Name System (DNS)   A service that matches IP addresses to names and vice versa. In DNS, collections of hosts are split into domains, for example sun.com, and then hosts appear within those domains; for example java.sun.com is the name of a machine in the sun.com domain. The DNS service is used on the Internet; for local naming services you can use DNS, NIS/NIS+, and others.

dot file   Files starting with a dot (period) are called dot files and are normally hidden from standard file lists. Dot files are used to hold configuration and preferences information. For example, *.profile* holds the preference script used to set up the environment in which you work when using the Bourne shell.

duplexing   A technique where information is simultaneously written to one online and one offline device. Often used in RAID systems where you need an instantly available backup disk in the event of a disk failure.

Dynamic Host Configuration Protocol (DHCP)   A protocol used by clients to request an IP address, gateway, DNS, and other information from a server dynamically from a pre-configured pool of addresses and information. Using DHCP negates the need to manage the individual IP addresses of a large number of hosts.

dynamic reconfiguration   A system ability that allows hardware to be connected and disconnected while the machine is powered and running. When the device is added, the hardware is identified and the corresponding device driver loaded.

DVD   Digital Versatile Disk, the next generation of CD-ROM capable of storing GB of information. DVD can be used both for computer storage and, because of its high capacity, for digital video.

Enterprise Volume Manager   A virtual disk management system.

Environment Variables   Every application, and especially the shell, has access to a list of variables called environment variables which hold useful information valid to all applications. Environment variables are used to store everything from the format used to display your command line prompt ($PS1), to the list of directories searched when you type in a command's name at the command prompt ($PATH).

Ethernet address A unique 48-bit address assigned to every Ethernet device. The Ethernet address is used to identify individual machines and other equipment on the network at the lowest network software level. Note that the Ethernet address is unique to each Ethernet device—if you have more than one Ethernet adaptor in your machine then it will have more than one Ethernet address.

Federated Naming Service (FNS) A name service that conforms to the X/Open Federated Naming Specification (XFN).

file A document or other collection of information stored as a single entity.

file server A server used to share files and directories over the network.

file system A logical collection of files and directories contained in a partition.

File Transfer Protocol (FTP) FTP is a network protocol specially designed for navigating directories and transferring files.

foreground An application that is running and generates its output to the terminal or interactively is said to be running in the foreground.

fork A process where a currently running application is duplicated, creating a parent and a child. Forked processes are often used by services that need to support multiple users concurrently. For example, a web server uses fork to create multiple copies of the web server application so that it can service requests from more than one client at a time.

Free Software Foundation (FSF) The FSF promotes the development and use of free software (in terms of copyright and distribution). See Appendix A, "Resource Guide," for more information.

gateway A point on the network where information is redistributed to another network. For example, an Internet gateway is used to connect your network to the Internet.

gcc The Free Software Foundation's C compiler (GNU cc).

Gibibyte (GiB) 1,024 Mebibytes. The proper NIST standard unit for referring to computer storage expressed as a multiple of the base 2 system.

Gigabit (Gb) 1,000 Megabits. Gigabits, Megabits, and Kilobits are used to refer to data transfer speeds, but not storage capacities.

Gigabyte (GB) 1,024 Megabytes. Also referred to as a 'gig.' Note that a strict interpretation is 1,000 Megabytes (or 1,000,000,000 bytes).

GNU GNU stands for the recursive GNUs Not Unix. It refers to a series of applications developed by the FSF, and designed to be a free implementation of the components making up the Unix operating system.

group A group of users. For example, you might create a group for all the people in a single department. Groups are also used to control security.

group account   A unique name and associated group ID used to manage a collection of user accounts.

group ID (GID)   A unique numeric ID assigned to a group account, used for group ownership and permissions.

hack   According to the dictionary this means "to write programs, code, or to use all your knowledge and skill to solve a problem in an interesting way." Note that it doesn't say "break into a computer" or "destroy files and data on a computer." *See also* cracker.

hacker   A person who toys and tinkers with computers, or who uses a computer to solve problems. *See also* cracker.

host   A computer system that provides resources to locally and/or remotely logged-on users.

hot plugging   A hardware capability that allows system components to be changed without powering down the system.

Hypertext Transfer Protocol (HTTP)   HTTP is the protocol that is used to transfer the HTML, graphics, and other files when you browse the Internet.

indirect map   A type of AutoFS configuration file that identifies partial pathnames to mount points and associated NFS resources. The partial pathnames are relative to the directory identified in the */etc/auto-master* file.

initialization file templates   Login and shell startup initialization files for each user account are copied from templates under the */etc/skel* directory when the home directory for the user account is created.

initialization files   A file that provides initialization and startup information for an application. The shells, mail software, *ftp* command, and many others have their own initialization files which set up information used by the application during its execution. The operating system also has its own set of initialization files which are executed during startup. These set vital information for the operating system and also start important applications such as web server and NFS services.

install client   A system that will be installed over the network. You must have a boot server and install server available to provide the necessary information and resources to the install client to start up.

install server   A network server that provides the distribution files necessary for the installation of the Solaris operating system on an install client during a network installation.

installation   The process of copying and configuring an operating system or application so that it can be used on a machine.

JumpStart   An automated installation process that uses standardized configurations based on system architecture and hardware to determine the system configuration to install.

JumpStart configuration directory   A directory that contains the files used to customize a JumpStart installation.

kernel   The software that contains the core elements of the operating system required to manage services, communicate with devices (including storage devices), and execute applications and other processes.

kernel modules   Rather than using one big kernel that contains all of the information for all the different hardware and services that you want to support, modern kernels are generally divided into a number of different modules. Only the modules required are actually loaded when the operating system requires them.

Kibibytes (KiB)   1,024 bytes. The NIST standard for referring to storage capacities in base 2.

Kilobits (Kb)   1,000 bits.

Kilobytes (KB)   1,024 bytes. Note that a strict interpretation of Kilobytes is 1,000 bytes, although tradition treats the value as 1,024 bytes as it is a power of 2.

Korn shell (ksh)   A version of the Unix shell developed by David Korn from AT&T Bell Labs and referred to as ksh.

Lightweight Directory Access Protocol (LDAP)   A protocol used to store and provide information about users, groups, machines, organizations, and other resources.

Local Area Network (LAN)   A collection of computers networked together within a relatively small area such as a home, office, or single building.

localhost   The loopback IP address for the local system; typically 127.0.0.1, but can be any address starting with 127.

logical device name   A naming convention used to identify devices using a logical structure rather than the specific technical structure used internally by the operating system. The real devices used by the operating system are available in the */devices* directory, the logical device names are made available in the */dev* directory. For example the real device */devices/ pci@0,0/pci9004,8078@c/sd@0,0:a* is more easily understood as the device 0, disk 0, partition 0 on controller 1 (*/dev/dsk/c1t0d0s0*).

m4 macro   A macro (interpreted by the m4 macro language) often used for configuring different applications and services.

man **page**   A page from the operating system manuals—all *man* pages for an operating system are available via the *man* command.

mandatory locking   A special file permission that prevents a program from reading or writing a file while another program has the file open.

Mebibytes (MiB)   1,024 Kilobytes. The NIST standard for referring to storage capacities in base 2.

Megabits (Mb)   1,000,000 bits.

Megabytes (MB)   1,024 Kilobytes. Note that a strict interpretation of Megabytes is 1,000,000 bytes, although tradition treats the value as 1,048,576 (1,024*1,024) bytes.

memory management   A service provided by the operating system which keeps track of and manages the memory (physical and virtual) of a machine.

metadevice   The basic virtual disk used by DiskSuite to manage physical disks.

mirroring   A technique where information is copied between an online and offline device in a RAID disk. The offline, mirrored disk contains an exact image of the online disk and can be instantly swapped with the online disk if it fails, without any break in availability of the information.

mount point   A directory in a mounted file system that serves as an access point for another file system.

mounting   The process of associating a file system (on a physical disk or a networked file system) with a mount point on the local file system.

multitasking   The ability to execute more than one process or task at a time.

multiuser   The ability of a system to support multiple simultaneous users.

name service   A network service that maps names to numbers. Primarily used for mapping host names to IP addresses (as provided by the DNS, NIS/NIS+, and LDAP services) although it can also relate to the user, group, and other table information shared by NIS/NIS+ and LDAP.

namespace   A collection of information regarding systems within the domain of a name service.

network client   A system that has little or no disk space, loading the operating system and applications from a network server.

Network File System (NFS)   A system for sharing a file system over a network.

Network Information Service (NIS)   A name service that stores user, group, email alias, host, and other information in a map, making it globally available to any clients.

Network Information Service Plus (NIS+)   An enhanced version of NIS supporting advanced security and authentication for accessing and updating the information.

non-volatile random access memory (NVRAM)   A memory chip available on Sun's SPARC systems that contains configuration information used by OpenBoot and also holds the current date and time.

Open Windows   A window manager that sits on top of the X Windows System and provides the menus, window decorations, and other information. OpenWindows was the old windowing system supported by Solaris; it has now been replaced by CDE.

OpenBoot   OpenBoot is the firmware used by Sun SPARC systems and holds the diagnostic applications for testing the hardware, the boot loader code to enable a SPARC platform to boot from a network server without a boot disk, and also provides an interface for modifying the configuration stored in NVRAM. On Intel systems the OpenBoot software is provided by a boot floppy (or installed on the hard disk when Solaris has been installed on the machine) but it only provides the basic boot loader information for booting the system and a hardware discovery system for identifying the physical equipment on the machine.

operating system release   The version of an operating system, such as 8 or 9 for Solaris.

operating system (OS) server   A network server that provides network clients with access to operating system files as required.

operating system (OS) service   A set of files needed to support a particular network client. An OS service is identified and configured for a combination of platform, system architecture, and OS release.

partition   A contiguous collection of disk sectors as defined by the partition table. A disk can be split into 8 logical partitions under Solaris. Each partition can hold a single file system.

partition table   A table on a disk which defines the location of each partition.

password aging   You can set passwords to automatically expire and require a new password. Using password aging is a simple way of increasing security as it requires users to change their password regularly.

Peripheral Component Interconnect (PCI)   A slot- and card-based bus mechanism used to connect video adapters, network cards, sound cards, and so on to a computer system. Intel PCs and newer SPARC systems use the PCI system, older SPARC systems use SBUS.

platform   The particular type of hardware—either SPARC or Intel x86 compatible.

privileged operation   A Solaris command that is executed with the UID or GID set to a privileged user.

process   A task or program currently being executed by the computer system.

pseudo file system   A memory-based file system. Pseudo file systems can be used to improve performance for certain operations—for example, if you are setting up a machine designed for software development it is a good idea to use a pseudo file system for the */tmp* directory, which gets used heavily during a compile sequence.

RAID   Redundant Array of Inexpensive (or Independent) Disks. RAID systems can be used to improve performance or provide redundancy in the event of a disk failure, or both, all through the use of relatively inexpensive disk drives and controllers.

remote authentication database   The database used to determine whether a remote host has the authority and is trusted to connect to the local machine. For example, the *rlogin*, *rsh*, and *rcp* commands make use of the */etc/host.equiv* and */.rhosts* files to determine authenticated hosts.

Remote Procedure Call (RPC)   A mechanism that allows a client to request a remote server to execute a procedure or process.

Request For Comment (RFC)   A document used to publish networking-related policies and protocols so that interested parties can submit comments and recommend changes. Most of the protocols (including HTTP, FTP, TCP/IP, and others), applications, and related technologies have been suggested, discussed, and improved upon through the use of the RFC mechanism.

Reverse Address Resolution Protocol (RARP)   A protocol used to map from an Ethernet address to an IP address.

role   A special type of user account provided by the Role-Based Access Control mechanism to grant a set of superuser privileges to perform some administrative tasks.

Role-Based Access Control (RBAC)   A mechanism used to grant access to privileged operations or commands to accounts as needed to perform a task.

run control (rc) script   A shell script (typically Bourne) written to start and stop various processes and services or to configure the preferences for an application. OS rc files are located in */etc/init.d* and configuration files for applications are either stored globally (typically in */etc*) or in a user's home directory as a dot file.

server   A computer that provides services to clients.

setgid   A special file access mode that sets the effective GID of the user account executing a program to the GID of the program group owner. You can use this to grant any user access to a directory or file *only* when they are executing this application.

setuid   A special file access mode that sets the effective UID of the user account executing a program to the UID of the program owner. You can use this to grant any user access to a directory or file or to provide superuser privileges *only* when they are executing this application.

SGML   The Standard Generalized Markup Language used to provide a generic method of encoding the contents of a document without associating it with a particular format. The forerunner to HTML and XML.

share   The process of making an NFS resource available for mounting by remote NFS clients.

shell   A software module that provides the interface between users and the core operating system. The shell allows a user to execute other programs and manipulate the file system. Most shells also include the ability to be "scripted" to allow repetitive sequences to be stored and later played back.

signal   A notification sent to a process to indicate an event or an action that should be performed. Signals are used through Unix to indicate different events to different processes. For example, you can terminate a process by sending the process the "kill" signal, or force a daemon to reload its configuration and data files by sending the process the "hangup" signal.

small computer system interface (SCSI)   A bus-based peripheral device connection mechanism used to connect devices to a computer. SCSI is primarily used for disk and tape devices but can also be used for scanners, printers, and other devices that need to transfer large quantities of information quickly. SCSI is available in a number of different versions, including Fast SCSI, SCSI-2, SCSI-3, and Wide SCSI. The different standards all use the same basic method for transferring information, but differ in their speed, bandwidth, and connectivity options.

software cluster   A logical grouping of software packages. Software clusters allow software to be installed from a number of distinct packages in a single sequence. For example, when you first install the Solaris operating system you select the cluster that you want to install; the cluster defines the collection of packages for the desired system such as development, server, or client. After the initial installation, clusters are most commonly used to distribute patches and updates to the operating system.

software configuration cluster   *See* software group.

software group   A collection of software clusters that hold the software packages for a particular platform and operating system combination.

software package   An easily installable collection of Solaris system and application software. The package consists of the files, an installation script to install them, and manifest information to identify the files and eventual locations of the files once they have been installed. Packages also contain information about the package and any other packages on which the software package contains relies. All of this information is used by the package management software to allow the software to be installed, uninstalled, or verified automatically.

software patch   An easily installable collection of file and directories intended to update or fix a problem with an installed software package.

SPARC   A computer architecture developed by Sun Microsystems. It uses a reduced instruction set (RISC) processor, which provides superior performance over processors that operate using a standard instruction set. Modern variants include the SuperSPARC, HyperSPARC, and UltraSPARC processors.

standalone system   A system that has its own hard disk which contains all the software required for the machine's operation. Standalone machines can be networked or free-standing, and they can act as servers or clients to other machines on the network.

sticky bit   A special file permission that, when set on a directory that allows write permission for everyone, allows only the user account that created the files and subdirectories under that directory to remove those files and subdirectories. A sticky bit is especially useful for the */tmp* directory, which is available from any user account.

sub disk   The basic unit used by the Volume Manager to allocate storage.

Suninstall   An interactive Open Windows installation program that can be used to install the Solaris operating system.

superuser   A special administrative account that provides the ultimate in terms of access to data and services, because it can override any file permissions on the system. By convention the only superuser account on a system is "root" although any user can potentially have superuser privileges.

swap space   Disk space used to augment the physical memory on a machine. Processes and data that are not currently in use are "swapped" to disk to make as much physical memory as possible available to running applications. These processes and data are swapped back into physical memory when they are required. Using swap space allows a machine to execute more processes than the physical memory alone would normally allow, while sacrificing some performance.

syslog   A central service on a machine used to log information and errors from daemons and applications. The syslog service can also accept log messages from other hosts on the network to allow you to centralize the errors and information from all of your machines. The configuration of the syslog service is handled by the */etc/syslog.conf* file.

syslog actions   The action that is performed when a syslog message of the identified source priority is received by the syslogd daemon.

syslog priority levels   A syslog message can be identified by priority level or severity.

syslog source facilities   Errors stored in the syslog service also contain a "source" string to help you identify which service and machine raised the error.

system profile   For user accounts that use sh or ksh as a login shell, commands in the system profile (*/etc/profile*) are executed before the user's login initialization file (*.profile*).

system run levels   The daemons and services supported by a machine are determined by the system's "runlevel" which is in turn defined by the contents of the */etc/inittab* file. The different runlevels run from single-user mode, which does not run any background daemons or services and is used for system administration tasks such as upgrades and file system repairs, through to the standard runlevels which run all standard services and other levels for shutting down and restarting the machine.

Transmission Control Protocol/Internet Protocol (TCP/IP)   TCP/IP is the primary protocol used to communicate between Unix machines and services and is also used as the communications protocol for the Internet. TCP is the transmission and communication portion. IP is the protocol used for identifying machines using an IP address.

UFS   UFS is the standard file system format (the layout of files and directories and data storage) for Solaris systems.

UFS file system logging   A system where updates to a UFS file system are logged in a file. In the event of a system failure the file system can be rebuilt by executing the entries in the log. This is quicker than using the *fsck* command and is more reliable as any pending updates will not have been lost.

user account   A unique name and user ID that control an individual's access to a computer and its resources.

user ID (UID)   A unique numeric ID assigned to a user account. The user ID information is stored along with files and directories and is used to identify users. If you change the mapping between the user ID and user name then the ownership will appear to change—even though the user ID has remained the same.

Veritas File System (vxfs)   The type of virtual file system supported by the Enterprise Volume Manager. Veritas file systems can be made up of multiple partitions from multiple disks to support very large logical file systems.

virtual disk management system   A software package that allows the use of physical disks in different ways that are not supported by the standard Solaris file systems. It can overcome disk capacity and architecture limitations and improve performance and reliability. In addition, manageability is enhanced by the use of a graphical management tool.

virtual file system   An enhanced file system that provides improved performance and data reliability.

Volume Manager (VM) disk   A physical disk partition or slice that has been assigned to the Enterprise Volume Manager.

volume table of contents (VTOC)   Contains the partition table and geometry data about a physical disk. The information is written to the disk as part of the disk label and is used by the operating system to identify partitions and ultimately file systems usable by the machine.

WebNFS   A protocol that allows web browsers to access NFS resources.

Web Start   An interactive installation method that uses a web browser interface.

Wide Area Network (WAN)   A network of computers that may be in distant locations. For example, a LAN in New York and another in London may be connected together to make a WAN.

x86 Intel compatible   A computer architecture based on a microprocessor originally designed by the Intel Corporation. X86 relates, generically, to the series of processors that includes the 8086, 286, 386, 486, and Pentium (586 and 686) processors.

X/Open Federated Naming Specification (XFN)   The specification for the Federated Naming Service (FNS) as defined by the X/Open Consortium.

zone   A portion of a domain delegated to a DNS server.

Index